Designs for Australian Leadlighting

By the same authors

Australian Leadlighting

Designs for Australian Leadlighting

❖

Paul Danaher & Dexter Jackson

Illustrations and designs by Julia Dunn

❖

VIKING

Viking
Penguin Books Australia Ltd
487 Maroondah Highway, PO Box 257
Ringwood, Victoria 3134, Australia
Penguin Books Ltd
Harmondsworth, Middlesex, England
Penguin Putnam Inc.
375 Hudson Street, New York, New York 10014, USA
Penguin Books Canada Limited
10 Alcorn Avenue, Toronto, Ontario, Canada M4V 3B2
Penguin Books (N.Z.) Ltd
Cnr Rosedale and Airborne Roads, Albany, Auckland, New Zealand
Penguin Books (South Africa) (Pty) Ltd
5 Watkins Street, Denver Ext 4, 2094, South Africa
Penguin Books India (P) Ltd
11, Community Centre, Panchsheel Park, New Delhi 110 017, India

First published by Penguin Books Australia Ltd 1995

10 9 8 7 6 5 4 3

Typeset in Galliard by Midland Typesetters, Maryborough, Victoria
Photography by Peter Suveges
Printed in Australia by Impact Printing, Melbourne

National Library of Australia
Cataloguing-in-Publication data

Danaher, Paul.
Designs for Australian Leadlighting.

Includes index.
ISBN 0 670 86342 4.

1. Glass painting and staining – Australia. 2. Glass painting and staining – Australia – patterns. I. Jackson, Dexter. II. Title.

748.502840994

www.penguin.com.au

The Lead Balloon
1240 Malvern Road
Malvern Vic. 3144
Tel: 03 9822 0686

Contents

Introduction

We would like to take this opportunity of thanking those people who read and enjoyed our earlier book, *Australian Leadlighting*. Your comments (thankfully mostly flattering) came from all round the country and were greatly appreciated.

Where we were able to talk to our readers we asked what they would have liked us to include in the first book. The most consistent replies were that we should have a more comprehensive section on the technique of copper foiling and, especially, more leadlight patterns and designs.

So here we go!

Designs for Australian Leadlighting is in three parts. The catalogue section updates the catalogue in *Australian Leadlighting*, describing and illustrating the range of tools and equipment available to leadlighters. Some tools are used in both copper foiling and leadlighting so, to make the catalogue section of this book complete in its own right, we have duplicated material from the earlier book where necessary. As well, some tools have been deleted as they are no longer available.

The next section explains the techniques of leadlighting and copper foiling in particular. We hope you find it informative. We decided not to include much in the way of detailed copper foil projects in the book, as this area is covered by a large range of books already available. However, all the window designs in the last section of the book can be constructed using copper foil or lead.

The last section of the book is full of Julia's good quality drawings, comprising a selection of Victorian, Edwardian, Art Nouveau, Federation, Art Deco and contemporary designs including Australiana.

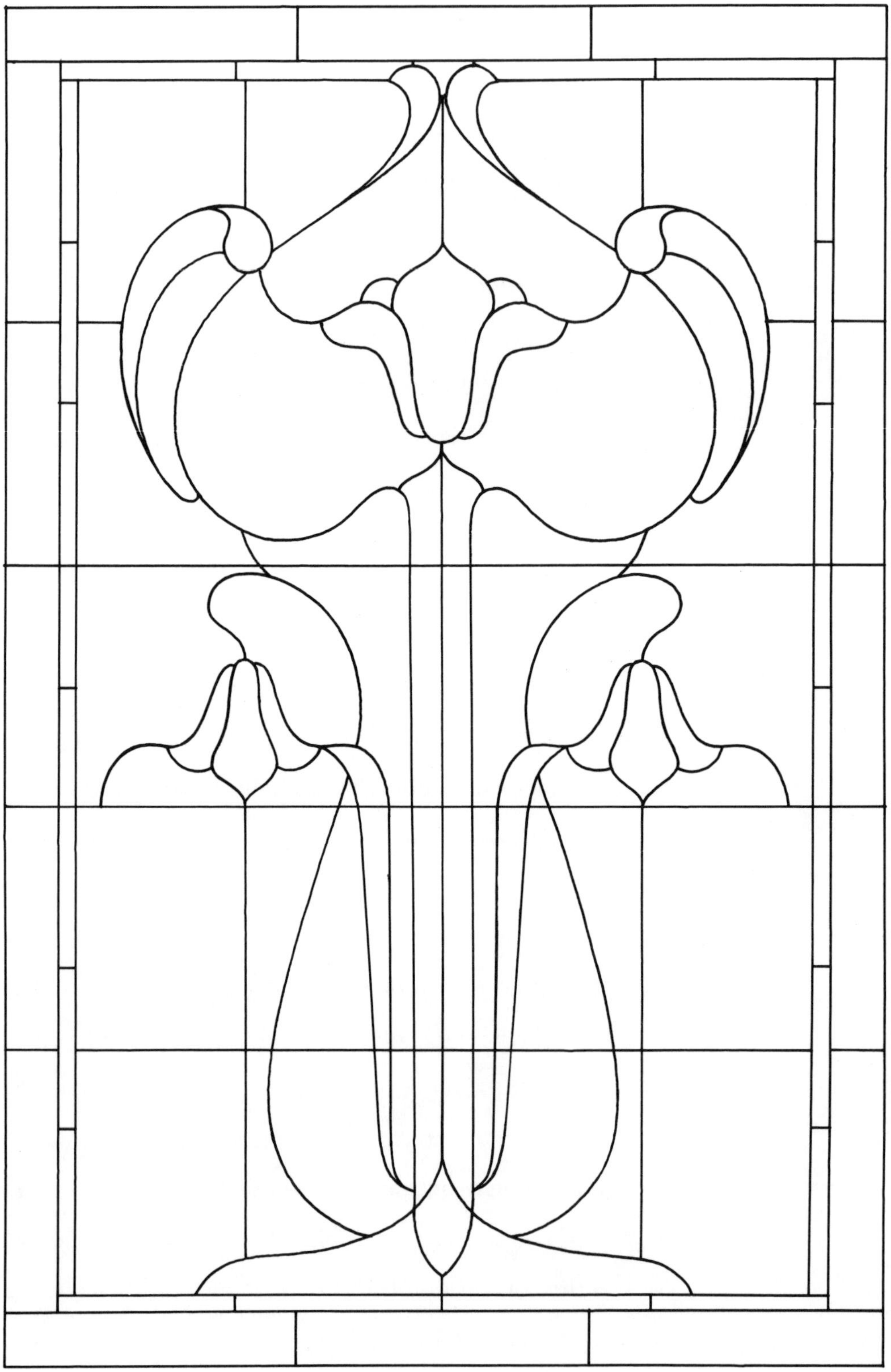

Copper Foiling – A Brief History

Copper foiling is a method of joining glass together by wrapping each piece of glass individually with a strip of copper adhesive tape, putting all the pieces of glass in their place over the pattern and then soldering them together all the way along the joins. When leadlighting, by contrast, the pieces of glass are held together by strips of lead – each piece of glass fitting into flanges in the lead – and only the joints are soldered; the glass is then puttied into place.

It is popularly believed that the copper foil method of window and lamp construction was pioneered by Louis C. Tiffany in the United States of America during the mid to late nineteenth century. Tiffany's business protagonist, John La Farge, is also sometimes credited with the early use of copper foil. Certainly, La Farge gained a patent on the manufacture and use of opalescent glass before Tiffany.

Both Tiffany and La Farge manufactured glass that varied in thickness. One particular glass that was much thicker than normal coloured glass was drapery glass, which was commonly used instead of stained or painted glass to represent the folding of material in gowns or dresses, for instance. Drapery glass might vary in thickness from 5 mm to 40 mm. The traditional method of constructing a leadlight window works well if the glass is uniform, but not if the thickness varies much (usually any glass thicker than 6 mm became a nuisance in lead work). A new technique was therefore pioneered: copper foiling.

Today the copper foil method of construction also allows easier and stronger manufacture of lampshades, mobiles, mirrors, clocks and jewellery boxes than does traditional leadlighting. This no doubt explains the popularity of copper foiling among professionals and hobbyists alike.

ADVANTAGES OF FOILING

- ❖ You do not have to putty your completed project.
- ❖ Copper foiled pieces tend to be more durable than those made using lead. The greater tin content of the solder used makes it inherently lighter and stronger than the solder suitable for lead work.
- ❖ Broken pieces of glass are not too complicated to replace or repair.
- ❖ Working with copper foil gives you the opportunity to make projects that have more than one dimension, such as lampshades, terrariums, jewellery boxes, etc.
- ❖ Small pieces of glass are less obscured with copper foil than with lead.
- ❖ If your soldering iron is too hot, you will not burn a hole in the copper foil as you can do with lead.
- ❖ If you want to improve the finish of your soldering it is possible to do so. You can keep going over your soldering until you are happy with the result.
- ❖ The foiling, even though a little tedious, can be done in front of the television or while sitting up in bed.
- ❖ There is a choice of finishes that can be applied to your finished projects. You can leave the solder in its natural silver colour and just polish it with a cleaning compound or, by applying black patina or copper patina as desired, the solder seams will change colour to black or copper respectively.

DISADVANTAGES OF FOILING

- ❖ The glass edges have to be reasonably smooth so as to accept the copper foil easily, and you should therefore consider buying a glass grinder if you are getting seriously involved in copper foiling.
- ❖ The solder joins or beads will be uneven in width. If you are extremely fussy and insist on all your joining lines being the same width, then copper foiling is not for you. You will go crazy trying to achieve an even width of solder.

  The original Tiffany windows and lamps have solder joins of uneven widths and if yours are uneven too, then you are in good company. Just do your best and that should be fine.
- ❖ Partners may complain that they cannot sleep when you are foiling in bed.

❖

1

Catalogue

The materials and tools in this catalogue section are only representative of the range of available products. We consider them to be the basic items required to make most projects, either using copper foil or leadlight techniques.

Any emphasis shown to one item over another does not mean that the less favoured product is inferior at all. If any bias does show it usually means that we have become used to that product or tool, and found it to be the most suitable for our needs. Better leadlight retailers will stock all the following items. If you do have trouble finding products, The Lead Balloon is happy to supply by mail.

Materials

Glass

The glass used in leadlighting is usually 2–4 mm thick. Glass that is mouth blown is known as 'antique glass' – so called because the method of manufacture is old, not the glass itself. Glass made by machine is called 'cathedral glass'. Antique glass comes mainly from England, France and Germany, while cathedral glass is generally made in England, Germany, Belgium and the United States.

The glass is coloured when it is made, various metallic oxides and chemicals being added to produce different effects.

When choosing glass for your project make sure you buy enough to complete the job. Batches of coloured glass vary and in some cases colours or textures may even be phased out. Ask the retailer if they will exchange or buy back any excess glass you may have at the end of the project; if so, buy more than you think you will need when beginning the piece.

Colour of glass	Metallic oxide
green	*copper and chrome*
black	*copper*
red	*selenium with cadmium and copper*
yellow	*selenium and chromium, with cadmium or sodium*
purple	*manganese and cobalt*
blue	*cobalt and chromium*
red/pink	*manganese and gold*

Antique glass

Antique glass is usually quite transparent. Some sheets have bubbles, or seeds, and others have striations, or grainy lines, that give the glass a 'fractured' or faceted look. The glass is coloured throughout its thickness – 'pot colour' – and the colour usually varies across the sheet. No two sheets of antique glass are ever the same.

Antique glass is relatively expensive, because of the individual care taken to make it, but it is generally an easy glass to cut although some of the selenium-coloured glass may be tough. It is more transparent than other coloured glass so is not used where privacy is desired.

Flashed glass

This is a form of antique glass where a thin layer, or 'flashing', of coloured glass is bonded during manufacture to the surface of a thicker base glass. The base glass may be clear or a different colour to the flashing. Flashed glass was used in Victorian windows with designs etched or sandblasted into the thin coat to reveal the base glass. It is used by contemporary designers also.

Flashed glass is expensive. It must be cut on the base glass side, not the flashed side.

Cathedral glass

*M*ade by machine, the molten glass is passed through rollers to form sheets. The colour and thickness are uniform in cathedral glass, and the glass can have varying textures on its surface depending on the type of roller used. It is not as transparent as antique glass, but it is considerably cheaper. There are various kinds of cathedral glass including those mentioned below.

Machined antique glass

A cathedral glass made to resemble antique glass.

Seedy glass

A machine-made glass that is smooth on both surfaces but has tiny bubbles trapped inside it. It is more difficult to cut than ordinary cathedral glass.

Glue chipped glass

A glass with a fern-like pattern. It is easy to work with and reasonably priced.

Opalescent glass

*M*ilky-looking glass. The base glass can be white, clear or coloured: then additional milky colour is mixed in during manufacture, usually producing a swirled effect. Opalescent glass was used by Tiffany in the late nineteenth century in the United States. It is now often used in copper foil projects.

Sundry glass items

*T*here are various interesting glass items that can be incorporated in copper foil and leadlighting designs.

Stained glass border and centre sets

*T*hese border and centre sets are painted and kiln-fired in the same manner as the stained glass birds. They are available in two designs: gum leaf and traditional. Both designs come in a variety of coloured glass. They can be used in conjunction with the stained glass birds or on their own, as shown in the Design section of the book.

CS
CN
BB
BN
MB
MN
SB
SN

GUM LEAF DESIGN TRADITIONAL DESIGN

TYPE OF GLASS	SET CONTAINS
SB and SN Border series	*4 straight pieces (190 x 20 mm each)* *4 curved pieces (135 x 20 mm each)*
MB and MN Border series	*5 medium pieces (100 x 40 mm each)* *5 small pieces (60 x 40 mm each)*
BB and BN Border series	*5 long pieces (175 x 40 mm each)*
CS and CN Centre series	*1 square (160 x 160 mm)*

Stained glass birds

These older-style stained glass medallions depict birds and plants. They are designed to be incorporated as a focal point in a traditional leadlight.

The medallions have been made in the same way for centuries. The picture is painted on glass, either light-coloured or plain, which is then kiln-fired. The resulting glass is easy to cut into shapes suitable for particular designs. Some suggestions for their use are shown in the Design section of this book.

Eastern Yellow Robin

Red-breasted Robin

Malurus cyaneus ♀
Superb blue wren

Superb Blue Wren female

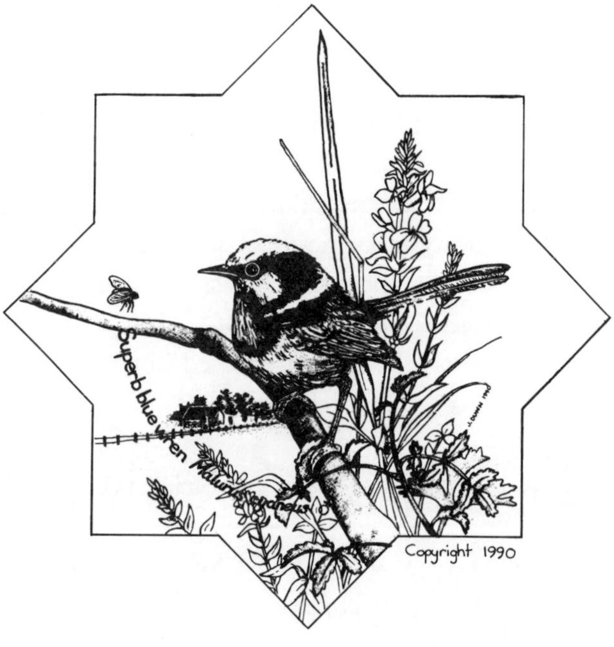
Superb blue wren
Copyright 1990

Superb Blue Wren male

STAINED GLASS BIRDS

Glass jewels

These are sometimes known as rondells, bevels or teardrops. They can be round, oval or square, faceted or smooth. They may be coloured or clear and are available in a range of sizes.

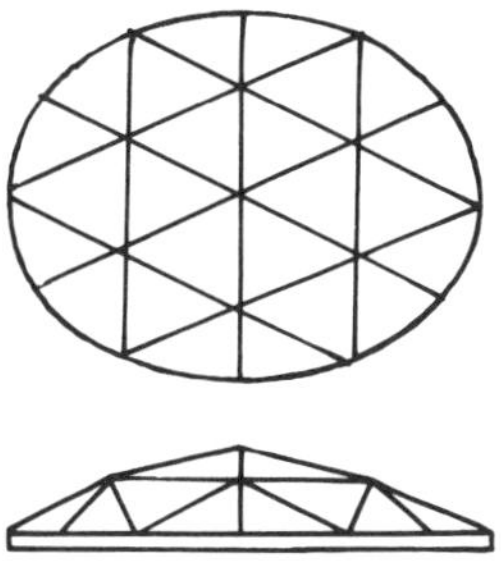

Faceted jewels

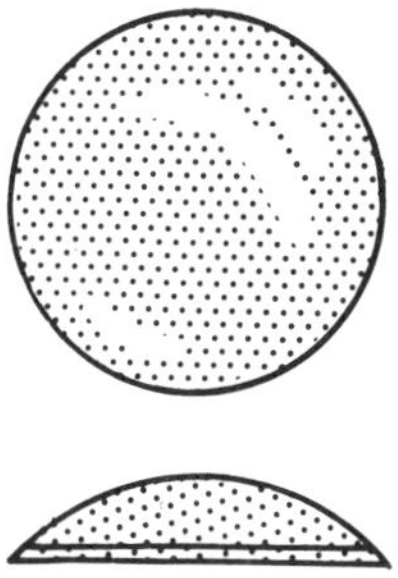

Curved head jewels

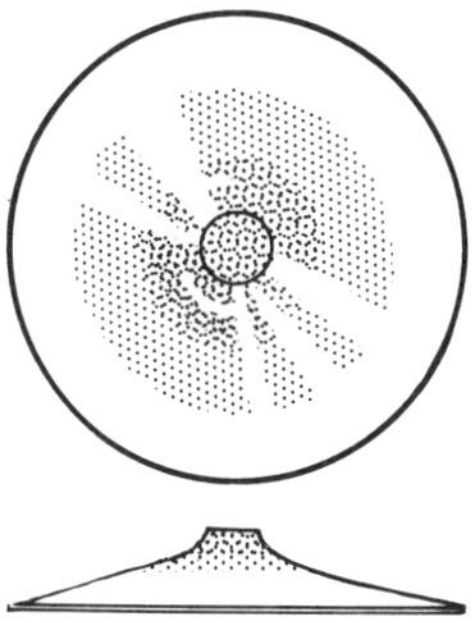

Hand-spun rondells

GLASS JEWELS

Filigree work

Some very intricate pieces of metal overlays can be bought. The dragonfly motif, with two pairs of wings, is used in lampshades and pendants, while poppy flowers and leaves, spiders' legs and vine branches are also available.

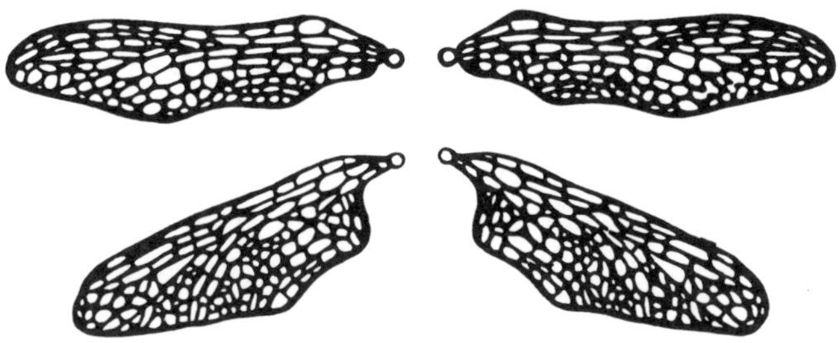

DRAGONFLY WINGS

LEAD

In leadlighting the strips of lead used to separate and support the glass are called 'cames' or 'calmes'. They come in a range of thicknesses and widths, but essentially consist of a solid centre heart, with channels to either side in which the glass fits. In cross-section the lead cames have an H-shaped appearance. The glass butts up to the centre. The height of came you will need will depend on the glass chosen for the project (remember to allow space for putty as well), while the width is more of a cosmetic choice.

Buy lead in small amounts as it quickly becomes heavily oxidised and then needs wire brushing before soldering.

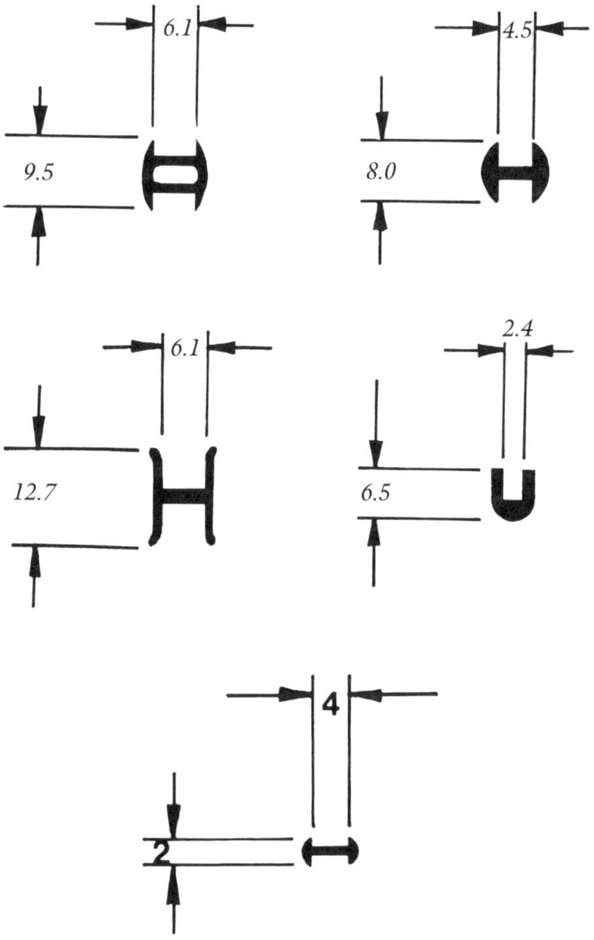
6.1
9.5
4.5
8.0
6.1
12.7
2.4
6.5
4
2

(all measurements are in mm)

A SELECTION OF LEAD CAMES, SHOWING DIFFERENT PROFILES

Copper foil

Copper foil is available in 5 mm, 5.5 mm, 6 mm and 10 mm widths. It is packaged in 30-metre rolls, with an adhesive backing covered by a removable paper strip. Copper foil is also manufactured with silver or black backing, for use with clear glass or mirror, to match the visible internal foil with the finished seams. With black backing black patina is used on the seams, while with silver backing no patina is used. Foil is obtainable with a crinkle or scalloped edge for decorative work.

The different widths and styles of copper foil can be mixed together with good effect, as long as the foil is always slightly wider than the thickness of the glass being used.

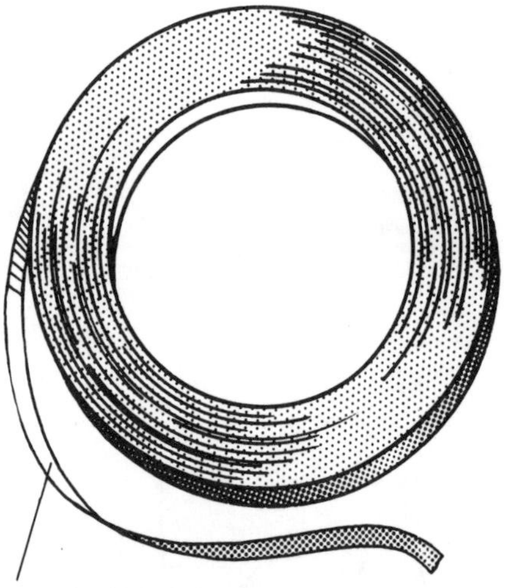
Remove paper backing before use

COPPER FOIL

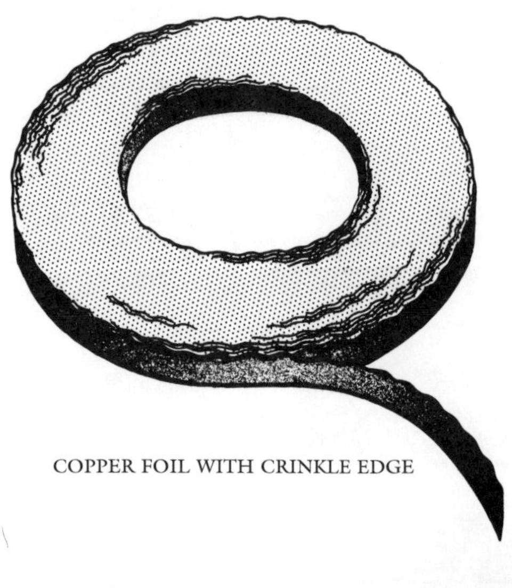

COPPER FOIL WITH CRINKLE EDGE

Solder

Solder is available in coils or stick form. The coils are usually extruded to a diameter of 3–4 mm and the sticks are 5–6 mm thick.

We suggest you do not use stick solder much thicker than 6 mm because too much of the heat generated by the soldering iron dissipates down the stick of solder and away from your leadlighting or copper foiling. This means that your soldering iron cools down too quickly, preventing you achieving a reasonable speed or level of proficiency when soldering.

STICK SOLDER

COILED SOLDER

The solder generally available from hardware shops has a resin core (an inbuilt flux) and is unsuitable for leadlighting or copper foiling. Use coreless or solid solder, and apply your own flux before soldering.

Solder is an alloy of tin and lead. Since tin melts at a lower temperature than lead, solder therefore melts at a lower temperature than lead alone. When soldering, allow your soldering iron to reach a temperature where it will melt the solder without melting the lead in your project.

The two most common tin/lead proportions in solder are 60/40 and 50/50. The first number in the combination indicates the percentage tin and the second the lead. 50/50 solder is usually cheaper than 60/40 and because there is no appreciable difference in strength or operation of join, it is most commonly used in leadlighting. 60/40 solder is more commonly used in copper foiling because it melts at a lower temperature than 50/50 and leaves a smoother, more rounded finish.

CHEMICALS

FLUX

All metals oxidise, that is, they react with the air and a layer of metal oxide forms on their surface. The role of a flux in leadlighting and copper foiling is to remove the oxides from the lead or copper so that the solder will flow on to, and bond with, the metal to which it is applied. You will not be able to solder successfully without first applying a flux.

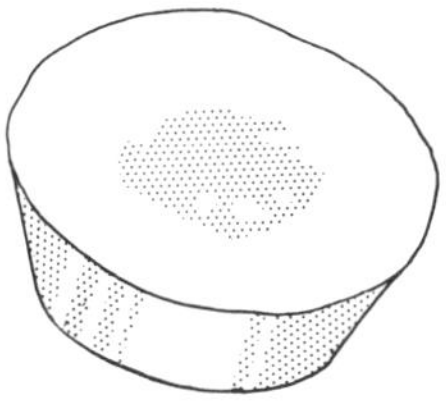

STEARINE FLUX
(solid flux for leadlighting)

The commonly used flux for lead is stearine (solid). In copper foil work a liquid flux is used. These both contain mild fatty acids that remove the oxide.

The solid, stearine flux is easily applied just prior to soldering by rubbing it on the lead joins and, even more important, is very easily removed after soldering by brushing with a wire brush.

For copper foil, a liquid flux or soldering paste are ideal as a flux; they are applied sparingly with a brush and removed by washing in soapy water.

LIQUID FLUX

NOKORODE
SOLDERING PASTE

SOLDERING PASTE

Important

Remove all flux from copper work by washing with soapy water and from lead work by brushing with a wire brush immediately after use.

Use reasonable caution when working with chemicals. All fluxes give off fumes when heat is applied. Work in a ventilated room and avoid breathing the fumes or wear a mask. Always wash your hands after using flux.

PUTTY AND CEMENT

These are used to waterproof and strengthen a leadlight window or panel by sealing the space between the glass and lead. They are not used with copper foil.

inland
Cement
system

CEMENT
(for sealing leadlights)

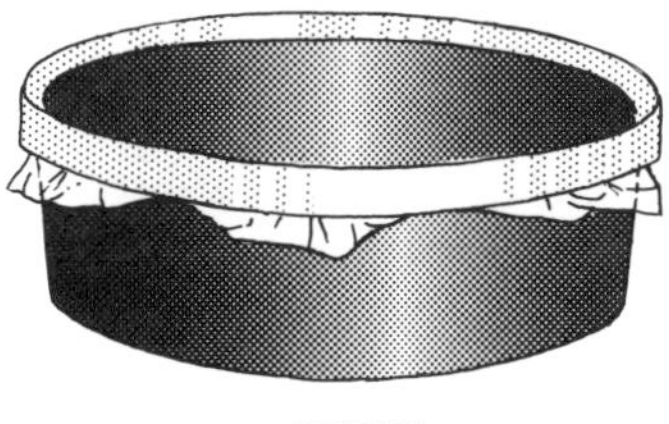

PUTTY

ENGLISH WHITING

English whiting is a fine, chalky powder applied to your leadlight window after puttying or cementing. It assists in removing the scum left on the glass and lead after puttying and absorbs any excess oil. It is also helpful in burnishing (darkening) lead and solder joins.

Apply sparingly, preferably outdoors, and wear a mask if you feel it necessary. It is removed by scrubbing vigorously with a natural bristle scrubbing brush.

PATINAS AND POLISHES

Patinas and polishes are not interchangeable. Stove polish will not work on copper foil, while patinas are not intended for use on leadlighting projects.

Important

Take care when using as these are toxic preparations. Follow the manufacturer's instructions on the bottle, and always scrub your hands after handling or wear gloves.

Silver protector

This is applied to the sides and back of mirror glass prior to copper foiling as it helps protect the silver surface during soldering.

Copper patina

Suitable only for copper foil projects. It gives the solder a warm copper finish. Copper patina works a little better if the solder seams are gently rubbed with steel wool before it is applied, to remove any oxides. Then use a toothbrush to cover solder with the patina.

Black patina

This is used only for copper foil projects. It changes the colour of the solder, through grey to black depending on the number of applications. It is applied with a soft brush. Take care using it – it is toxic.

To blacken brass fittings such as lamp caps and finials mix 1 tablespoon black patina with 1 teaspoon kitchen salt, then apply as above.

Finishing compound

This product gives bright, even and durable finish to both lead and solder seams. It polishes and protects against tarnish and waxes glass to a brilliant shine. It also restores shine to tarnished surfaces.

Stove polish

Stove polish is suitable only for leaded projects, not copper foiled. It will blacken your leads to a deep shiny finish. Apply several days after puttying and use very sparingly. Polish with a soft brush to obtain a deep shine.

Over the years lead will oxidise gradually, thus eventually darkening. Using stove polish means you don't have to wait years to see the lead blacken.

COMPOUND

BLACK PATINA SILVER PROTECTOR FINISHING COMPOUND COPPER PATINAS

PAINTS AND STAINS

There are two kinds of paints and stains. Cold paint is a solvent-based, transparent paint that does not need firing in a kiln. Other stains and enamels require kiln firing so they fuse into the surface of the glass. These kiln-fired paints are used in traditional painted work and we use them to produce our stained glass birds and borders.

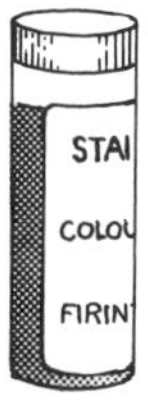

KILN-FIRED PAINT

VITRAIL

COLD PAINT

SAL AMMONIAC

This is used for cleaning and tinning soldering iron tips. Used regularly it will prolong the life of the soldering iron's tip and ensure that good, smooth solder joints are easily achieved. Most new soldering irons must be tinned before use.

Sal ammoniac is imported from America and therefore is bought in 8 oz blocks.

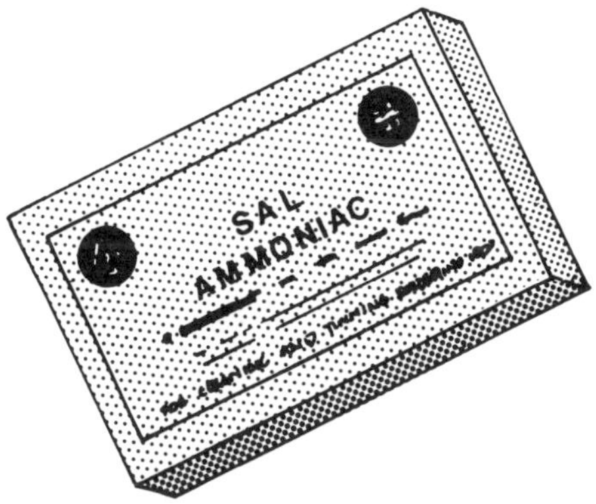
SAL
AMMONIAC

SAL AMMONIAC

TOOLS

GLASS CUTTERS

Diamantor glass cutter

German all-purpose cutter with a small steel cutting wheel and wooden handle. Cheap and disposable, but a good cutter to begin with.

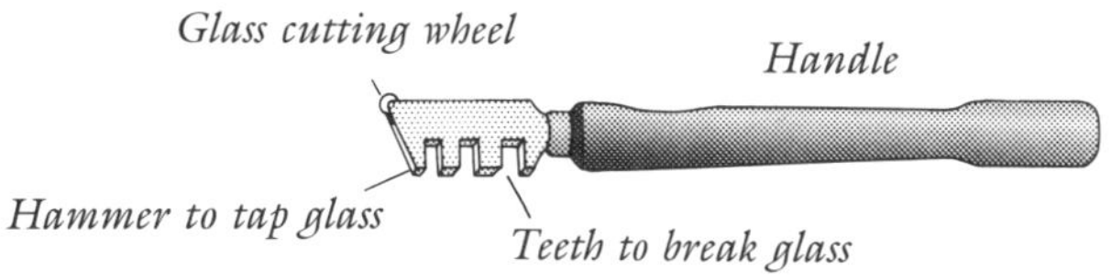
Glass cutting wheel
Handle
Hammer to tap glass
Teeth to break glass

DIAMANTOR GLASS CUTTER

Red devil and Fletcher glass cutters

American cutters with steel handles. These range from disposable models with steel wheels to those with tungsten-coated wheels.

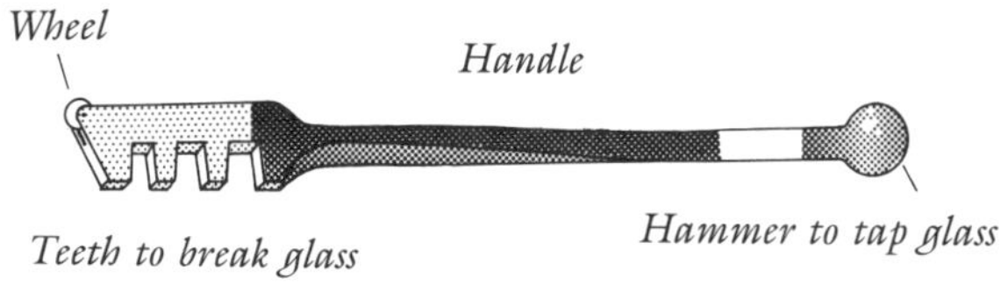
Wheel
Handle
Teeth to break glass
Hammer to tap glass

RED DEVIL AND FLETCHER GLASS CUTTER

OIL GLASS CUTTERS

Oil cutters are good quality and long-lasting tools that should be the first 'good tool', any serious copper foiling or leadlighting student purchases. Both the oil cutters described below are top of the range, but are well worth the money. Should the cutting wheel wear down replacement heads are available.

Pencil grip oil cutter

A self-lubricating Japanese cutter with tungsten steel wheel and a plastic or metal reservoir to hold the lubricating solution.

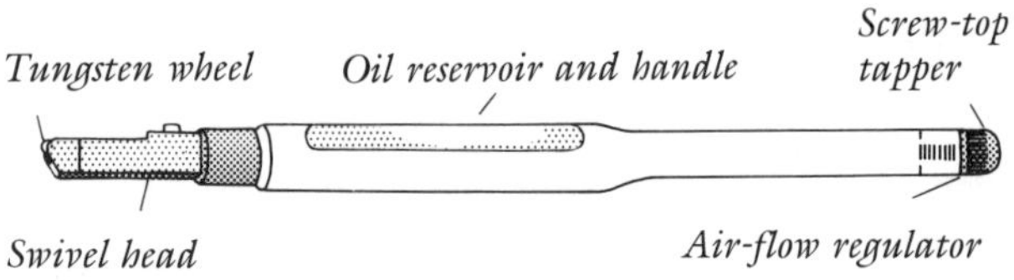
Tungsten wheel
Oil reservoir and handle
Screw-top tapper
Swivel head
Air-flow regulator

PENCIL GRIP OIL CUTTER

Pistol grip oil cutter

*T*his is similar to the pencil grip oil cutter, but with the oil reservoir shaped to fit the grip of the hand comfortably. It is ideal for those who cannot achieve enough pressure to cut the glass cleanly with pencil-type cutters.

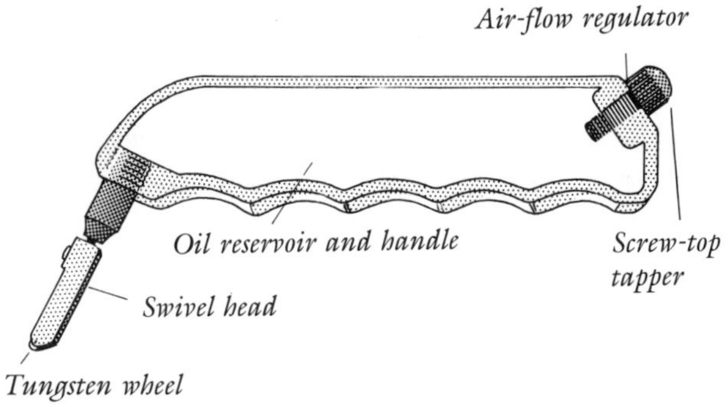
Air-flow regulator
Oil reservoir and handle
Screw-top tapper
Swivel head
Tungsten wheel

PISTOL GRIP OIL CUTTER

GLASS PLIERS

*G*lass pliers are specifically designed for the task of grozing. When the jaws are closed, they meet only at the nose of the pliers so that it is possible to grip the glass on a scoreline without crushing the glass between the scoreline and the edge.

Used as an extension of the hand, they allow you to remove glass too small or too dangerous to grip by hand.

There are several kinds of glass pliers.

Breaking pliers

*T*hese are single purpose tools used only for breaking out scorelines (breaking apart glass that has been scored by a cutter). The smooth jaws render them useless for grozing (nibbling away the irregular edges of the glass).

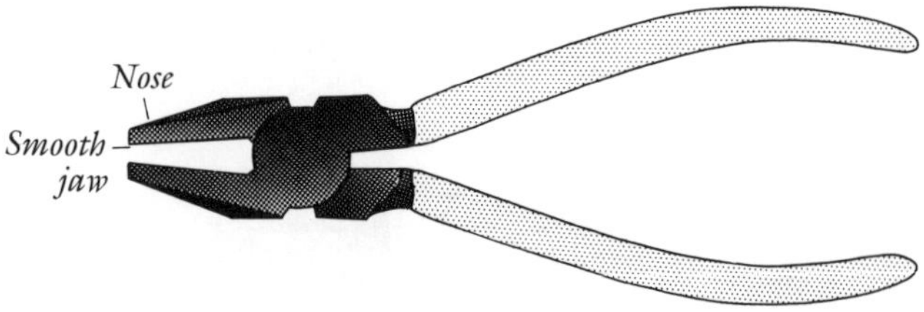
Nose
Smooth jaw

BREAKING PLIERS

Combination breaking/ grozing pliers

*M*anufactured with serrated jaws, these are designed to break out the glass along a scoreline (see breaking pliers), to clean up the jagged edges of some glass and, if used properly, to shape such lines as inside curves. They should be held with the curved jaw underneath.

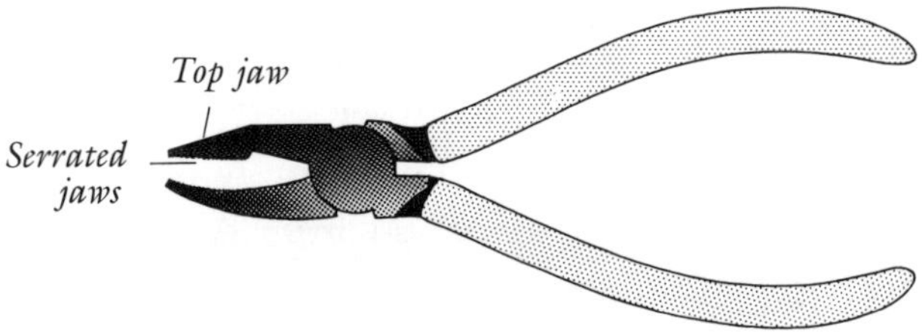
Top jaw
Serrated jaws

COMBINATION BREAKING/GROZING PLIERS

Running pliers *(Snappers)*

*U*sually made of plastic, these pliers are designed to break out the glass after the score has been made. Breaking out glass is made a great deal easier with them because they give you increased control. They work by placing upward pressure directly under the scoreline while also placing downward pressure either side of the scoreline on the upper surface.

RUNNING PLIERS/SNAPPERS

LEAD CUTTING KNIVES

These are required for cutting the lead to size when assembling a leadlight project.

When purchasing look for a knife with a thin tapering blade, without shoulders. Such a shape allows for smoother cutting without buckling the lead and it is easier to sharpen. A lead-weighted handle is also most useful.

All the lead knives below can be bought without a weighted handle, but this means you have to use a separate hammer on horseshoe nails and for tapping glass into position, which involves you constantly picking up and putting down tools. A waste of time.

No matter how expensive the lead knife you purchase, or whatever the shape of the blade, frequent sharpening of your knife is the basis for achieving professional work. Regular application of block stearine flux on the cutting edge of the blade will also aid in smoother cutting.

Note

We recommend that you do not use a Stanley-type knife or razor blade for cutting lead. They are not designed for this purpose; additionally the blades are brittle and are likely to snap and fly off dangerously. They are also difficult to control and there is a good chance that an accident could occur.

Australian style

The knife has a weighted handle and a good, thin sharp blade without wide shoulders. Good for cutting acute angles without squashing or buckling the lead. The weighted handle is made of soft lead and is ideal for tapping glass into place and hammering horseshoe nails into your work surface. A good combination tool.

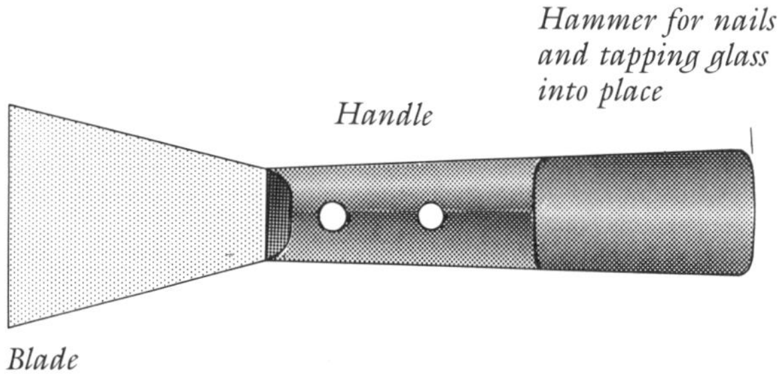
Hammer for nails and tapping glass into place
Handle
Blade

AUSTRALIAN STYLE LEAD KNIFE

American style

Have weighted handles. They are hard to sharpen. The substance used to weight the handle is very hard and tends to break the glass too frequently if used to tap pieces into place.

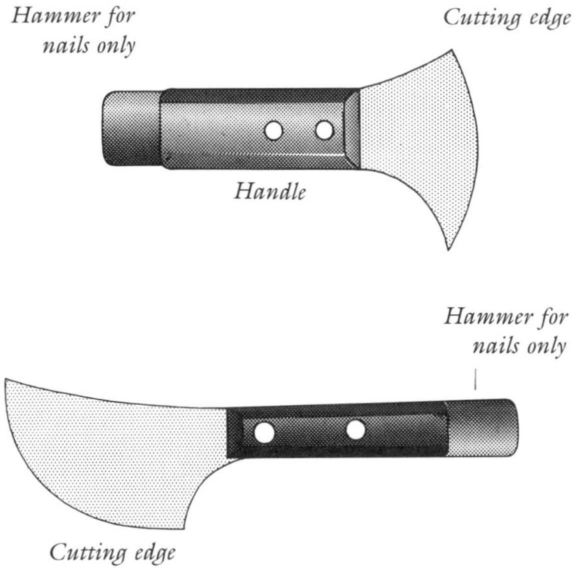
Hammer for nails only
Cutting edge
Handle
Hammer for nails only
Cutting edge

AMERICAN STYLE LEAD KNIVES

LEAD CUTTING PLIERS

This is not as versatile a tool as the lead knife, which we use for cutting lead.

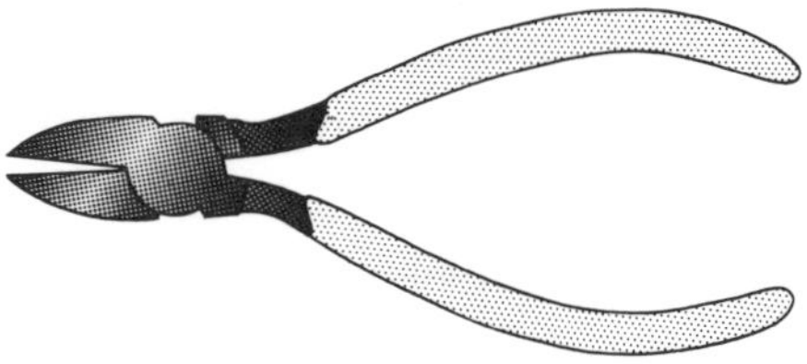

LEAD CUTTING PLIERS

PATTERN CUTTING SHEARS

When cutting glass, two methods are used. If the glass is transparent it can be placed on top of the pattern and the glass shapes cut freehand. However, when the glass is heavy opalescent or very dark, or if a light box is not available, it may not be possible to see the pattern clearly through the glass. A copy must then be made of the pattern. It is cut into pieces with pattern shears and the individual pieces, or templates, are placed over the glass; the glass is scored around them.

The pattern shears, being three-bladed, will remove the thickness taken up by the heart of the lead or the copper foil. The shears are available in two sizes: for copper foil work the third blade removes 0.5 mm, and for lead work it removes 2 mm.

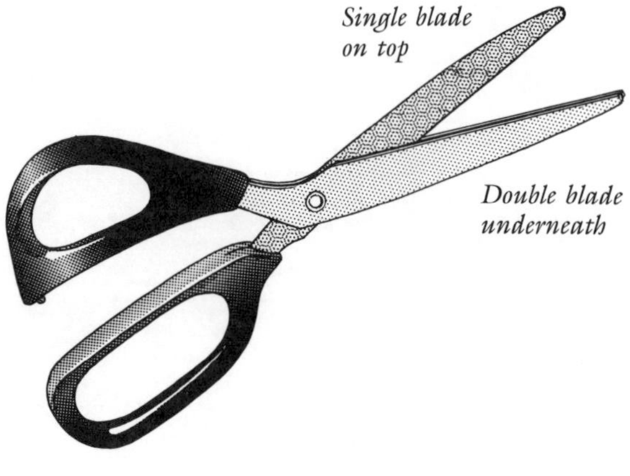

Single blade on top
Double blade underneath

PATTERN CUTTING SHEARS

SOLDERING IRONS

A number of good-quality soldering irons are available at leadlighting suppliers. Irrespective of the brand, an 80-watt iron is ideal for both copper foil and leadlight work. Look for easy maintenance when purchasing (e.g. check for removable tips and on the availability of replacement parts). Some irons tend to be too heavy and cumbersome for easy use. We find that a bent tip is invaluable when leadlighting – your supplier may be able to bend the tip for you if he only stocks straight tips.

We illustrate two irons here, but there are others just as good.

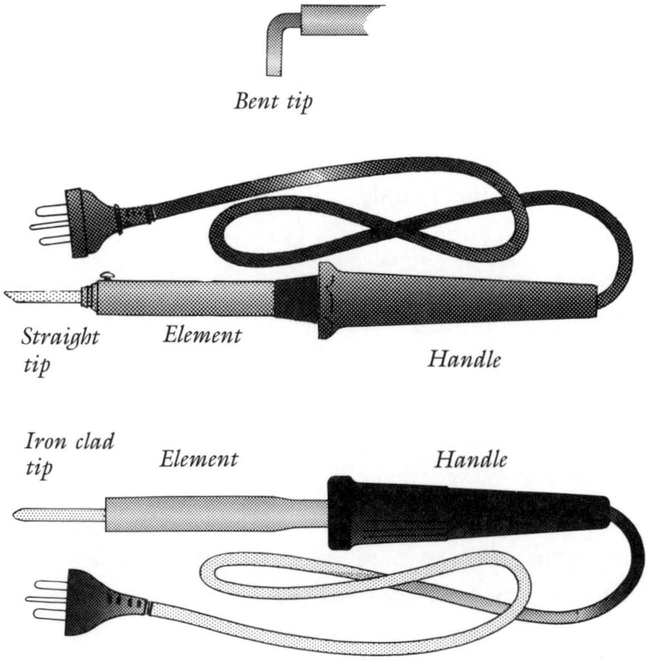

Bent tip
Straight tip
Element
Handle
Iron clad tip
Element
Handle

SOLDERING IRONS

LEAD VICE

Used to grip one end of the lead while the other is held with pliers and stretched.

Feed at least 50 mm of lead into the vice to give the jaws something to grip on to, and remember that the idea is to straighten the lead and not to try to stretch it out. Lead fatigues and

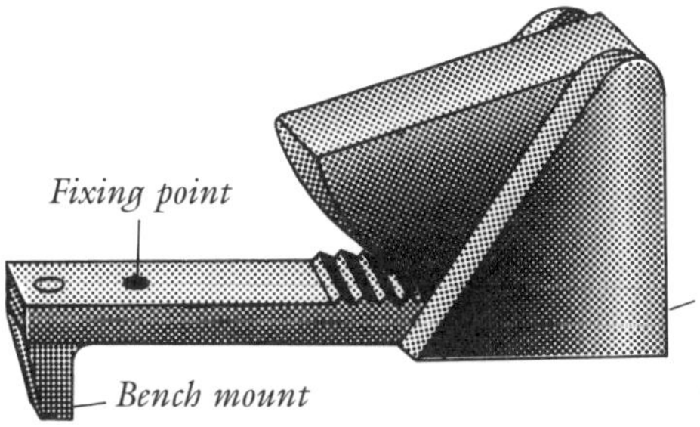
Fixing point
Feed came between base and top clamp for stretching
Bench mount

LEAD VICE

snaps easily, so plant your feet firmly apart while stretching, just in case.

LATHEKIN

A plastic tool used for opening the leaves of the lead after stretching. It is essential that it be used on both sides of the wider exterior window lead came, so that the lead doesn't buckle over while the window is being constructed.

Tip Rub stearine flux on the lathekin's blade so that it slips through the lead without sticking.

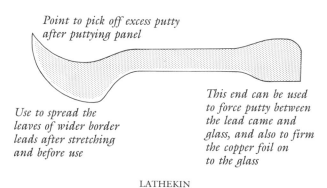

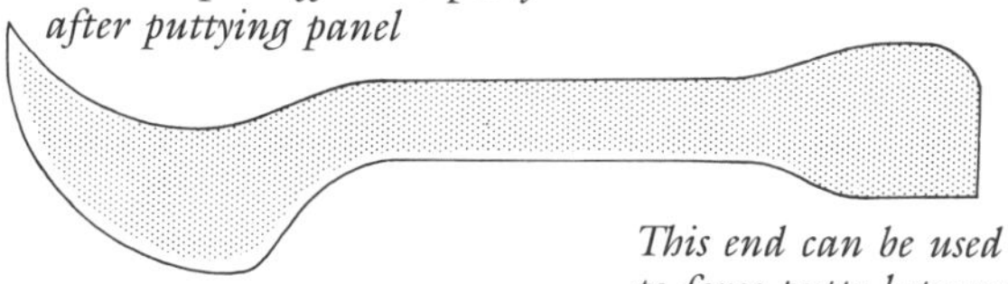
Point to pick off excess putty after puttying panel
Use to spread the leaves of wider border leads after stretching and before use
This end can be used to force putty between the lead came and glass, and also to firm the copper foil on to the glass

LATHEKIN

FOILERS

Hand foiler

A tool used to apply foil to the edge of a piece of glass, automatically centring it.

Foil applied to glass here
Foil feeds in here and backing is removed

HAND FOILER

Glass foiler

*T*his is a great time saver for the serious copper foiler. It accepts all foil sizes, and separates the foil, wraps it round the glass and crimps as you go. These foilers take a little getting used to but, once you master them, they work well. Several brands are available.

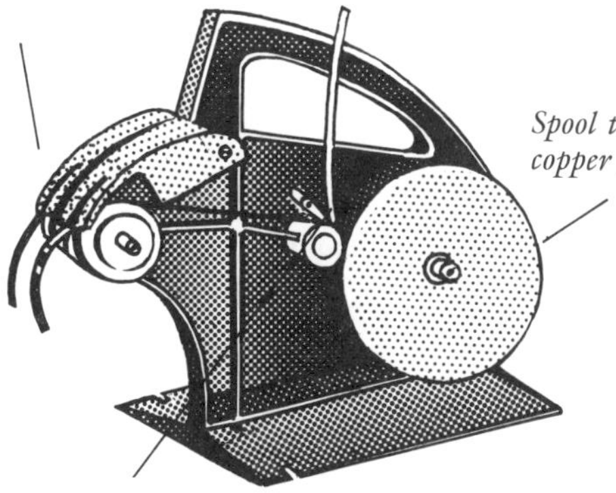
To wrap the pieces of glass with foil feed them through rollers
Spool to hold copper foil
Separation of backing paper from foil

GLASS FOILER

STRAIGHT EDGE
(Non-slip rule)

*T*hese felt-backed straight edges are great. Cut glass using the high side of the ruler rather than the bevelled side. Practise on some scrap glass to get used to it, then see how much time you save. Straight edges are available in 600–1000 mm lengths.

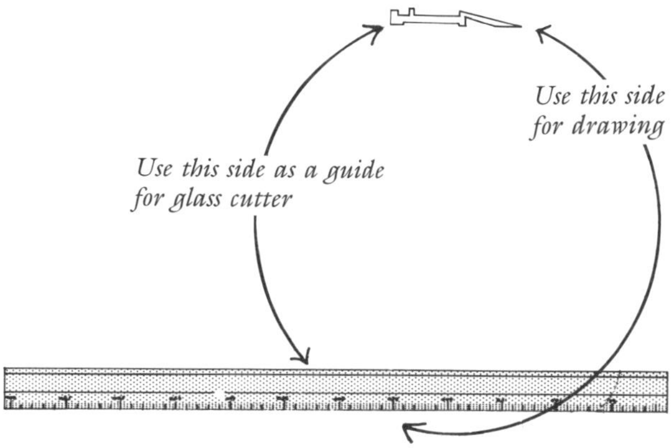
Use this side for drawing
Use this side as a guide for glass cutter

STRAIGHT EDGE (NON-SLIP RULE)

COMBINATION CIRCLE/ STRIP CUTTER

A good quality tool. The circle cutter scores perfect circles 76–610 mm (3–24 in) in diameter. It has a three-pointed non-slip centre base. Remove the pivoting base and insert the guide, and you have a strip cutter effective for repetitive straight cutting of borders, rectangles, squares and diamonds, 12–305 mm (½–12 in) wide. The head comes complete with six interchangeable cutting wheels.

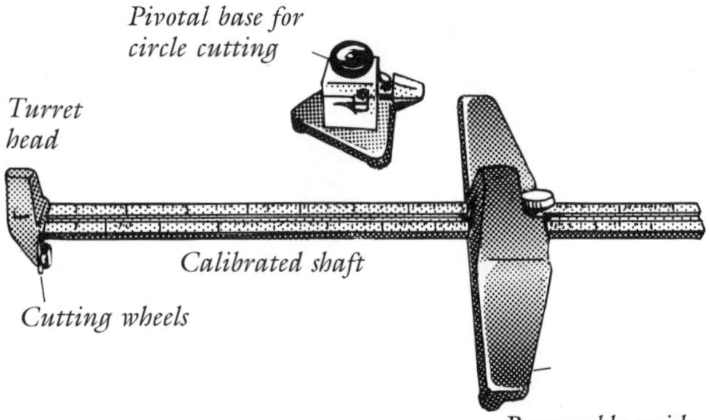
Pivotal base for circle cutting
Turret head
Calibrated shaft
Cutting wheels
Removable guide (for strip cutting)

COMBINATION CIRCLE/STRIP CUTTER

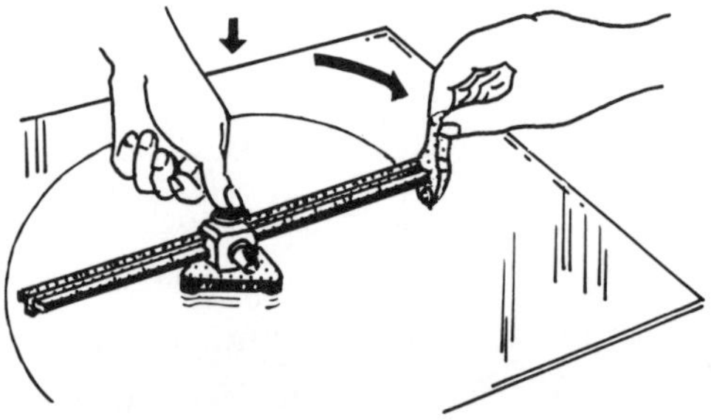

CIRCLE CUTTER

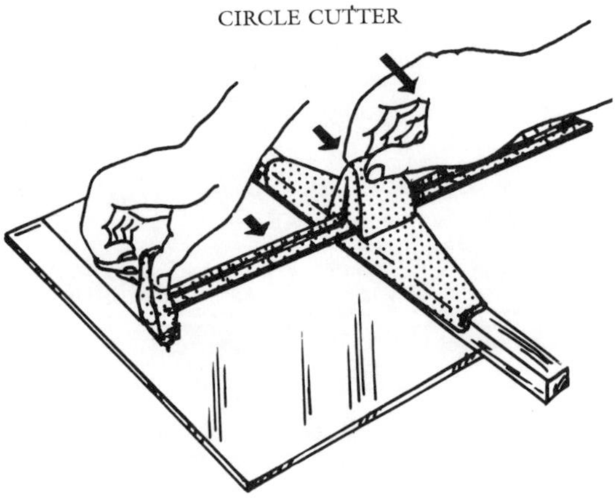

STRIP CUTTER

CIRCLE CUTTER
(Lens cutter or disc cutter)

*U*sed for cutting circles under 152 mm (6 in) diameter. The cutter pivots on a suction cap that should be moistened before being placed on the glass. It is a handy tool if your work requires you to cut more than a few circles. The head also comes with six spare cutting wheels.

Teeth for breaking glass
Replacement wheels in handle
Suction pad
Glass cutting wheel

CIRCLE CUTTER

GLASS CUTTING SQUARE

A quick and easy way of squaring off ragged edges. The square anchors against the base of the glass and, being plastic, will not scratch the glass. Cuts to 610 mm (24 in).

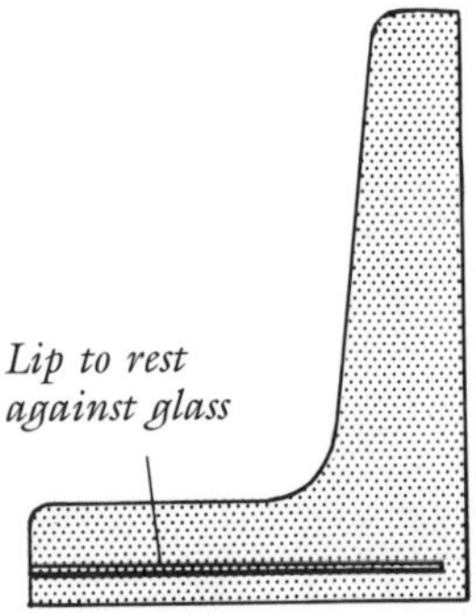
Lip to rest against glass

GLASS CUTTING SQUARE

FLUX BRUSH

*T*o apply liquid flux on lead and soldering fluid on copper foil.

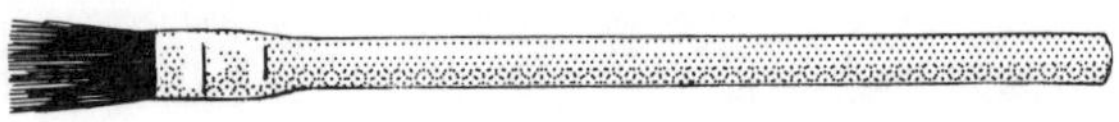

FLUX BRUSH

SCRUBBING BRUSH

A bristle brush is used to remove excess putty and scum from the window after whiting has been applied during the puttying or cementing process. Nylon brushes are not recommended.

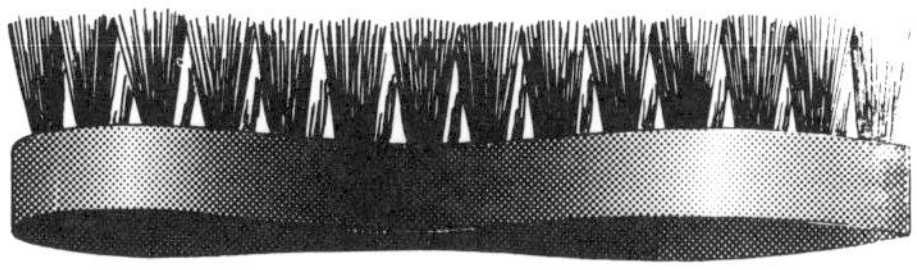

SCRUBBING BRUSH

WIRE BRUSH

*U*sed only in leadlighting. Large or small, use whichever feels comfortable to remove stearine flux from solder joins after soldering and before puttying. Do not use wire brush attachments that fit on to electric drills as they tend to damage the lead.

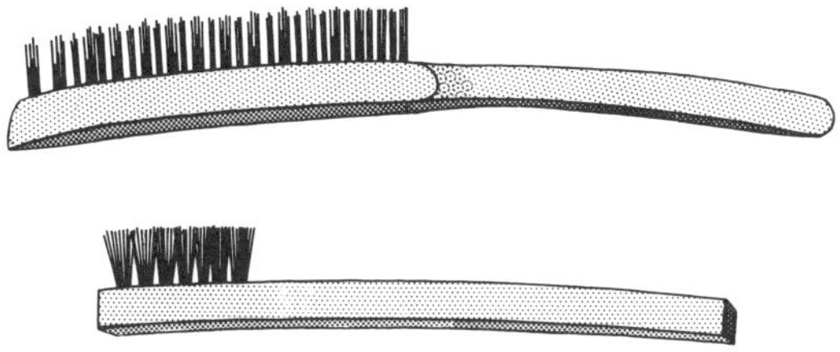

WIRE BRUSHES

HORSESHOE NAILS
(Farrier's nails)

*T*hese are used to hold pieces of glass or lead came in place as the project is being assembled over the cartoon. Their sharp points mean that very little hammering is required to fix them into position and their flat sides ensure that you don't accidentally shell your glass or mark the lead.

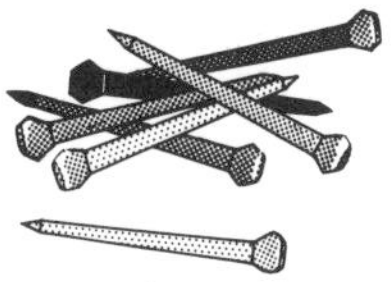

HORSESHOE NAILS

GLASS GRINDER

*A*bsolutely invaluable for the copper foiler and the serious student. As with the soldering irons, various companies produce grinding machines, and they are pretty well all as good as each other.

The grinders come complete with diamond grit heads that, if used properly, will last a long time. There is a sponge behind the head that draws the water up out of a water reservoir and on to the head, to ensure that it is always cool and moist. It is important that the grinding head is always kept moist while in use. Change the sponge frequently as it soon becomes clogged and ineffective. Clean the glass dust out of the water reservoir regularly – it tends to gather under the sponge and lift the sponge above the water level.

We know you will have fun with the grinder.

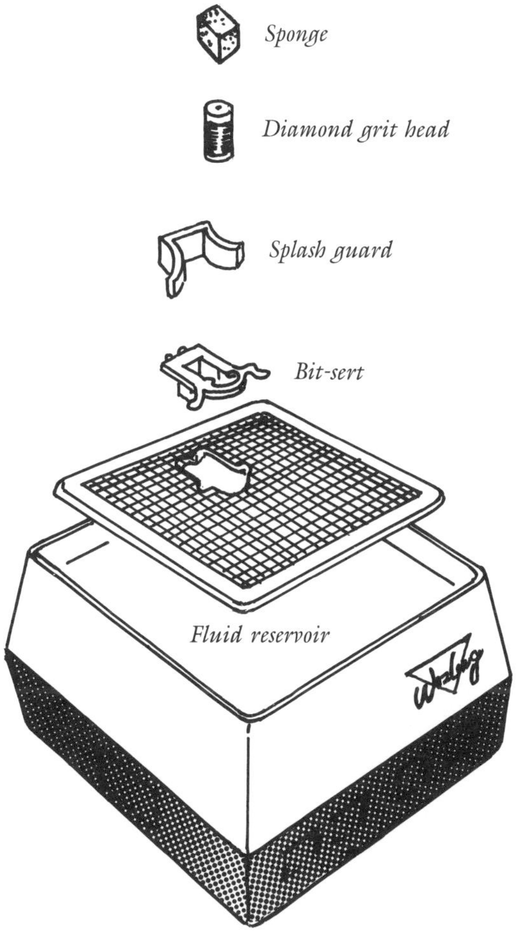
Sponge
Diamond grit head
Splash guard
Bit-sert
Fluid reservoir

GLASS GRINDER

Glass grinder accessories

Replacement heads

These vary in size between 6–25 mm (¼–1 in) for standard grinding. A replacement head is also available for drilling 6 mm (¼ in) or larger holes.

Eye shield

Some form of eye protection should be used when using the grinder. If you do not buy an eye shield then make sure you wear safety glasses. Check with your retailer for the current range of accessories.

GENERAL ACCESSORIES

DIMMER SWITCH

Used by some to keep their soldering irons from overheating. Overheating should not be a problem once you become proficient with your soldering iron.

REINFORCING OR STRENGTHENING BARS (*Saddle bars*)

These are placed at intervals across your design to prevent early wear and tear, sagging and buckling. Bars are generally used for any panel larger than 600 mm (24 in), and the reinforcement is added at least every 600 mm (24 in).

Bars come in varying shapes for differing uses. All windows should be reinforced on the interior side (away for the weather) and preferably across the shortest span. They may be used straight across or bent, to follow a lead line or hidden inside the lead.

Rods

Traditionally made of steel and either soldered directly on to the panel or tied on with copper ties. Used in varying diameters, 6–12 mm (¼–½ in), depending on the span to be covered and the number of rods being used.

Bars

Soldered directly to your panel, edge on rather than face on. Bars and rods are available in steel, brass and copper.

Reinforcing lead

A reinforcing bar is inserted through a specially designed lead came and built into the window while it is being assembled.

COPPER TIES

Used when reinforcing with external saddle bars. They are soldered on to the joins of a window in the workshop, and tied around the saddle bar after glazing.

ETCHING PEN

This pen has a tungsten carbide tip. Ideal for signing your work on the glass.

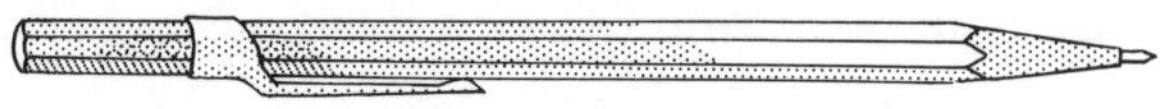

ETCHING PEN

MARKING PEN

A marking pen is invaluable when you are drawing the cartoon. Any brand that produces a line as thick as the heart of the lead came being used is suitable. A thinner pen is needed for the cartoon of a copper-foil project.

Draw your design in pencil first, and when you are happy with the design go over it with the marking pen.

ROD AND TUBE HINGE SET

Copper foil projects can be three-dimensional and many people like to make small jewellery boxes, etc. Hinges are needed for the lid.

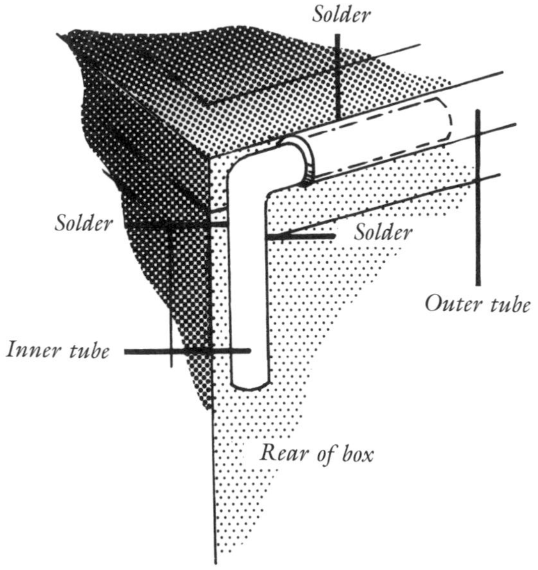
Solder
Solder
Solder
Outer tube
Inner tube
Rear of box

ROD AND TUBE HINGE SET

COPPER FOIL CLOCK WORKS

Clocks are popular projects as they look extremely attractive and are really functional. You first make a clockface using the copper foiling method, leaving a small hole in the centre. The quartz clock movement is thin and fits snugly behind the face. It runs on a single AA size battery. You can buy sets of either roman or arabic numerals in a bright brass finish with an adhesive backing, and hands are available in plain or decorative styles.

Books and patterns are available for making clockfaces.

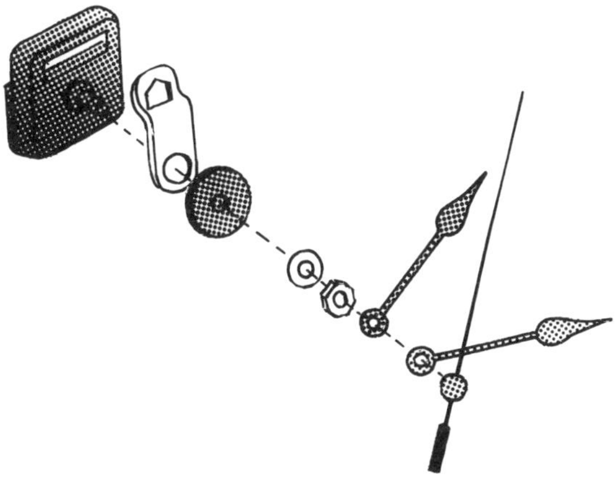

CLOCK MOVEMENT KIT

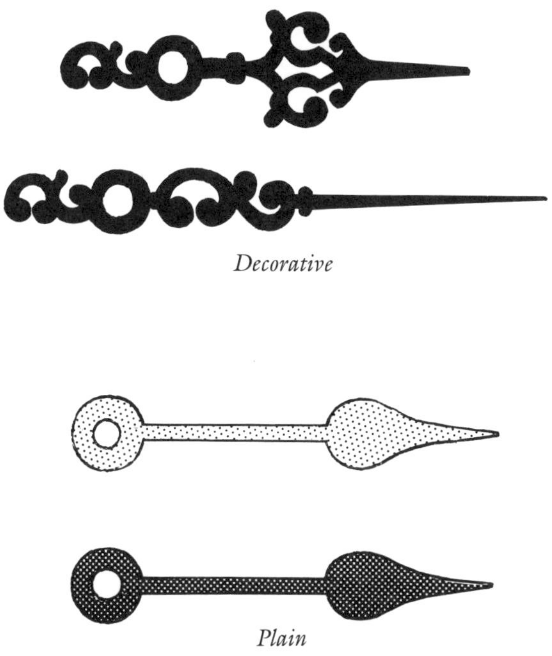
Decorative
Plain

CLOCK HANDS

SELF-ADHESIVE LEAD STRIP

This is used to create a leadlight look without glass cutting or soldering. The adhesive strip is sold in 10-metre rolls, and in widths of 3.5 mm, 4.5 mm and 6 mm.

To apply, first clean the glass thoroughly. Test that adhesion between the lead strip and glass is good (if your glass is cold or damp you may have to use a hair dryer on it before placing the lead). Use the boning tool that is supplied with the strip to firm the lead on to the glass, being especially careful at cross-over points to ensure no air is trapped behind the strip.

This adhesive lead is also suitable for use on mirrors and cabinet windows.

SELF-ADHESIVE LEAD STRIP

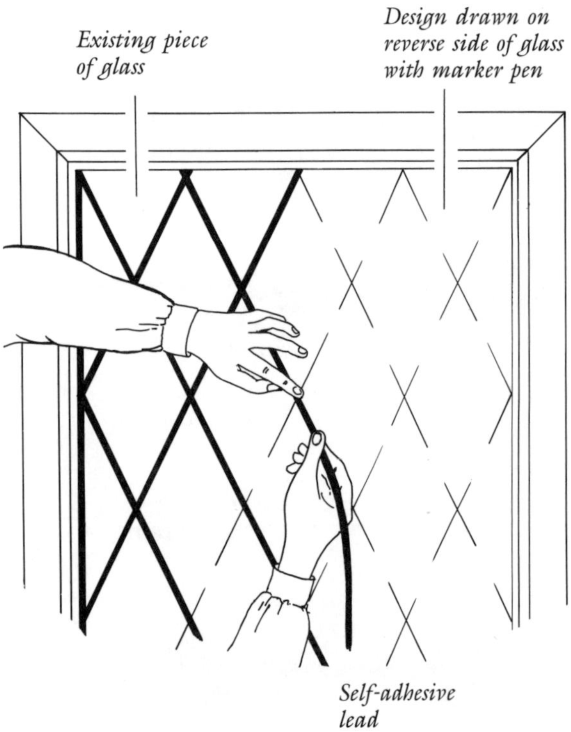
Existing piece of glass
Design drawn on reverse side of glass with marker pen
Self-adhesive lead

SELF-ADHESIVE LEAD TAPE PLACED ON GLASS OVER DESIGN

TIFFANY-STYLE LAMPSHADES

If you cannot afford to own an original Tiffany lampshade (and if you could you wouldn't be reading a 'how to do it yourself book'!), then make one for yourself.

With correctly chosen colours and textures they look absolutely exquisite. You should use only the copper foil method of construction. For the student they are the culmination of your glass-cutting skills and well worth the hours of toil. Given as a gift you have friends for life.

Tiffany lampshades are made using purchased moulds to construct the lampshade's shape. There are two brands available: Worden and Whittemore-Duggan.

THE WORDEN SYSTEM

These lampshades are always constructed over a mould or form. They feature old lamp designs, including original Tiffany lamps, reproduced and adapted to sectional form (mould) construction.

The lamp is made in sections, usually one sixth at a time, over a polystyrene form and the sections are then joined together to complete the shade. A cartoon is supplied for cutting and assembly.

We think the Worden system is most suitable for beginners. A good range of designs, shapes and sizes is available.

THE WORDEN SYSTEM'S SHAPES

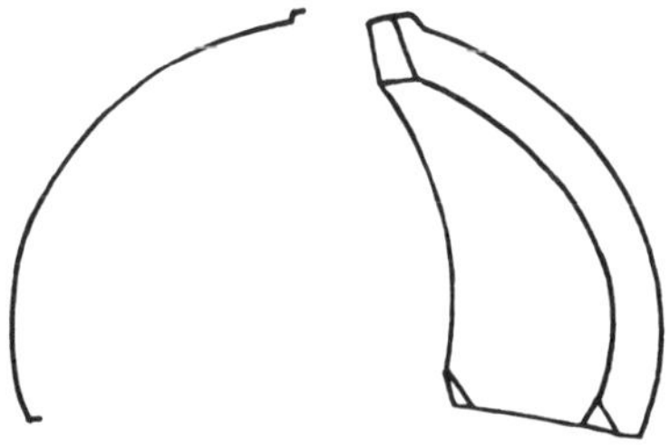

Globe
495 mm (19½ in) diameter
305 mm (12 in) high

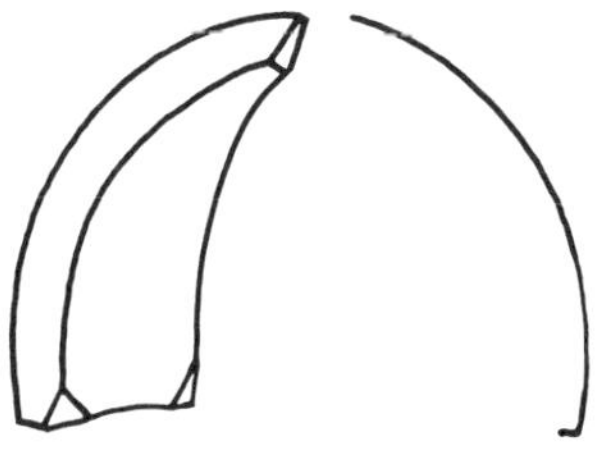

Globe
406 mm (16 in) high
292 mm (11½ in) high

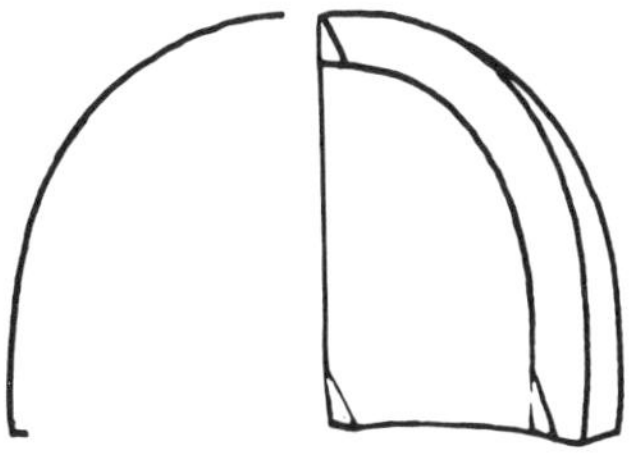

Globe
330 mm (13 in) diameter
254 mm (10 in) high

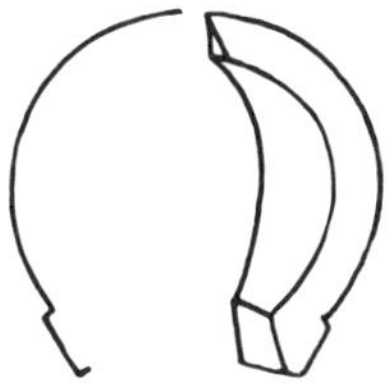

Globe (can be used as terrarium)
292 mm (11½ in) or 241 mm (9½ in) diameter
267 mm (10½ in) high

Terrarium dish
51 mm (2 in) high

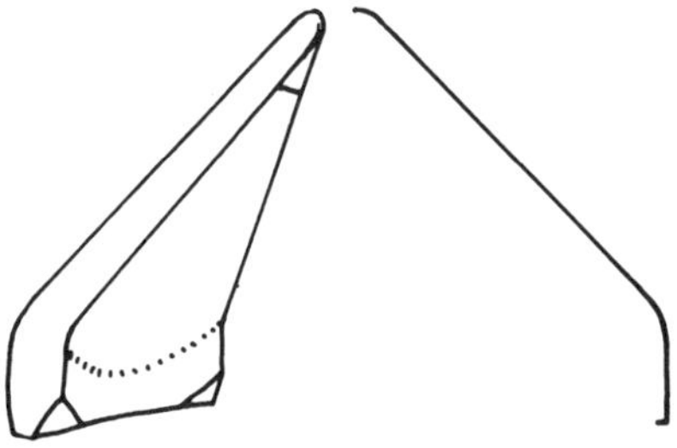

Cone
508 mm (20 in) diameter
305 mm (12 in) high

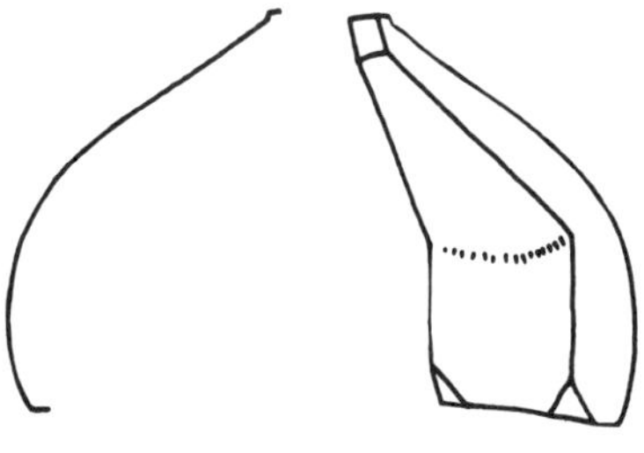

Modified cone
508 mm (20 in) diameter
305 mm (12 in) high

THE WORDEN SYSTEM'S SHAPES

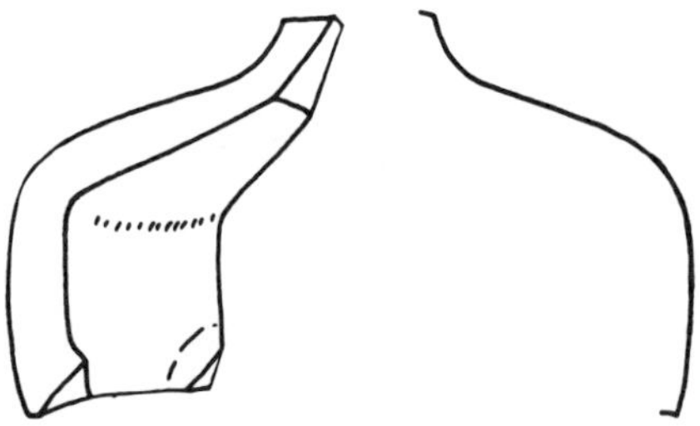

Reversed fruit lampshade
559 mm (22 in) diameter
305 mm (12 in) high

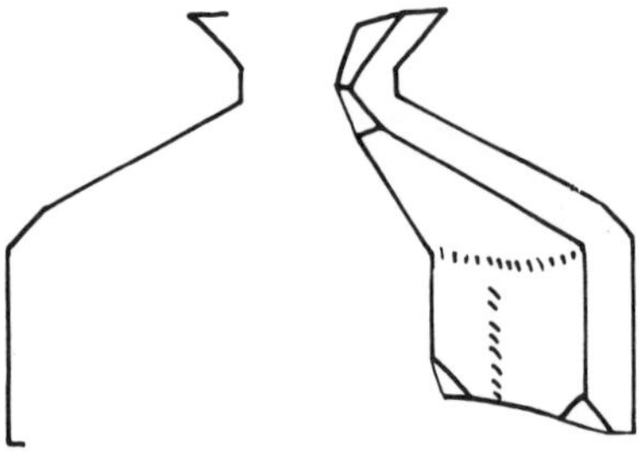

Build-in band and crown
508 mm (20 in) diameter
330 mm (13 in) high

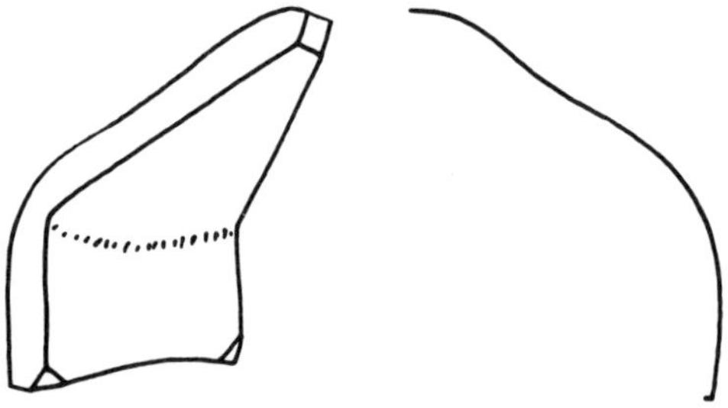

Bell shape
610 mm (24 in) diameter
305 mm (12 in) high

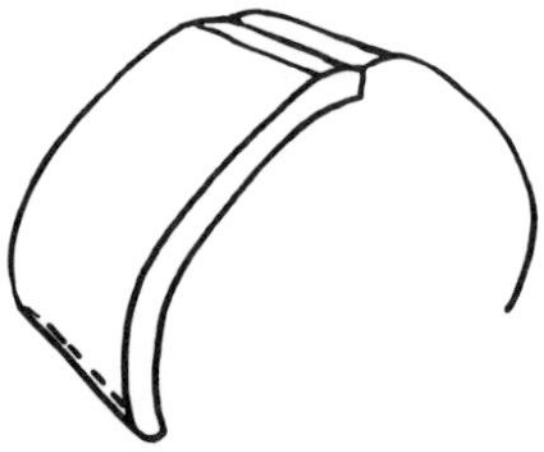

Awning and oblong lamp panel
260 mm (10¼ in) wide

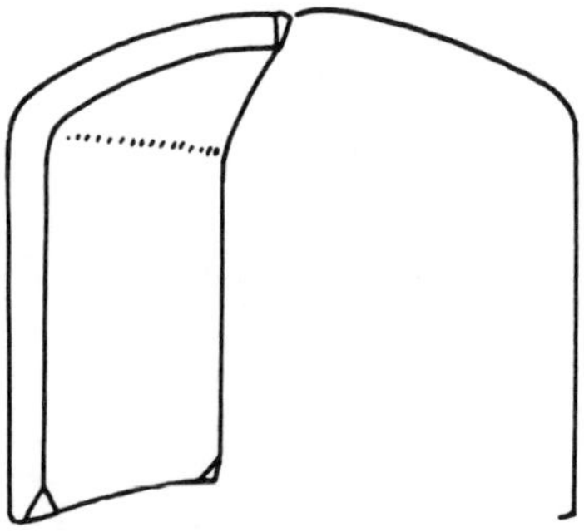

Wisteria shape
457 mm (18 in) diameter
419 mm (16½ in) high

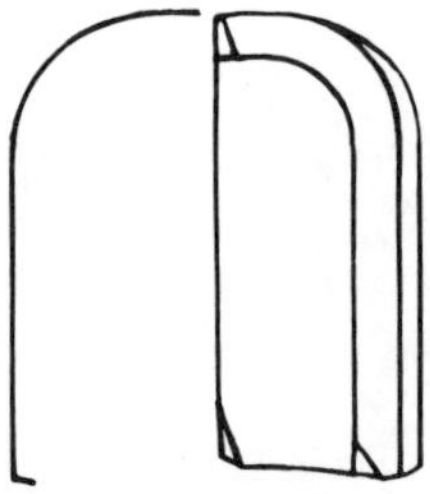

Wisteria shape
254 mm (10 in) diameter
279 mm (11 in) high

THE WHITTEMORE-DURGIN SYSTEM

*U*sing this system, you purchase a sturdy reuseable form, then choose from a large variety of patterns that can be used with that particular form. A copy of the pattern is stuck on to the form for assembly, and another copy is used for cutting the glass.

A full range of both old and new patterns is available.

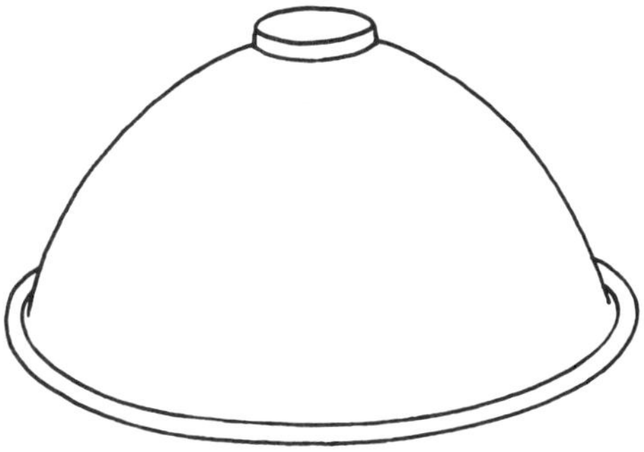

Form no. 2350, 406 mm (16 in) diameter
Form no. 2351, 508 mm (20 in) diameter

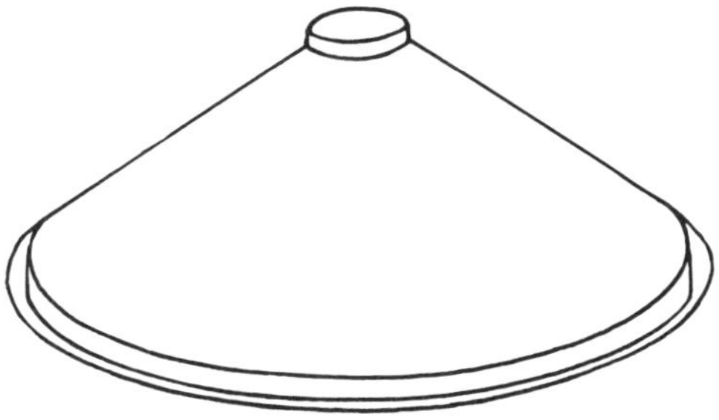

Form no. 2352, 457 mm (18 in) diameter
Form no. 2353, 559 mm (22 in) diameter

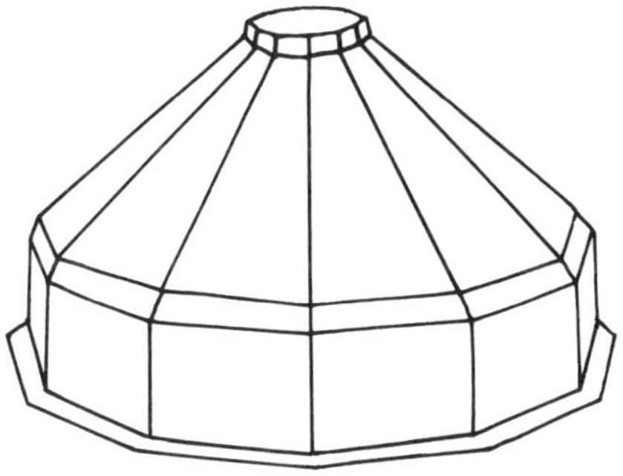

Form no. 2354, 381 mm (15 in) diameter

THE WHITTEMORE-DURGIN SYSTEM

LAMPSHADE ACCESSORIES

LAMP FASTENERS *(Spiders)*

*T*hese come in a variety of shapes and sizes. When soldered inside a finished lampshade they enable the shade to be properly mounted on a base or hung from the ceiling, as required.

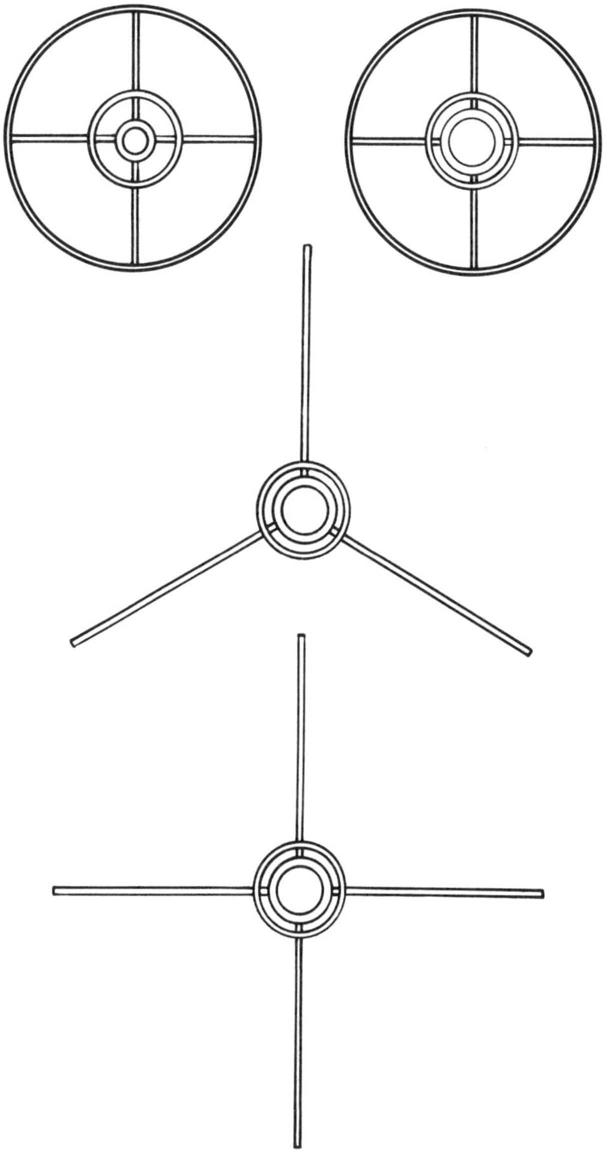

LAMP FASTENERS (SPIDERS)

LAMP HARPS

*H*arps also come in a variety of sizes and are used in conjunction with the spiders to mount lampshades on to lamp bases.

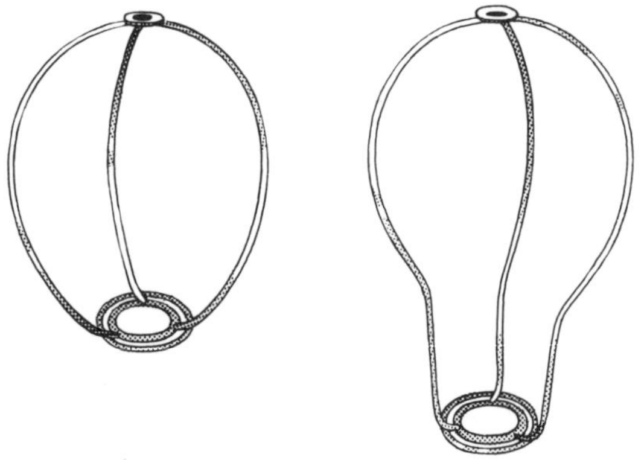

LAMP HARPS

LAMP CAPS
(Vase caps)

*T*hese are for use on lampshades where there is no crown. Available in unfinished brass or copper and can either be used in their natural finish or darkened with patina. Shapes and sizes vary.

Vented lamp caps can also be used where it is considered necessary to allow the heat of the globe to escape through the top of the shade.

Brass lamp caps

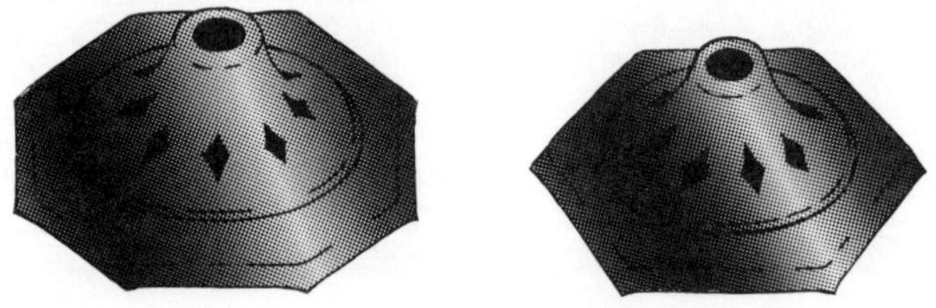

Vented lamp caps

LAMP CAPS

ASSORTED FINIALS, NUTS AND BOLTS

*U*sed to finish and bolt together the various components when assembling a lampshade.

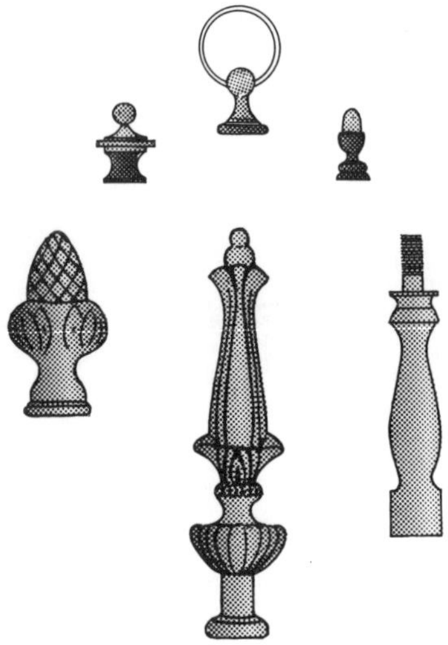

ASSORTED FINIALS

CEILING CANOPY AND CHAIN SET

*T*he set is used for attaching a hanging lampshade to the ceiling. The canopy covers any mess (hooks and wiring) at the ceiling.

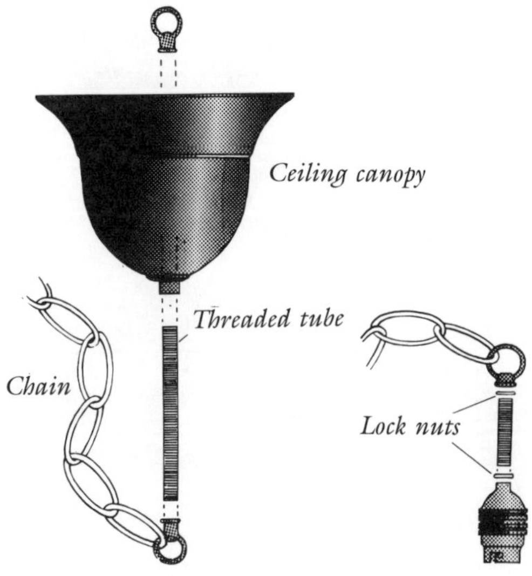
Ceiling canopy
Threaded tube
Chain
Lock nuts

CEILING CANOPY AND CHAIN

2

TECHNIQUES

A Copper Foil Project

*A*s one of the aims of this book is to give more details about copper foiling we have used the design and construction of a mirror with a copper foil decorative surround as an example in the following instructions on techniques. The mirror sits under the copper foil overlay, with both the overlay and mirror being held together in a picture frame.

The techniques involved in making the mirror are the same that are used in making any other copper foil project, so you can experiment if you wish.

Your Workshop

*Y*our workshop does not need to be large, but must be well organised. You need a bench area for working and a separate storage area. The floor should be timber, tiled or concreted for easy cleaning.

The bench should be about crutch height, solid and with a surface of chipboard or particle board. A bench that is accessible from all sides is more useful than one up against a wall. Although our work benches are chipboard we always place another piece of chipboard on top to construct panels on; this can be put away and stored with work in progress if necessary, making you much more flexible.

In the work area you will need a light box, either built into the bench or separate, but if the latter it should be at the same height as the bench. The light box is used for tracing and cutting dark or opaque glass. It should have a 6 mm (¼ in) sandblasted plate glass top, for good diffused light, a fluorescent tube as light source (so the work surface does not become too hot) and the inside of the box should be painted white or lined with mirror.

In the storage area you will require racks for storing glass. Ideally they should be close to natural light so you can check the colour and texture of each piece easily. The racks should be well constructed, and partitioned every 100–150 mm (4–6 in). They should never be crammed full as this results in the glass breaking and scratching.

Different sized lead should be stored separately in a way that means you do not have to pull them

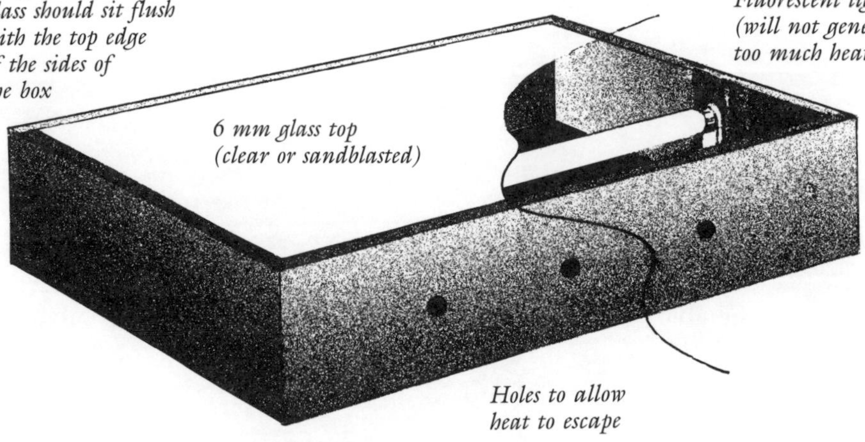
6 mm rebate to rest glass on: glass should sit flush with the top edge of the sides of the box
Fluorescent light fitting (will not generate too much heat)
6 mm glass top (clear or sandblasted)
Holes to allow heat to escape

LIGHT BOX

out by the ends, because they tangle and bend.

Chemicals should always be kept safely out of the reach of children, and should be easily identifiable.

Separate rubbish bins should be used for glass and lead – the lead can be sold to scrap metal dealers, of course. Glass is heavy and the bins become awkward to handle if they are full, so don't completely fill the glass bins.

SAFETY

*M*ost safety aspects are based on good old common sense. We feel it important, however, to list them, and suggest that you read them from time to time to ensure your standard of safety is high.

❖ Wear proper footwear while working and, preferably, an apron.
❖ Use a brush to clean the bench of glass regularly. Do not use your hands to clean surfaces. Try not to stir dust from the floor.
❖ Ideally, dusty work should be done outside.
❖ Wear gloves when handling chemicals and read and follow the manufacturer's safety instructions.
❖ Wash your hands thoroughly after working with lead.
❖ Do not leave glass hanging over the edge of your workbench. If glass drops do not try to catch it.
❖ Be careful when carrying glass. Make sure you are aware of people around you; carry the glass with both hands; hold it vertically and to your side, never horizontally or in front of you.
❖ Do not buy sheets of glass larger than you are comfortably able to handle. Ask your supplier to cut the glass to a suitable size when you purchase it.
❖ When breaking out glass, only go ahead if you are confident. You must be in control of the glass. Never trust to luck.
❖ Switch off soldering irons not in use.
❖ Keep a first-aid kit close to your working area, equipped with suitable treatments for minor cuts and burns. An eye wash and eye bath is useful, as is a mild hand cream, as skin can become dry with the frequent washing necessary.

DESIGNING

*W*hether you intend to make a leadlight panel for a door or a copper foil clockface, the first decision that must be taken is about the design. The third part of this book is full of designs that can be adapted to various shapes, and you might like to use them. You will always need to enlarge these designs to a suitable size. Some leadlight studios and suppliers will stock patterns, too.

We give detailed advice on how to make your own designs in our book *Australian Leadlighting*. If you are intending to design your own window or panel take the time to read it.

You can also copy existing leadlight work by taking a rubbing. Tape some heavy quality paper over the panel to be copied and with a piece of lead came rub over the paper where the leadlines are, and they will show through. You then use a marker pen to ink the lines in and they can be traced on to your pattern.

DRAWING THE CARTOON

*T*he design for your project is called a pattern, cartoon or sketch. It is a full-size working drawing. Use a reasonably heavy weight of paper, one that will not crinkle or distort but that will allow light through for use on a light box if necessary.

Either use an enlarging photocopier to make an existing pattern full size on the paper, or draw

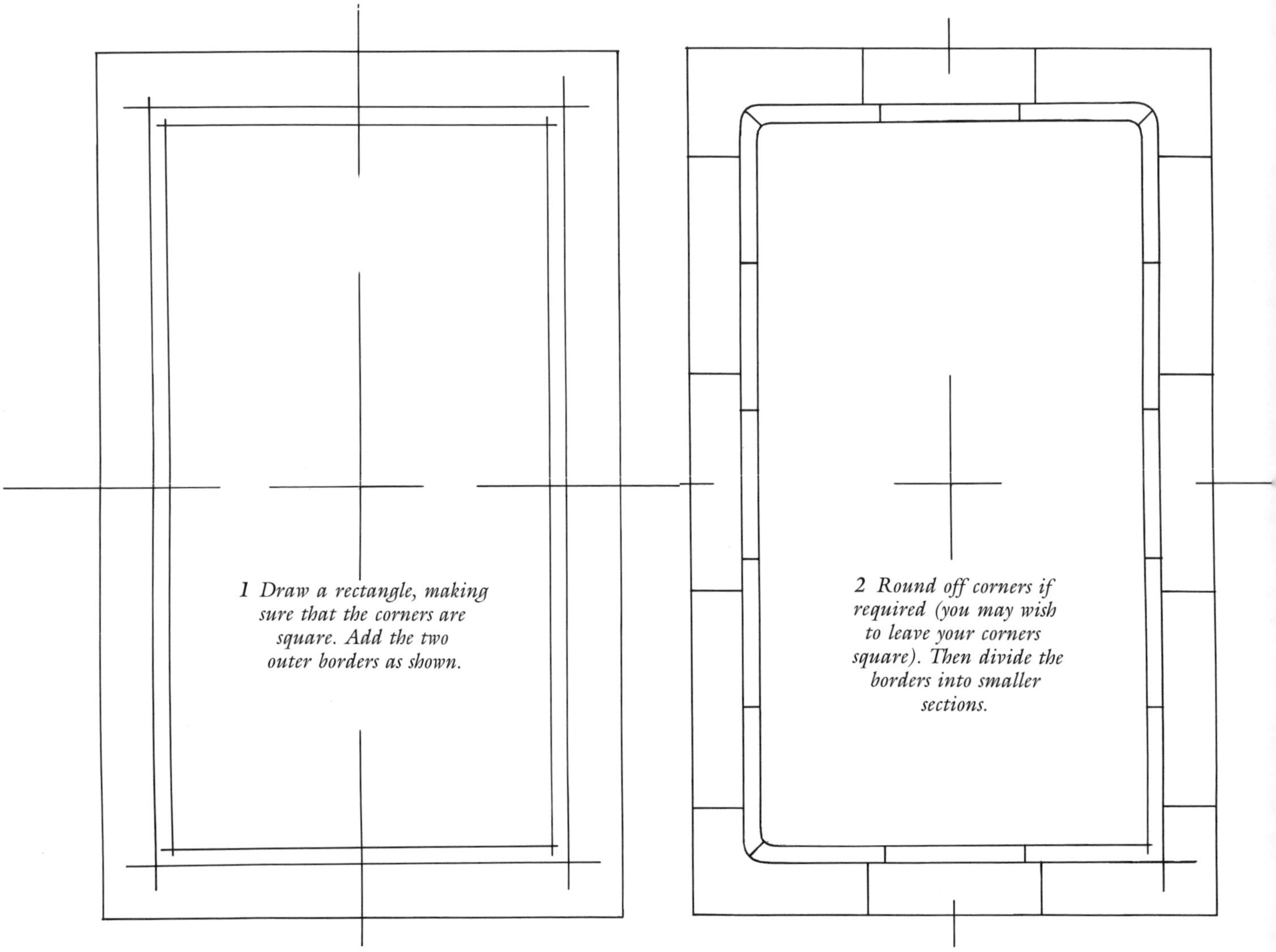
1 Draw a rectangle, making sure that the corners are square. Add the two outer borders as shown.
2 Round off corners if required (you may wish to leave your corners square). Then divide the borders into smaller sections.

DRAWING A CARTOON FOR A COPPER FOIL MIRROR OVERLAY

your own cartoon. If you choose to draw your own the following diagrams show the order in which to proceed. (The same order is usually followed when designing windows.)

Draw your cartoon design in pencil and when you are happy with the result draw over the pencil with a felt-tip pen that leaves a line 0.5 mm wide for copper foiling and 1.5–2.0 mm wide for a leadlight project. The width of this line represents the heart of the lead, or the thickness of the foil. In copper foiling the finer the gap between the pieces of glass the finer will be the finished solder join, as the bead of solder not only has to cover the exposed foil but also the gap between the glass pieces. Remember, however, that no matter how good you are at copper foiling, the widths of the beads of solder in your project will vary slightly – this is normal.

If you need help with the design or are not sure about any aspect of your project, have a word with the leadlight studio where you purchase your material. They should be pleased to help. However, if all else fails, some full-size cartoons are available from The Lead Balloon (many are illustrated on pages 44–50), who also offer a complete design service.

3 Add the leaves and any finer details.

CHOOSING GLASS

Your choice of glass is as important a part of your project as choosing the cartoon and should be a considered decision. It should also be good fun, for the range of colours and textures in both cathedral and opalescent glass is extensive.

Be mindful of how the different colours and textures will react with each other as well as how they may complement the situation in which they are going to be displayed. For example, if you are making a mirror it will probably live on someone's wall or dressing table and thus will not have as much light transmitted through it to show off the glass's colours and textures as would a window.

Most opal and streaky glasses work well in mirror overlays as they do not rely on back lighting to show off their colours. Light coloured glass and heavy textured clear glass can also be used to good effect in mirrors.

Opalescent glass is manufactured in either single or multi-coloured sheets. It can be solid opal, heavily swirled, or light and misty. It is also sometimes available with an iridescent finish on one surface, giving it a look similar to oil on water.

If your chosen glass has a directional pattern running through it and you wish to keep the direction running the same way in your project, when you are buying you must take into account how much waste you may have. You could also think of adjusting your cartoon to make maximum use of the sheet size and pattern direction of the glass.

After choosing your glass for the copper foil mirror project, and before you start cutting it out, place the glass over a piece of mirror just to see what the effect will eventually be when the light is reflected off the mirror and back through your glass. Now is the time to make changes if you are not happy with your choice. Most leadlight shops will not mind swapping your glass over.

GLASS CUTTING

Take your time when cutting and aim for accuracy but, most of all, be in a good mood. If you are having one of those days where nothing seems to be going well, put your glass cutting off to another time and go kick a ball instead. Cutting is done in two stages: scoring and breaking.

SCORING THE GLASS

We give detailed instructions on how to cut glass in our book *Australian Leadlighting,* and suggest that if you have never cut glass before you should read the advice there carefully. However, here are some tips.

- ❖ Use a good quality glass cutter. If you can afford it, buy a cutter with an oil reserve. Otherwise you have to grease the cutting wheel constantly by dipping it in oil.
- ❖ There are various grips for holding the cutter. Choose one that you are comfortable with, but always try to hold the cutter at 90 degrees to the glass.
- ❖ Use an offcut of glass to practise on first. Begin the first score with the glass cutter about 3 mm (⅛ in) from the edge furthest away from you, as if you start right on the edge the cutter often skids off.

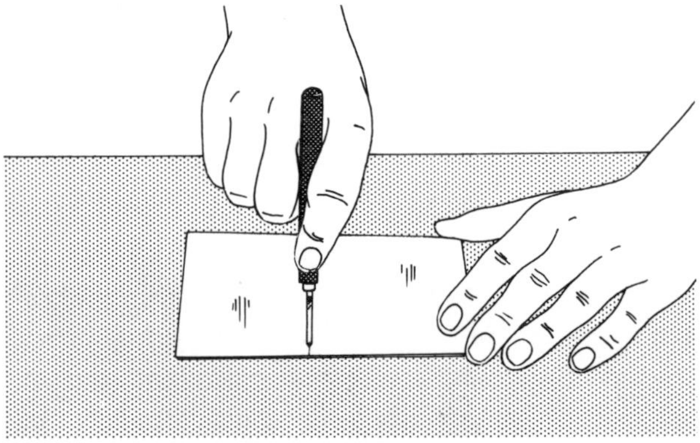

CORRECT GRIP FOR PENCIL CUTTER

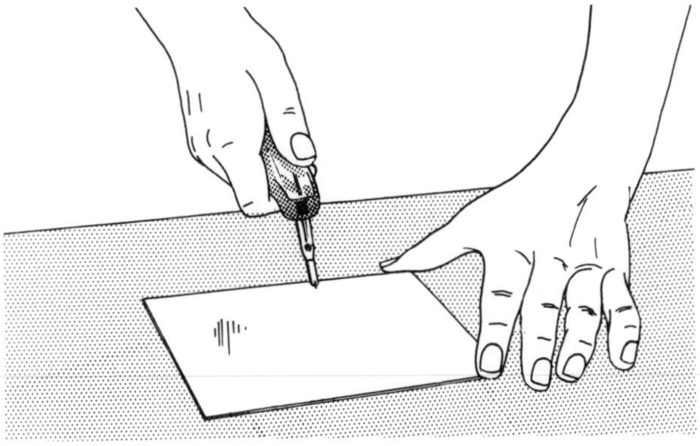

CORRECT GRIP FOR PISTOL GRIP CUTTER

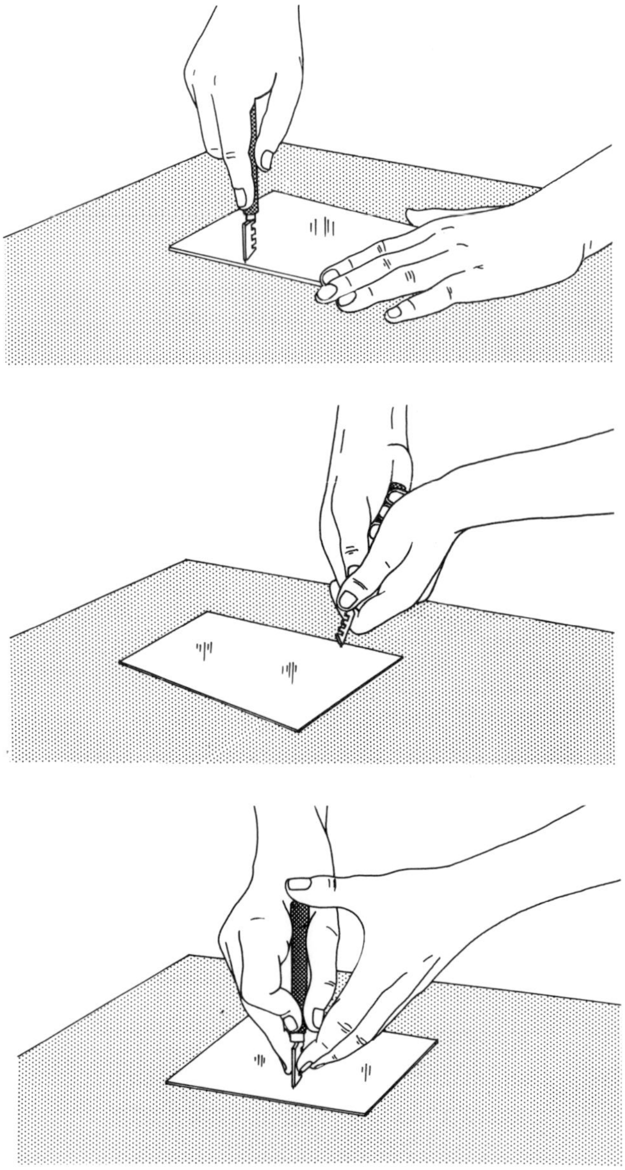

THREE VARIATIONS ON HOLDING A PENCIL CUTTER

- ❖ Draw the cutter slowly and evenly towards you, without stopping until the cutter rolls off the edge nearest you. You should hear a light 'hissing' sound while scoring.
- ❖ A good score should look like a thin, even line on the glass. If the line is patchy you might not have been applying enough pressure while scoring. Regular gaps in the score mean a flat spot on the cutting wheel and it must be replaced.
- ❖ A score that is whiter than normal is a sign you

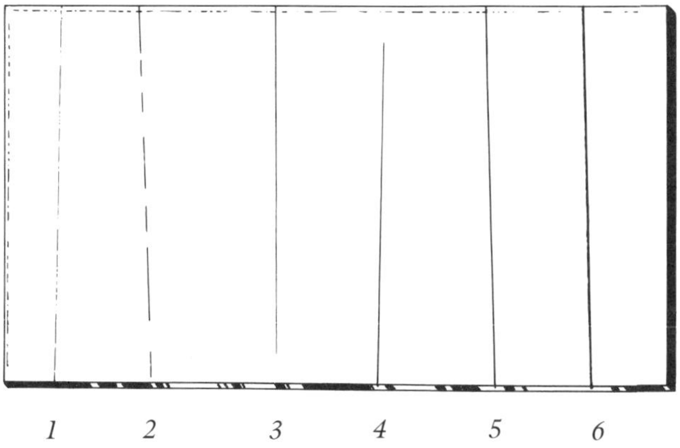
1
2
3
4
5
6

1 Not enough pressure applied 2 Wheel on glass cutter has flat spot – you need to get new cutter 3 Pressure was eased before edge of glass reached 4 Not enough pressure at start of score 5 Good, even scoreline 6 Cutter has scratched instead of scored the glass

SOME PRACTICE GLASS SCORES

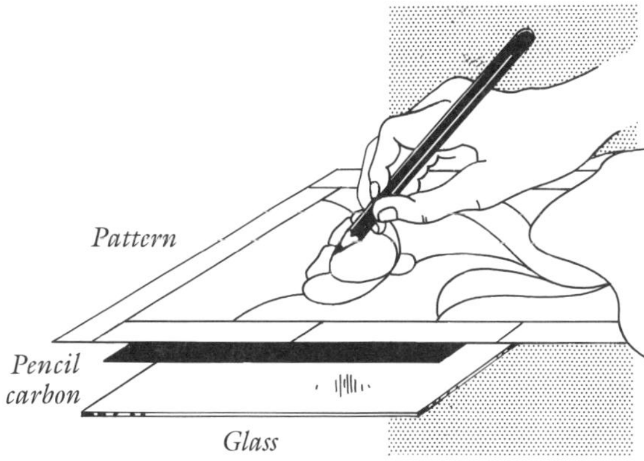
Pattern
Pencil carbon
Glass

Carbon imprint on glass (cut on the inside edge of the line)

TRACING PATTERN ON TO GLASS USING CARBON PAPER

are dragging the cutter rather than letting it revolve, or that the wheel has seized.

❖ Always score textured glass on the smoother of its sides.

Once you have mastered the technique of scoring using scrap glass you are ready for the real thing. If you are cutting straight lines you will be able to use a straight edge as a guide (see Catalogue), while for circles you can use a circle cutter.

There are three methods of cutting the pieces of glass to the cartoon's shapes: freehand (where the glass is put over the cartoon and you just cut inside the line of the pattern); using a carbon; or using a template. If you are using opalescent or darker coloured glass that is difficult to see through and are cutting freehand you will probably need to score your glass using a light box under the cartoon. A 6 mm thick piece of glass as the light box top is a sufficiently strong surface on which to cut the glass.

If you do not have access to a light box you can use carbon paper to make an imprint of the shape you wish to score. First, clean your glass with methylated spirits. Allow to dry and place a piece of pencil carbon over the glass. Position your cartoon on top. Trace the shape you wish to cut out with a pencil – the imprint should be left on the glass. Cut just on the inside edge of the imprint line.

If you prefer, you can use a template and pattern cutting shears. With this technique you need two copies of your cartoon. The first, on thin cardboard, is cut into separate pieces, using the shears, so that you have individual templates of all your glass. Put the templates on the glass and cut round them. You assemble your project on the copy.

Pattern cutting shears are like scissors with one blade on top but two blades underneath. The idea is that the shears remove a thin strip of paper equivalent to the thickness of the foiling and provide you with correctly sized templates ready for glass cutting. Make sure you don't accidentally use pattern cutting shears designed for lead work when copper foiling. These shears will remove too wide a strip from your cartoon and your pieces of glass will all be too small.

Mirror glass can only be cut on the side you see yourself in, and is as easy to cut as clear glass. Cutting squares or rectangles out of mirror is easy using a straight edge and a measuring tape, but for cutting shapes you will need to use pencil carbon or cutting shears, as described above, since you can't see any cartoon through it! Even though mirror itself is easy enough to cut, you must take extreme care that your work bench or cutting surface is very clean and free of glass splinters, etc., as the silvering or backing of the mirror is liable to scratch and mark easily.

BREAKING OUT THE GLASS

*H*aving scored the glass you have to 'break it out'. This means to apply pressure under the score so that the glass breaks cleanly at exactly that line. First practise using scrap glass: make just one scoreline and break it out. Pick up the scored glass by the edge nearest you; hold glass and scoreline as close to vertical as possible, with the scoreline facing away. Clench both hands and place the fingers under the scoreline and the thumbs on top. Keep the knuckles of one hand in contact with the corresponding knuckles on the other hand. Then twist your wrists up and apart, so upward pressure is applied on the scoreline. Your right fist should twist clockwise and the left counter-clockwise. You should now be holding two pieces of glass.

First master breaking out straight scores, then try gentle curves. You can run the break gradually all the way through to the edge of the glass by moving your hands along the scoreline and exerting slight breaking pressure as you do so.

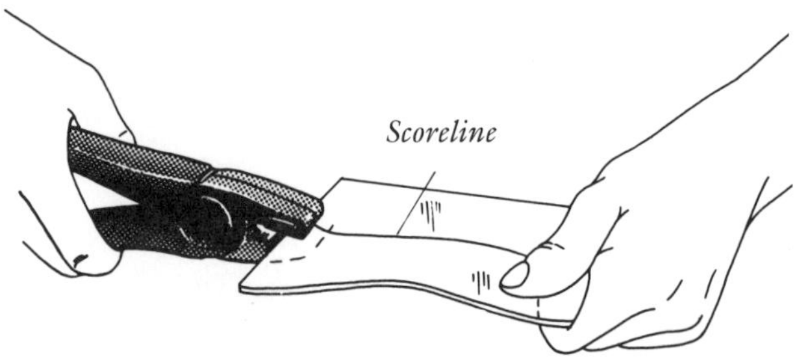
Scoreline
Grip glass so when it breaks in two you can comfortably hold both pieces

BREAKING OUT GLASS WITH RUNNING PLIERS

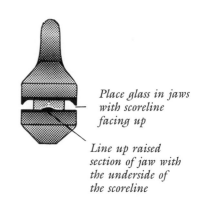

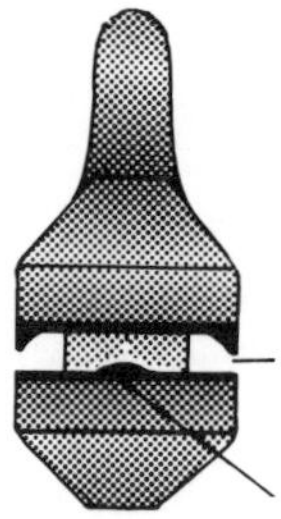
Place glass in jaws with scoreline facing up
Line up raised section of jaw with the underside of the scoreline

RUNNING PLIERS

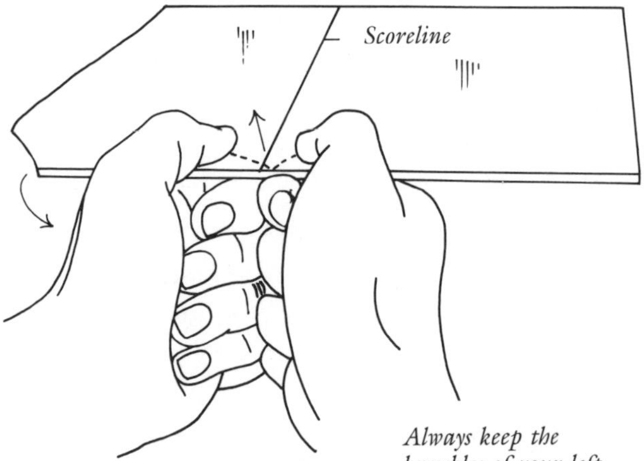
Scoreline
Always keep the knuckles of your left hand in contact with those of your right hand

BREAKING OUT GLASS BY HAND

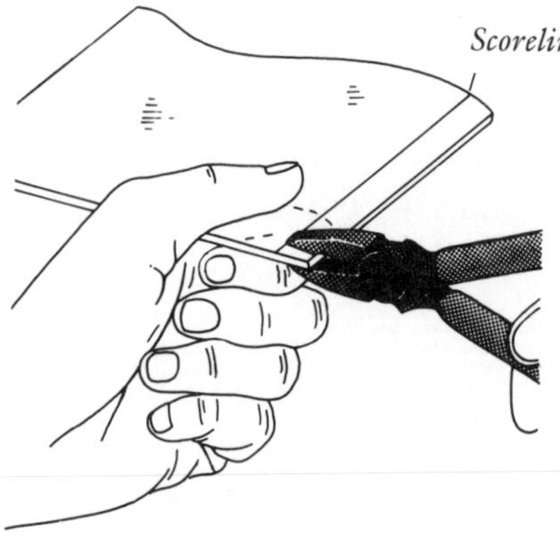
Scoreline

BREAKING OUT GLASS WITH GROZING PLIERS

If you are very tense or unsure about breaking glass out by hand you can use a tool. Running pliers are best for medium or large pieces of glass: hold the glass with one hand so that when the pliers break it out you can comfortably and safely hold both pieces, and apply pressure with the pliers at the other end of the scoreline. To remove a strip of glass thinner than 20 mm (¾ in) use grozing pliers instead.

Finally, for complex shapes you need to tap the glass out. Try to hold the glass either side of the scoreline and tap the underside of the score using the hammer on the reverse side of the glass cutter's head. The break should run in the same way

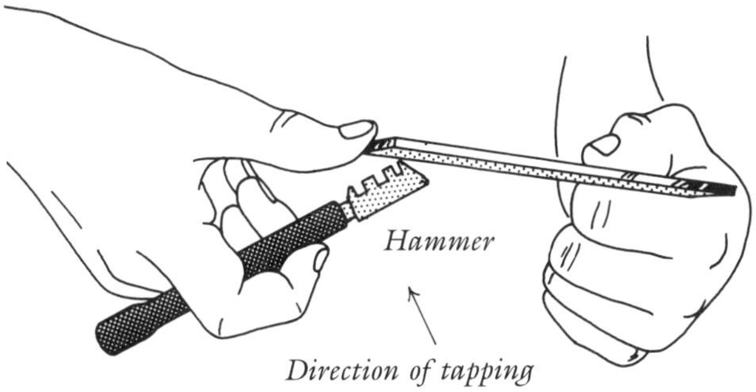
Hammer
Direction of tapping

HOW TO HOLD GLASS AND CUTTER WHEN TAPPING UNDER THE SCORELINE

as it does when hand-breaking gentle curves. Be careful not to try to score shapes with sharp angles, however, as they will not tap out satisfactorily and even if it were possible to produce the glass piece it would be extremely weak and likely to break during the construction of the project.

As you finish cutting and breaking your glass, place the cut pieces back on to your cartoon to make sure they fit reasonably. Reasonably is the operative word. If they are too small, then you must cut them again. If they miss the line by a little here and there, they should be okay. If the pieces are too large you will certainly have to trim them back or, if you are lucky enough to have a glass grinder, you can grind the edges back. A grinder is also invaluable in removing jagged edges, burrs and the like from the edges of your glass. This will also make it a lot easier to wrap the foil around the pieces.

FOILING

Now, clean the edges of your glass. Wipe with methylated spirits to remove dust and, especially, oil deposited from the oil cutter. If you do not clean the glass edges the foil may not adhere properly. After cleaning, if you still have problems getting the foil to stick to the glass, try foiling near a heater or warming your pieces of glass a little, especially if the air is cold or damp; you should find this helpful.

Any mirror glass that is to be foiled should first be coated with a silver protector. Apply the protector to the side and back edge of the mirror before foiling and it will help protect the silver backing while soldering.

Copper foil comprises a roll of thin, ductile copper tape coated with a layer of heat-resistant acrylic adhesive, which is covered by a removable paper backing strip. Once the protective backing is removed, the edge of each piece of glass is wrapped with the foil. The edges of the foil are crimped over onto the back and front of the glass.

Available in widths of 5 mm, 5.5 mm, 6 mm and 10 mm, the copper foil is packaged in 30-metre rolls. The width of the copper foil chosen depends largely on the thickness of glass used. Foil that allows for a 1 mm overlap on each side is ideal, so if you are using 3 mm thick glass for your project 5 mm foil should be used. If you use foil that is too wide, the overlap on the glass will be larger and the resulting seam of solder joining the glass pieces will also be on the wider side; most people prefer thinner seams of solder.

To wrap the foil around the glass, you can either use a copper foil machine, or a hand foiler, or even just your fingers to wrap the foil. Whatever you choose, each piece of glass has to have its edges wrapped in copper foil.

Peel away the protective backing to expose the adhesive side of the foil. Place one edge of your glass in the centre of the adhesive side of the foil.

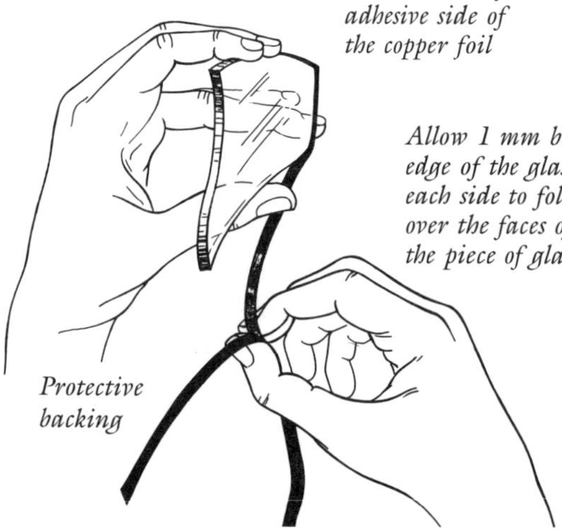
Edge of glass placed in the centre of the adhesive side of the copper foil
Allow 1 mm beyond edge of the glass on each side to fold over the faces of the piece of glass
Protective backing

WRAPPING THE FOIL BY HAND

If you wrap the foil towards yourself, you will be able to look down the length of the glass and foil and it will be easier for you to centre the glass on the foil. Take your time, and wrap the entire outer edge of the piece of glass in the foil, overlapping the start of your foiling by at least 10 mm; cut the foiled piece of glass away from the roll of foil with scissors.

Now, with thumb and forefinger, crimp the foil over so that it sticks to each face of the glass. With your fingernails, pinch the corners so that a mitred effect is achieved. Finally, press the foil down firmly with a plastic lathekin or the handle of your glass cutter. This will flatten any air bubbles.

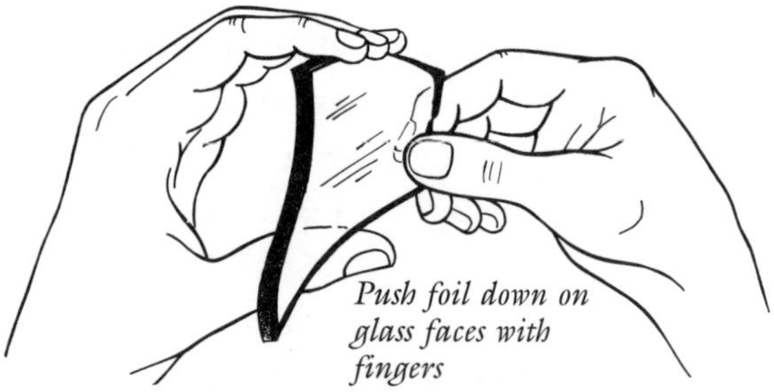
Push foil down on glass faces with fingers

CRIMPING THE FOIL

Take it easy when foiling tight inside corners. If you stretch your foil too tightly it will split, so just nurse it slowly along the inside curves.

It is also easy to break the foil when you are pulling it around the corners of your piece of glass. If you have a grinder, you may like to touch the corners of your glass pieces lightly on to the grinding head. This will lessen the chances of the foil splitting.

Whether you are foiling by hand or using one of the foiling machines, copper foiling will be slow and awkward to begin with, but it shouldn't take you long to get used to it.

ASSEMBLY

You have wrapped all your pieces of glass with copper foil. Now you will need a piece of chipboard – or any flat surface – on which to assemble your work. It should be at least 100 mm longer and wider than your cartoon. If your design is square or rectangular the chipboard should have four timber battens nailed down to form a frame around the cartoon. It is vital the corners are exact right angles.

Begin assembling from the edges, by placing the pieces of glass in their place on the cartoon, then placing the centre pieces of glass in position. For the mirror project, at this stage you only place the copper foiled glass for the overlay, not the mirror base.

If your pattern is a freeform design, then battens will not be necessary. In this case use horseshoe nails (with the flat side of nail against the glass) to hold your glass in position instead.

When you are happy that your pieces of glass fit reasonably on the cartoon, you can begin soldering.

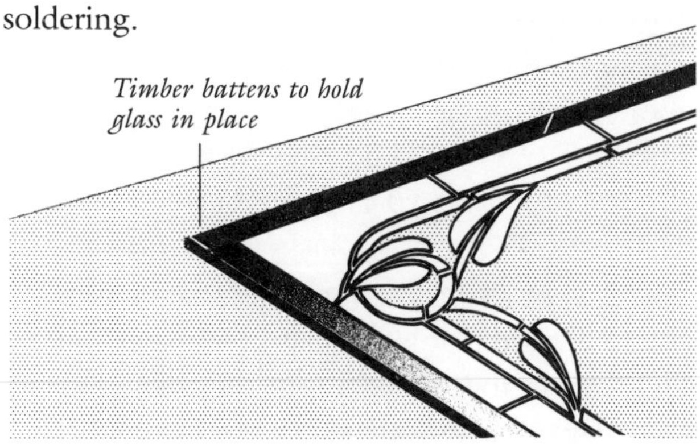
Timber battens to hold glass in place

FOILED GLASS ASSEMBLED OVER PATTERN

SOLDERING

SOLDERING IRON

*U*nlike leadlighting, you will not be able to burn a hole in your copper foil by mistake, so a hotter soldering iron is usually used.

Anything less than an 80-watt iron tends to run out of heat after a while and leaves your solder seams looking rough and pointed, but we find that 80 watts is a useful power level, and recommend it for copper foiling.

Some people use a soldering iron with a chisel-shaped tip and others work equally well with a bent, hook-nose tip. Whatever your preference you must ensure that the tip is kept well tinned and clean.

Tinning refers to plating your soldering iron with a thin layer of solder, which must be done before you can solder properly. First coat the tip of your cold iron with flux. Plug the iron in and allow it to heat. Melt some solder on to the tip and it should flow over the area coated with the tinning agent in a smooth and even manner. Maintain the tinning on your soldering iron by rubbing the tip on a block of sal ammoniac from time to time to remove dirt and other rubbish.

If your soldering iron comes with a pre-tinned or iron-coated tip, then tinning should not be necessary, nor should you use abrasives or tinning agents as they tend to damage the iron coating. Instead wipe the tip of your soldering iron across a damp sponge from time to time to keep your tip clean.

SOLDER

*S*older is an alloy of tin and lead that melts easily so can be used to join two pieces of metal. It holds your copper foiled pieces of glass together.

Sold in sticks or in rolls, the mixtures available for copper foiling are 50/50 or 60/40, the first number representing the tin percentage and the second the lead percentage. 60/40 solder is more commonly used for copper foil as it melts at a lower temperature, solidifies a little quicker and is perhaps a little easier to form into a rounded a beaded join. 50/50 solder can also be used for copper foiling but is more frequently used in leadlighting. Try both and see which one you prefer.

Do not use resin-core solder.

FLUX

*F*lux is an agent that removes any oxide that has formed from the surface of the copper foil, thus allowing the solder to bond to a clean surface. There are many brands available, in either paste or liquid form. You should look for a brand that claims to be not too toxic and that also washes off with water. Follow the manufacturer's safety instructions.

Flux is applied with a small brush or cotton bud to the exposed edges of the copper foil. Try not to use too much. Use it sparingly and you will produce fewer fumes. There will also be less of a tendency for the solder to bubble and spit and leave pock marks if you use minimal flux.

SOLDERING

*N*ow heat your soldering iron and apply solder to the corners of each piece of glass to 'tack' your panel together. This will stop the pieces moving around when you are trying to solder them. Always start tacking and soldering the pieces furthest away from you, working back towards yourself. You are less likely to burn yourself this way.

Once the panel is tacked together, begin soldering. Some people 'feed' the solder under the tip, while at the same time gently moving the soldering iron along the foiled edges; others dab solder onto the joins in a quick, repetitive movement. You use whatever method you wish, but the idea is to achieve a bead of solder that is raised and half rounded along all your joins.

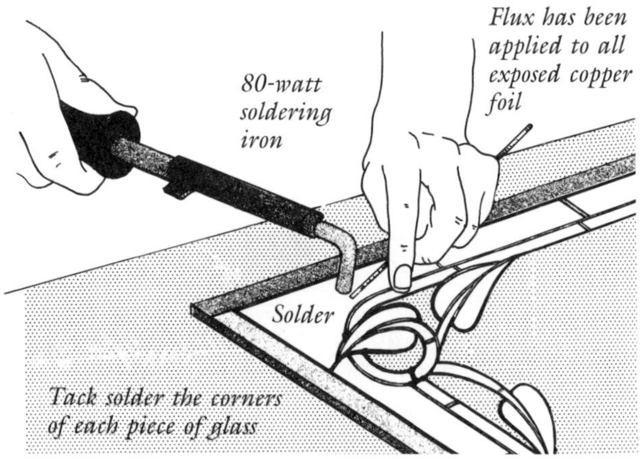
Flux has been applied to all exposed copper foil
80-watt soldering iron
Solder
Tack solder the corners of each piece of glass

TACK SOLDERING

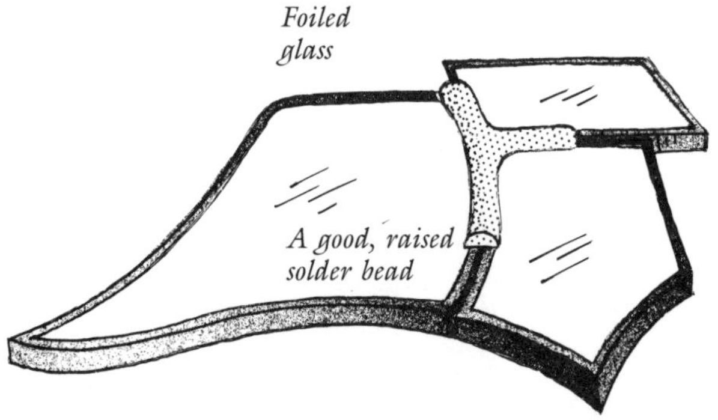
Foiled glass
A good, raised solder bead

SOLDERING

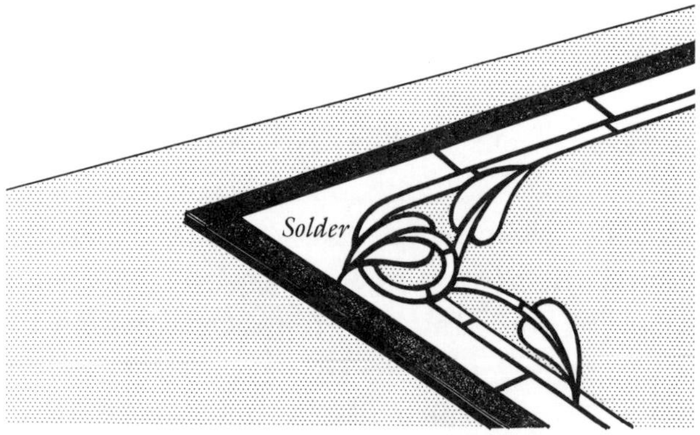
Solder

SOLDERED PANEL

Solder a section at a time, and don't go on until you have completed that section, otherwise you tend to find that you are going to and fro over your work, continually tidying up.

One advantage that copper foiling has over using lead is that if you are not happy with your soldering, you can re-solder without fear of damaging the copper.

Like all new things, it may take a little while to solder neatly, but with some practice you should be all right. Remember that if you have large gaps between your pieces of foiled glass, the resulting bead of solder will also be wide. It is also worthwhile repeating that your seams of solder will not all be the same width. This is the nature of the beast and shouldn't cause you concern. Just do the best you can.

When you have finished soldering the first side, turn the panel over, apply flux sparingly to the copper foil and follow the same procedure as for the first side.

Lastly, coat the outer edges of your panel with solder. It will not be practical to bead the edges, and a thin coating of solder to cover the foil will be sufficient.

If your project is a regular shape (square, rectangle, circle or oval, etc.), a U-section lead came can be wrapped around the outside edge for a neater appearance. The U-section lead should be soldered to your project whenever a beaded join touches it.

Soldering problems

❖ *The solder will not float and form a bead.*
You have not applied flux to this section. Apply flux and try again.

❖ *The solder won't run smoothly and leaves pointed peaks.*
Your soldering iron is not hot enough. If you are using a low-wattage iron (one that is under 80 watts) you may have to pause from time to time to allow the soldering iron to heat up sufficiently.

❖ *You keep applying solder to an area and it seems to disappear through to the other side of your work without beading up.*
It could be that the area you are soldering has become too hot and the solder therefore cannot cool down quickly enough to solidify

and form a bead. You should allow the area to cool considerably and then begin soldering again.

❖ *There is a gap between the pieces of glass that is difficult to fill with solder.*
Don't tell anyone, but plug the hole with copper wire, coat the area again with flux and re-solder.

Cleaning

When all soldering is finished and looking good, give yourself a pat on the back.

The panel now has to be cleaned to remove both the excess flux and the small balls of solder that tend to accumulate on the glass. A good scrub with soapy water and a sponge should do the trick, but remember not to disturb the outer edges of your project.

Rinse with clean water and allow to dry before finishing.

FINISHING

There are several patinas that can be used on your solder to change its appearance. These treatments should be applied soon after you finish soldering so that the solder doesn't have a chance to oxidise too badly. If your solder does oxidise you may have to rub it gently with steel wool before applying patina.

Of course, you may decide to leave your solder in its natural finish. Whether you use a patina or not, the last job is to apply a finishing compound. This will clean and polish both glass and solder and leave your project looking good.

When using patinas, finishing compounds, flux or any of the chemicals associated with copper foiling, be sure to read and follow the manufacturer's instructions and, where prudent, wear gloves.

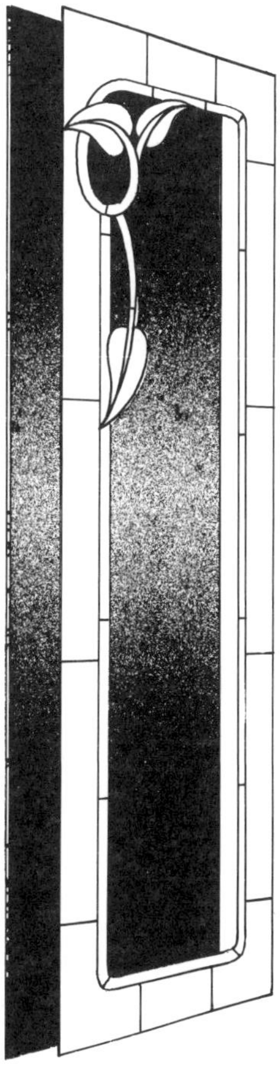
Finished copper foil overlay
Mirror

PLACING OVERLAY ON MIRROR

Now place your finished overlay on top of a piece of mirror the same size, with the textured side of the overlay facing out. Both mirror and overlay can now be fitted into a frame and hung on the wall . . . *Well done!*

COPPER FOIL REPAIRS

It has happened to all of us. You are just admiring your finished project when all of a sudden you see that one of your pieces of glass has cracked. Sometimes the heat from the soldering iron can cause a piece of glass to crack, but not often.

Don't worry, though, copper foil repairs are not too complicated, so you might as well repair the broken glass. First you need to remove the cracked piece of glass. If the project has been assembled you will need to dismantle it. With your glass cutter, score the cracked piece of glass on the smooth side as you would normally. Run your first scorelines away from each corner and then criss-cross the rest of the piece of glass as shown.

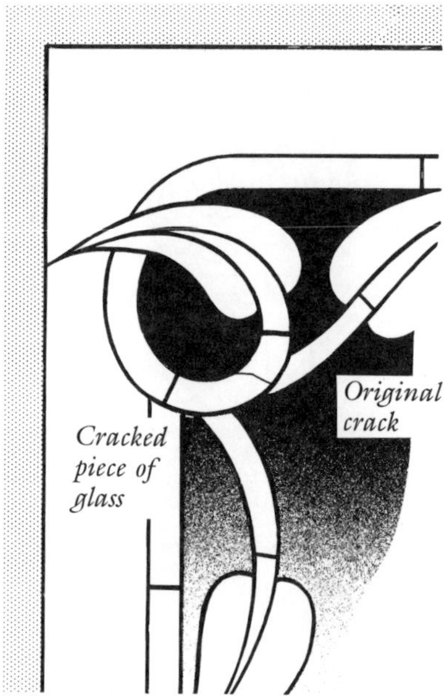
Original crack
Cracked piece of glass

CRACKED GLASS

Next, tap the underside of the glass directly beneath the scorelines. This should result in the glass breaking into smaller pieces that can be removed with your grozing pliers or a horseshoe nail or whatever. Be careful, when tapping the underside of the broken glass, that you don't tap one of the adjacent pieces and break it. Not very good for the sense of humour.

After you have removed all the glass fragments from the foil, you then have to remove the foil that was originally wrapped around the broken glass. Let your soldering iron heat up and slowly run it over the solder bead covering the foil that is to be removed. This should get rid of a lot of the excess solder. Then with your grozing pliers gently remove the foil while at the same time holding the soldering iron on the same piece of foil. Let the heat of the soldering iron separate the foil more than the tug of the pliers.

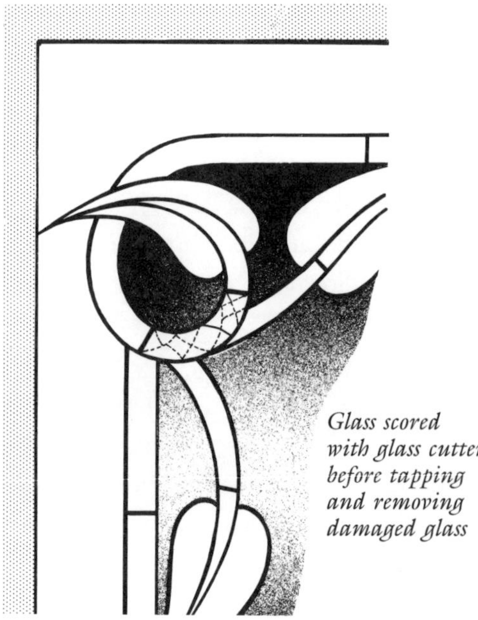
Glass scored with glass cutter before tapping and removing damaged glass

REMOVING BROKEN GLASS

The foil to be removed should slowly part company with the foil wrapping the adjacent pieces of glass. Continue this action until all the unwanted foil is removed, but once again remember not to pull too hard. Let the heat from the soldering iron rather than the tug of the pliers do most of the separation or you will damage the foil wrapping the adjoining pieces of glass.

Now for the new piece of glass. You can cut it using your original cartoon, or by placing a piece of glass under or on top of the damaged section

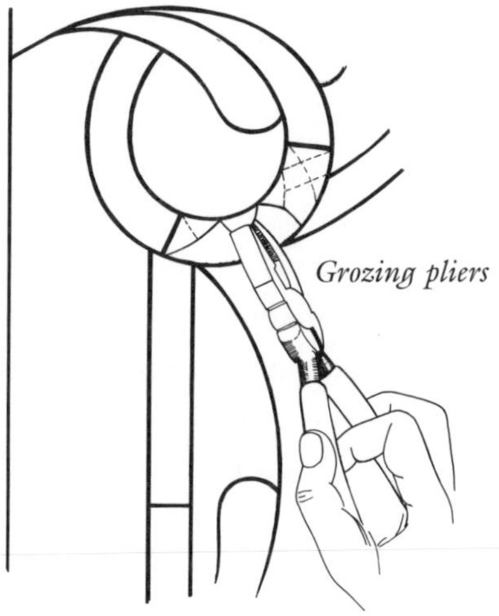
Grozing pliers

USING PLIERS TO REMOVE FRAGMENTS

and tracing the shape to be cut with a Texta pen. Cut the piece of glass, make sure it fits, clean the edges and wrap it with foil. Fit the glass in place and re-solder both sides. Clean the damaged area and reapply patina if required.

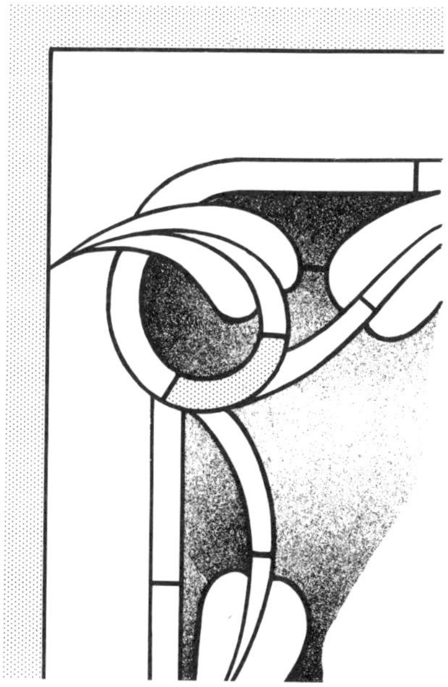

FINISHED REPAIR

THREE-DIMENSIONAL PROJECTS

Copper foiling is ideal for making three-dimensional projects – lampshades and jewellery boxes, for instance – as it produces rigid and strong joins between the pieces of glass.

Leadlight suppliers stock a large range of Tiffany-style lampshade moulds and cartoons. These come with detailed instructions about construction. You will also need lampshade accessories – see the Catalogue section for details, and ask the advice of the retailer.

Small boxes are made by finishing all the sides, top and base first, and then they are assembled. Accuracy is important as all corners must be right angles. The sides are soldered on to the base, and then the top is attached to the back of the box with hinges. Again, see the Catalogue section for details of hinges and how they are soldered on.

Clocks are also popular copper foil projects. The clockface is made to whatever shape is desired, but a small hole must be left in the centre. The clock workings can then be attached to the back and the hands and numerals to the front. Quartz clock workings are slim so the clock face will not stand out from the wall much. The clock is fixed to a wall by a ring mounted on the clock workings.

LEADLIGHTING

We give detailed instructions on leadlighting in our previous book, *Australian Leadlighting*, and so only outline the technique here.

Scoring and cutting the glass is done in exactly the same way as in copper foiling. However, the glass is joined in a different way, using strips of lead came.

All lead and glass is put together over the cartoon. First the outer lead is positioned: lead the length of the side of the project is stretched to straighten it and then cut off; its sides are opened slightly with a lathekin to allow the glass to fit in snugly. It is put against the batten on the chipboard. A second piece is put on an adjoining side. Then the first piece of glass is placed in the corner. Its edge is slipped into the outside leads and it is tapped home gently using the weighted end of your lead knife.

Now place a strip of lead, a little longer than is required, on the edge against which the second piece of glass is to be placed. Insert the second piece and tap gently into position. Trim the lead back so there will be no overhang when the next piece of inside lead is placed at that join. Continue, and in this way piece by piece the glass is joined by the lead 'seams'.

In leadlighting all lead joins are soldered, but not the entire 'seam' as you do for copper foiling. Solid stearine flux is rubbed over the joins and then the soldering is done. As with copper foiling the panel is turned over and the joins then soldered again on the second side. If the project is larger than 600 mm (24 in) in any direction you will have to solder reinforcing saddle bars across the back unless you have already inserted bars as part of the design (you can obtain lead came with a hollow centre through which you put a steel bar for reinforcing).

Now you have to putty the glass into the lead came with cement. This is a messy job, but unavoidable. Force the putty under the lead with your lathekin or thumb. When this is completed clean excess putty off, then spread a small amount of whiting over the panel. Take a scrubbing brush and scrub the window well all over. The lead lines will remain crisp and neat and the excess putty will be removed. Turn the window over and repeat the procedure.

Now store the window for a couple of days to let the putty harden. You can then finish by applying stove polish to the lead and solder to blacken them.

❖

3

Designs

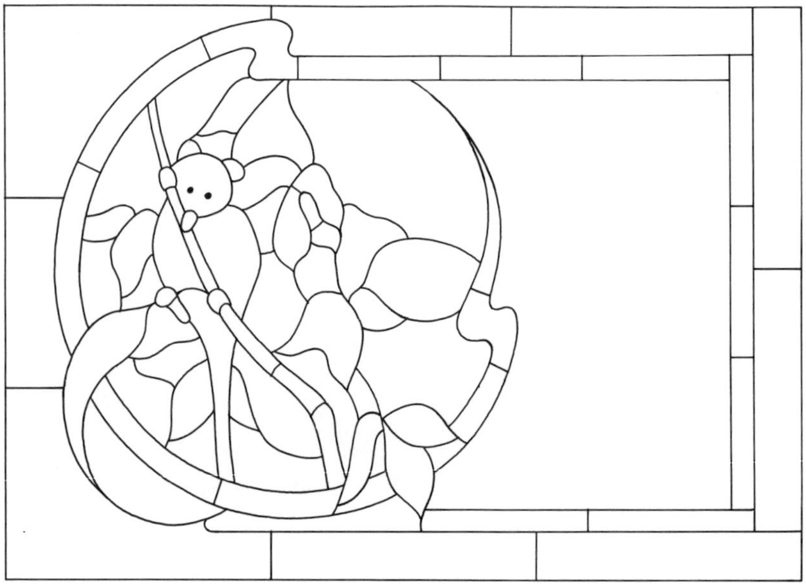

POSSUM WINDOW OR MIRROR SURROUND
(full size pattern approx. 500 x 400 mm)

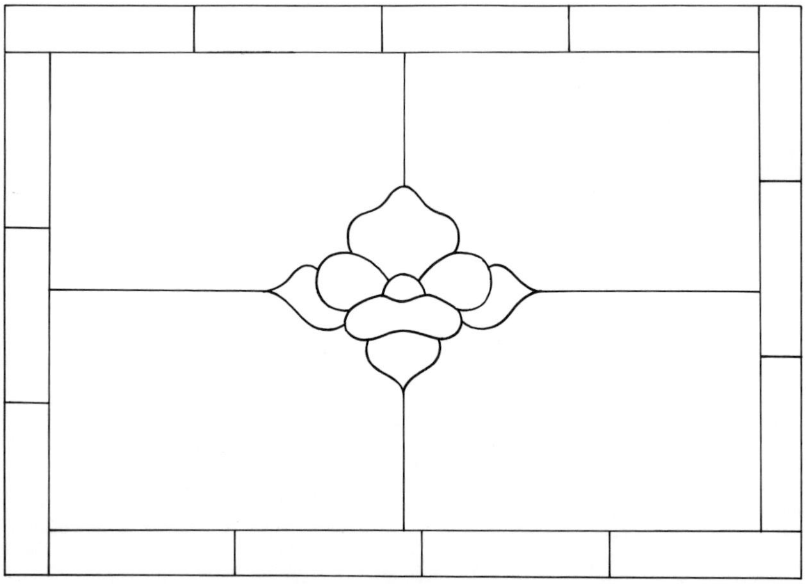

CONTEMPORARY WINDOW OR DOOR PANEL
(full size pattern approx. 500 x 400 mm)

Designs available as full size patterns

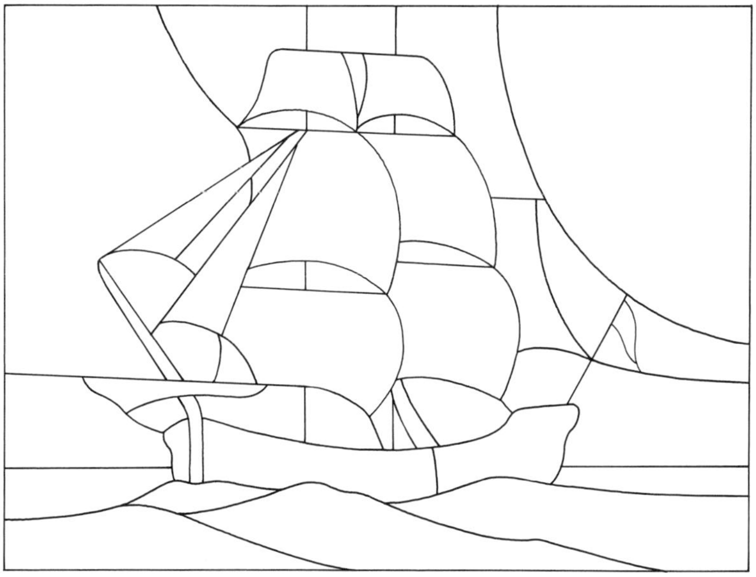

SAILING SHIP
(full size pattern approx. 500 x 400 mm)

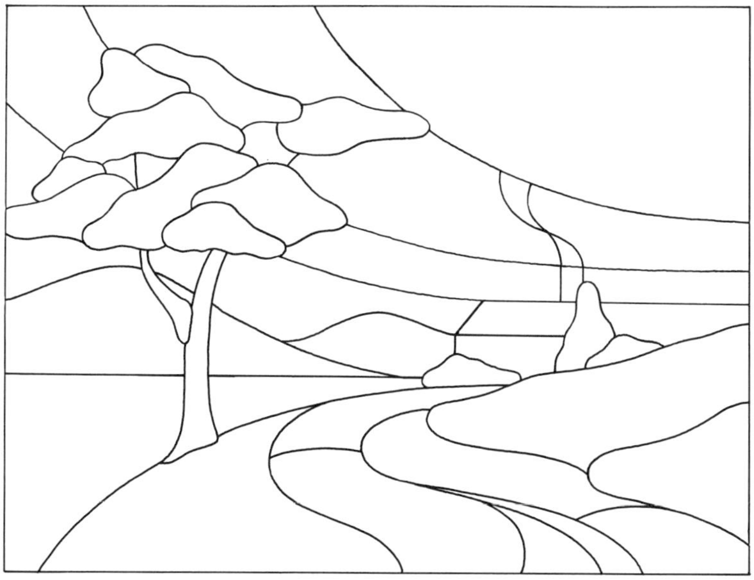

BUSH SCENE
(full size pattern approx. 500 x 400 mm)

Designs available as full size patterns

BUTTERFLY
(full size pattern approx. 400 x 500 mm)

ROSELLA
(full size pattern approx. 400 x 500 mm)

STEVO THE CLOWN
(full size pattern approx. 400 x 500 mm)

Designs available as full size patterns

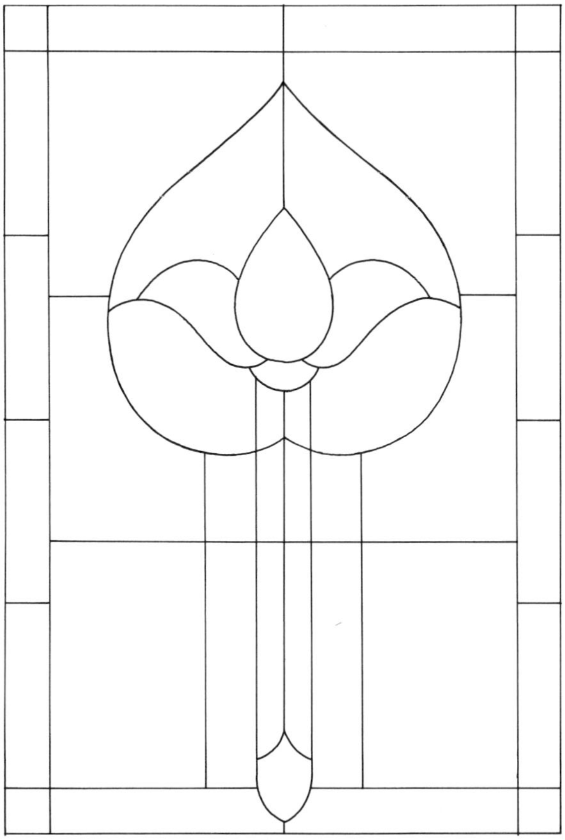

TRADITIONAL WINDOW OR DOOR PANEL
(full size pattern approx. 400 x 500 mm)

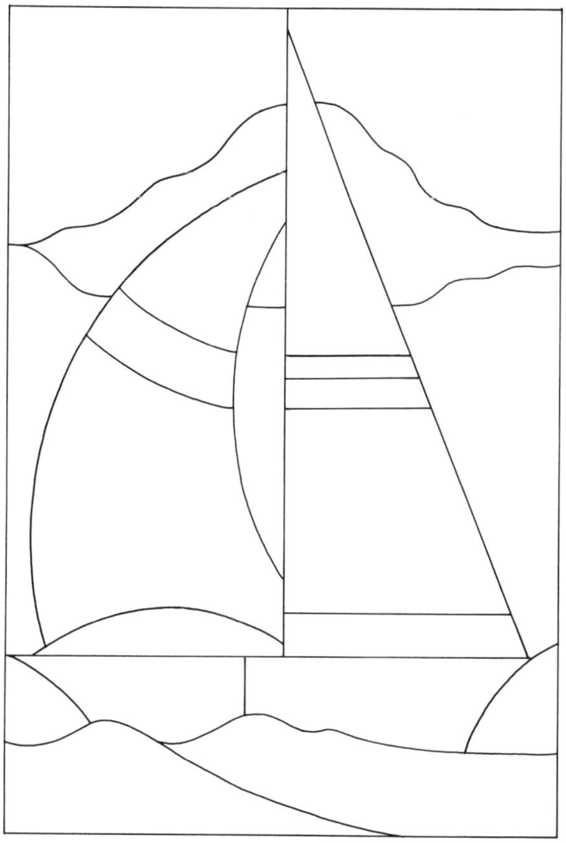

YACHT
(full size pattern approx. 400 x 500 mm)

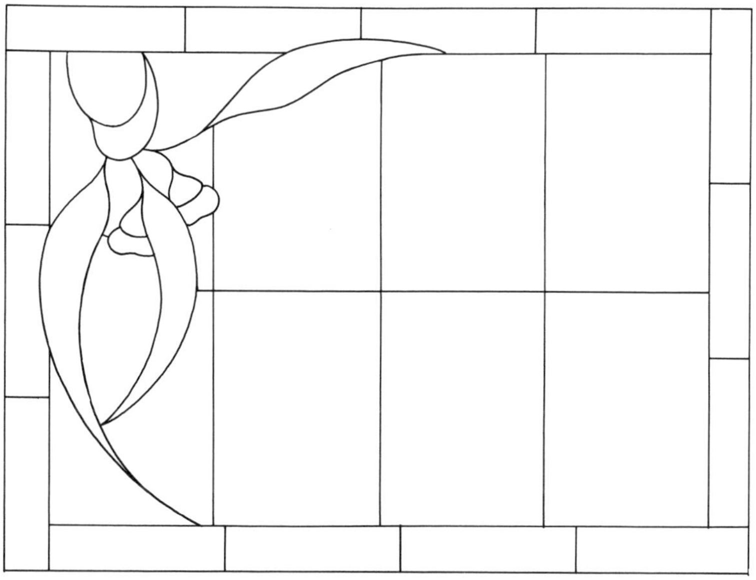

GUM NUT AND LEAVES WINDOW, DOOR PANEL OR MIRROR SURROUND
(full size pattern approx. 400 x 500 mm)

Designs available as full size patterns

POSSUM
(full size pattern approx. 450 mm diameter)

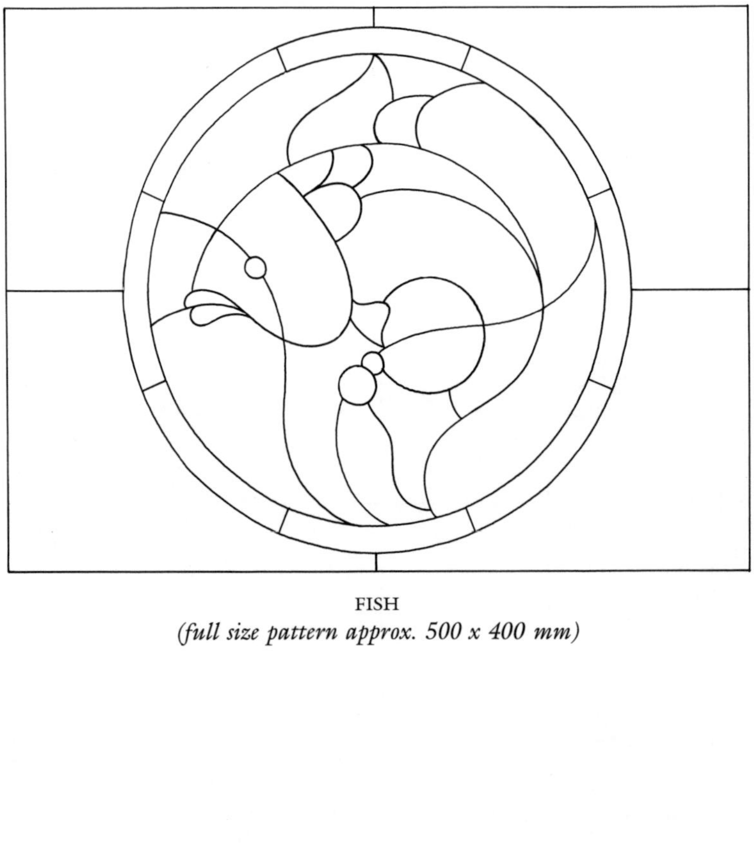

FISH
(full size pattern approx. 500 x 400 mm)

Designs available as full size patterns

MAGPIE
(full size pattern 580 x 910 mm)

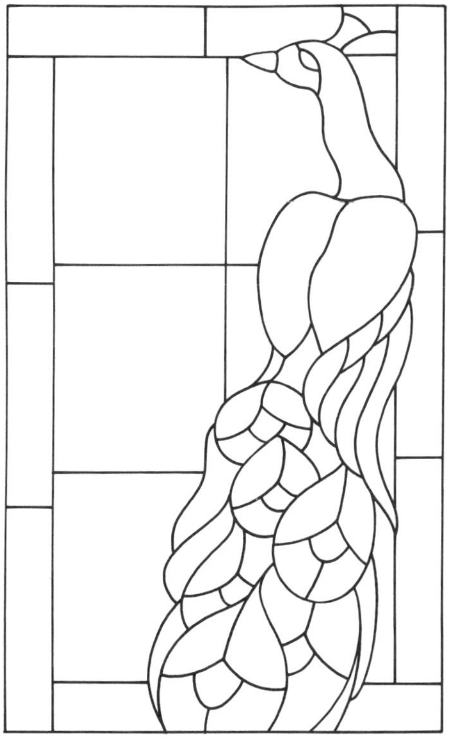

DESIGN SUITABLE FOR WINDOW OR MIRROR
(full size pattern 580 x 910 mm)

JAPANESE LADY
(full size pattern 580 x 910 mm)

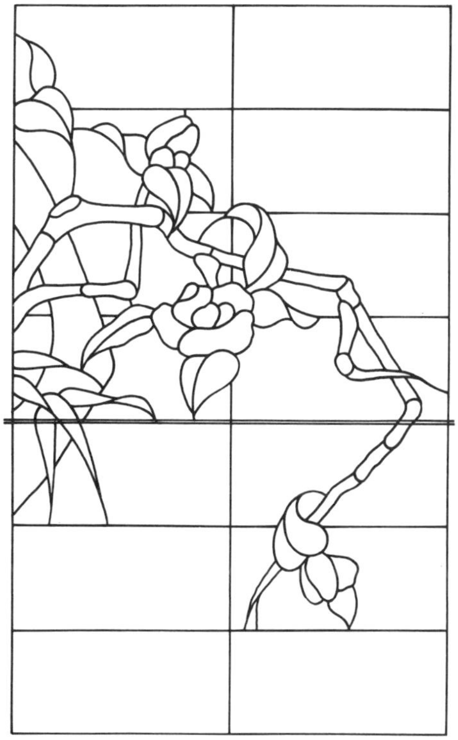

ORIENTAL INSPIRED WINDOW
(full size pattern 580 x 910 mm)

Designs available as full size patterns

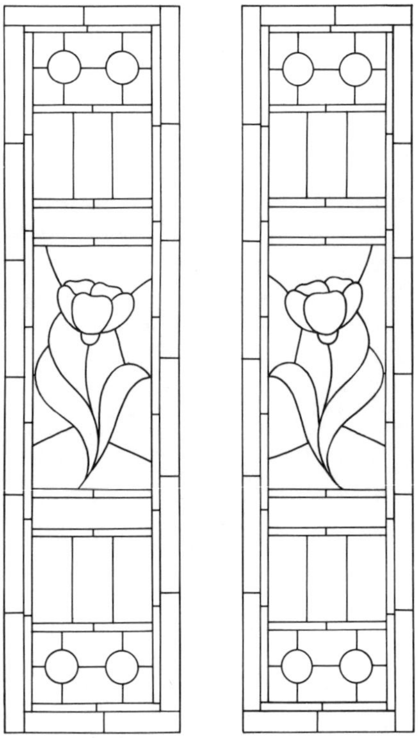

VICTORIAN FRONT ENTRY PANELS
(full size pattern 1000 x 270 mm)

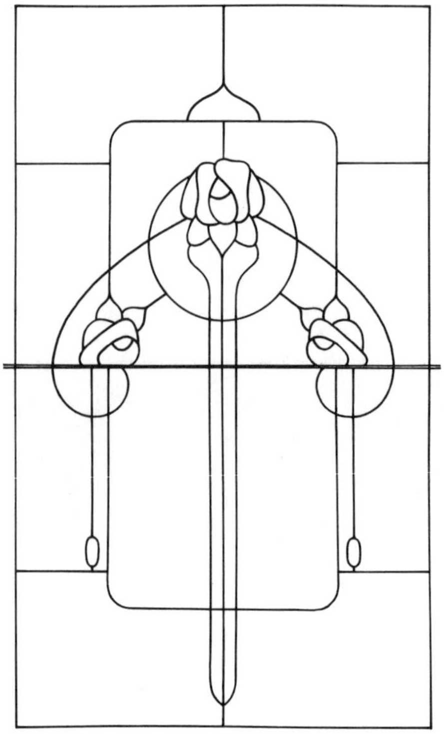

ART NOUVEAU FEATURE PANEL
(full size pattern 580 x 910 mm)

ART NOUVEAU FEATURE PANEL
(full size pattern 580 x 910 mm)

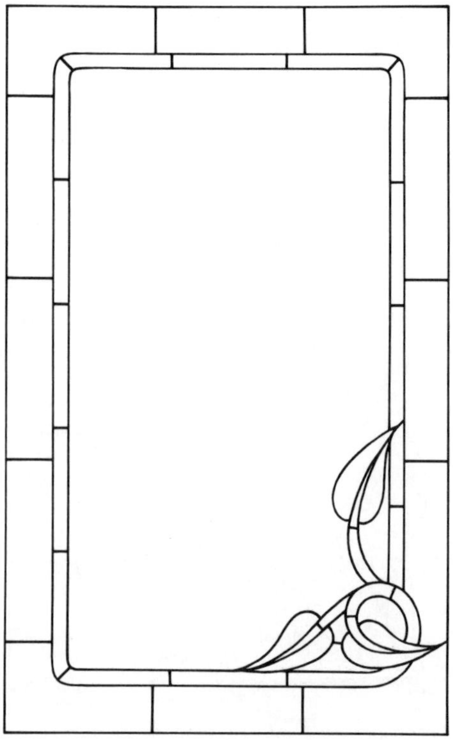

DESIGN SUITABLE FOR WINDOW OR MIRROR
(full size pattern 580 x 910 mm)

Designs available as full size patterns

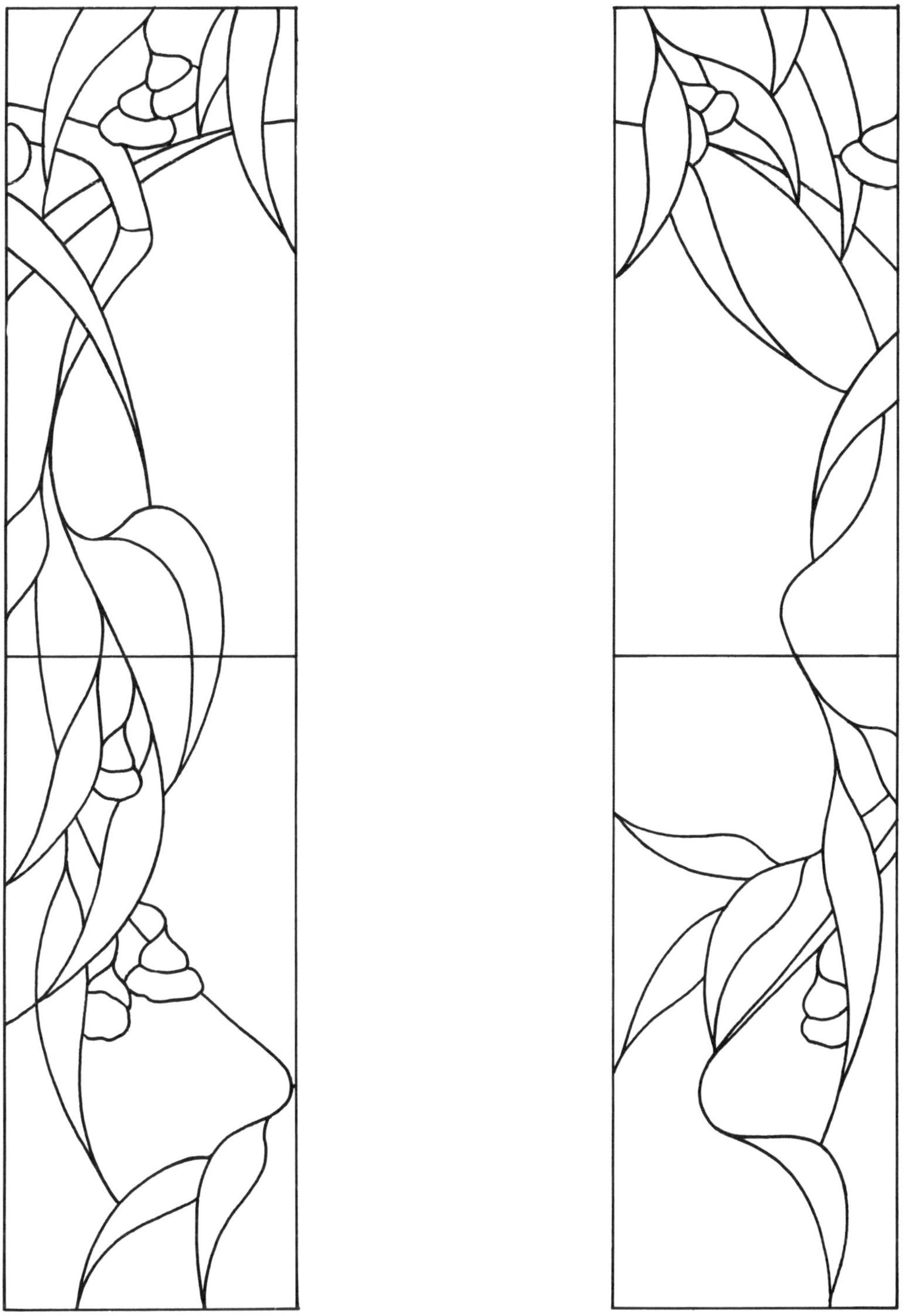

GUM NUTS AND LEAVES DOOR OR FRONT ENTRY PANELS

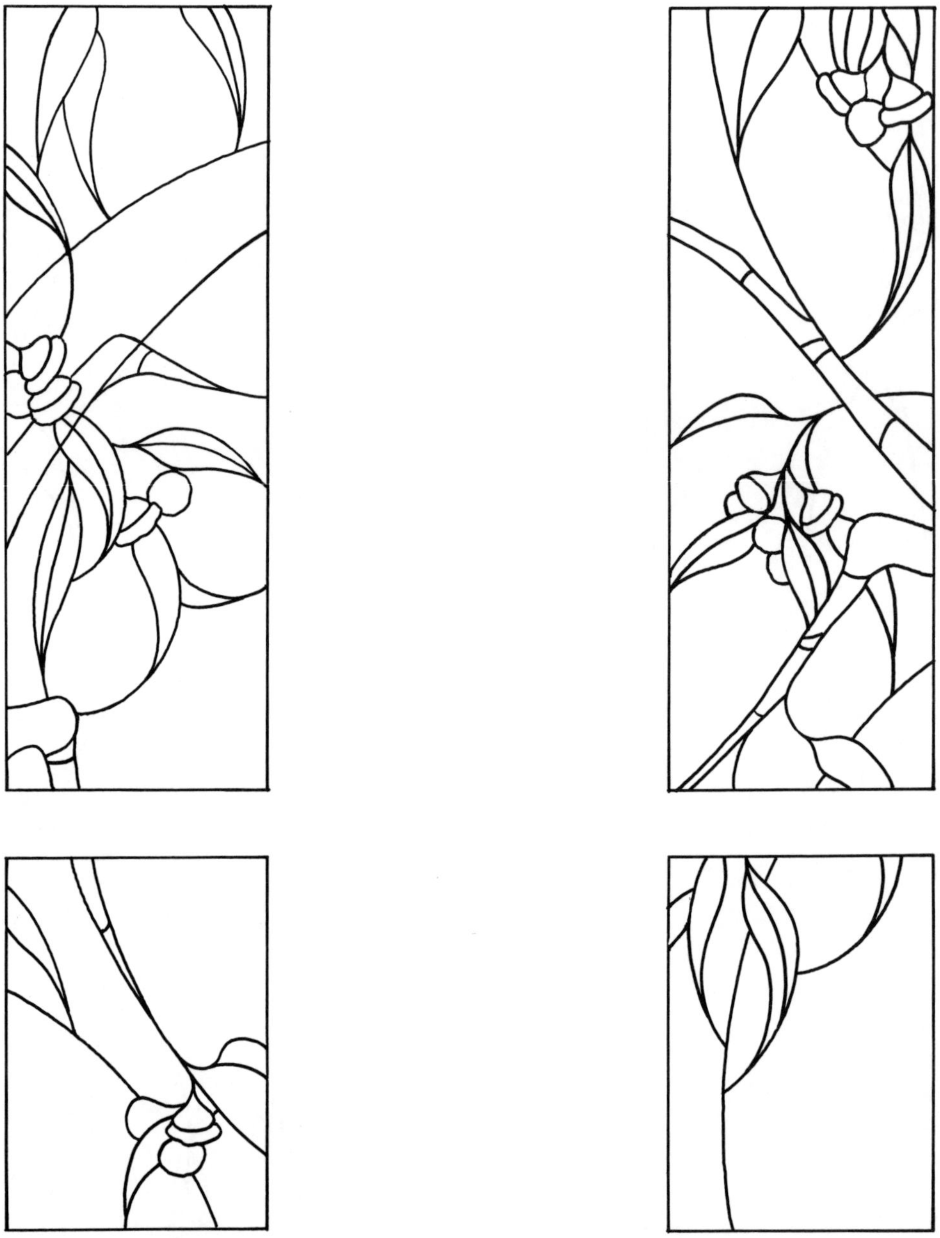

GUMNUTS AND LEAVES FRONT ENTRY PANELS

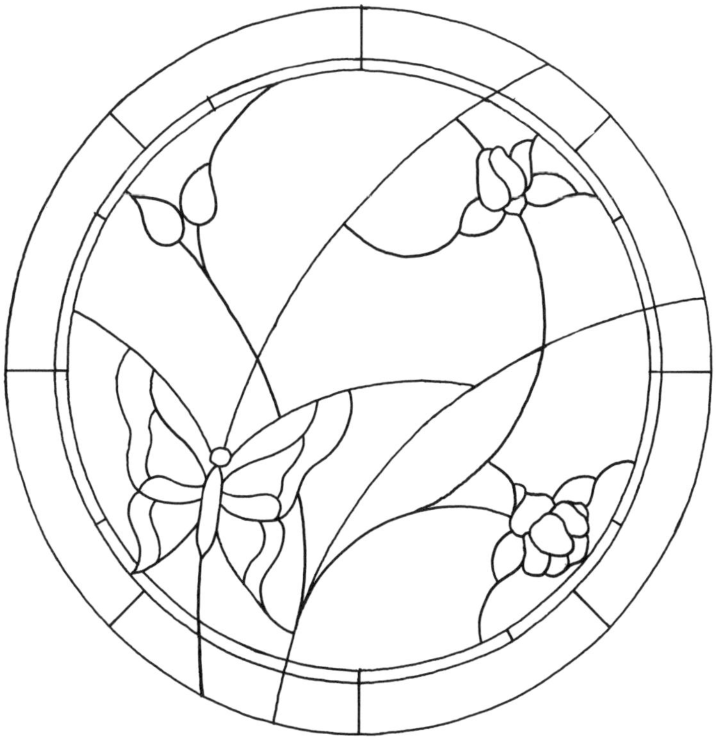

BUTTERFLY PORTHOLE WINDOWS
(see colour plates)

SEAFARING FRONT ENTRY PANELS OR WINDOWS

MATADOR

JAPANESE LADY

GRAND PIANO

SAILING AWAY

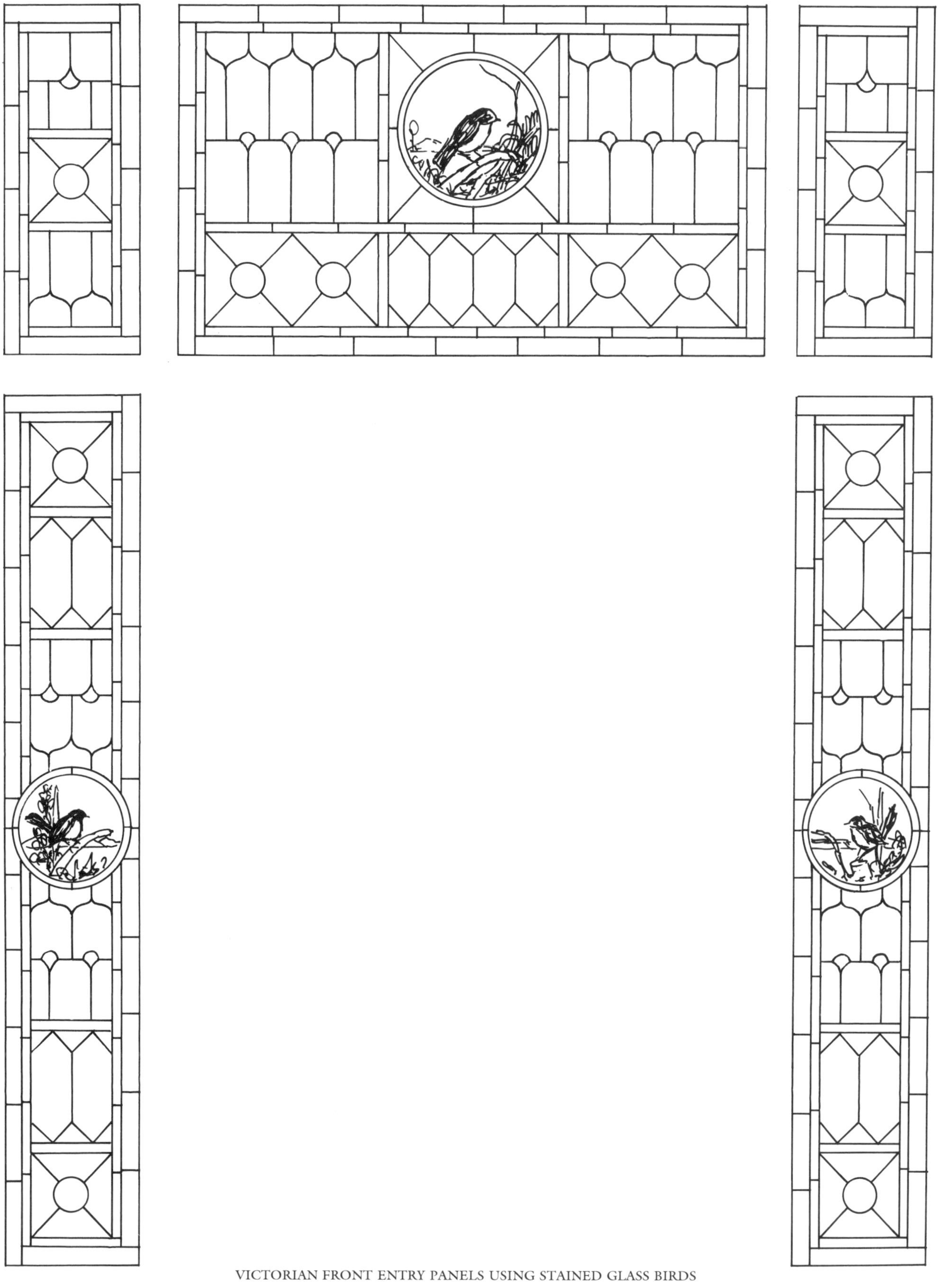

VICTORIAN FRONT ENTRY PANELS USING STAINED GLASS BIRDS

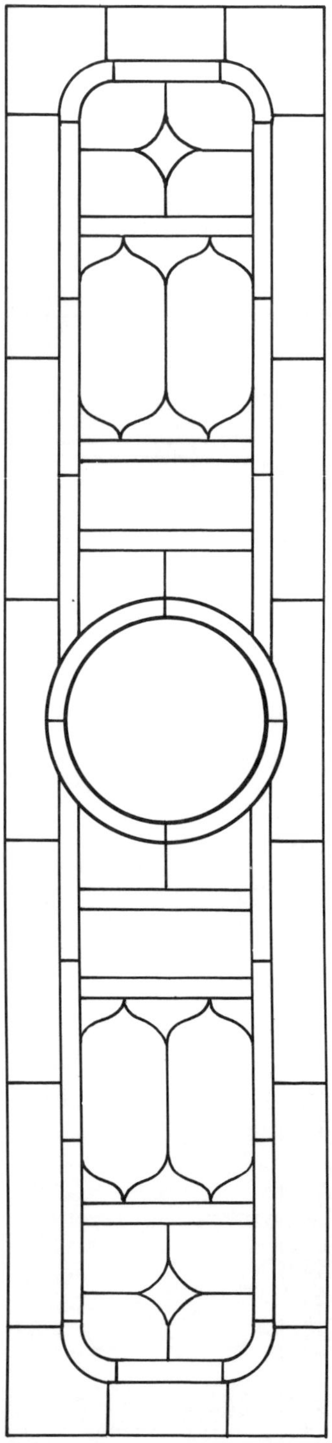

FRONT ENTRY PANELS USING STAINED GLASS BIRD AND BORDER

FRONT ENTRY PANELS USING STAINED GLASS CENTRE AND BORDER

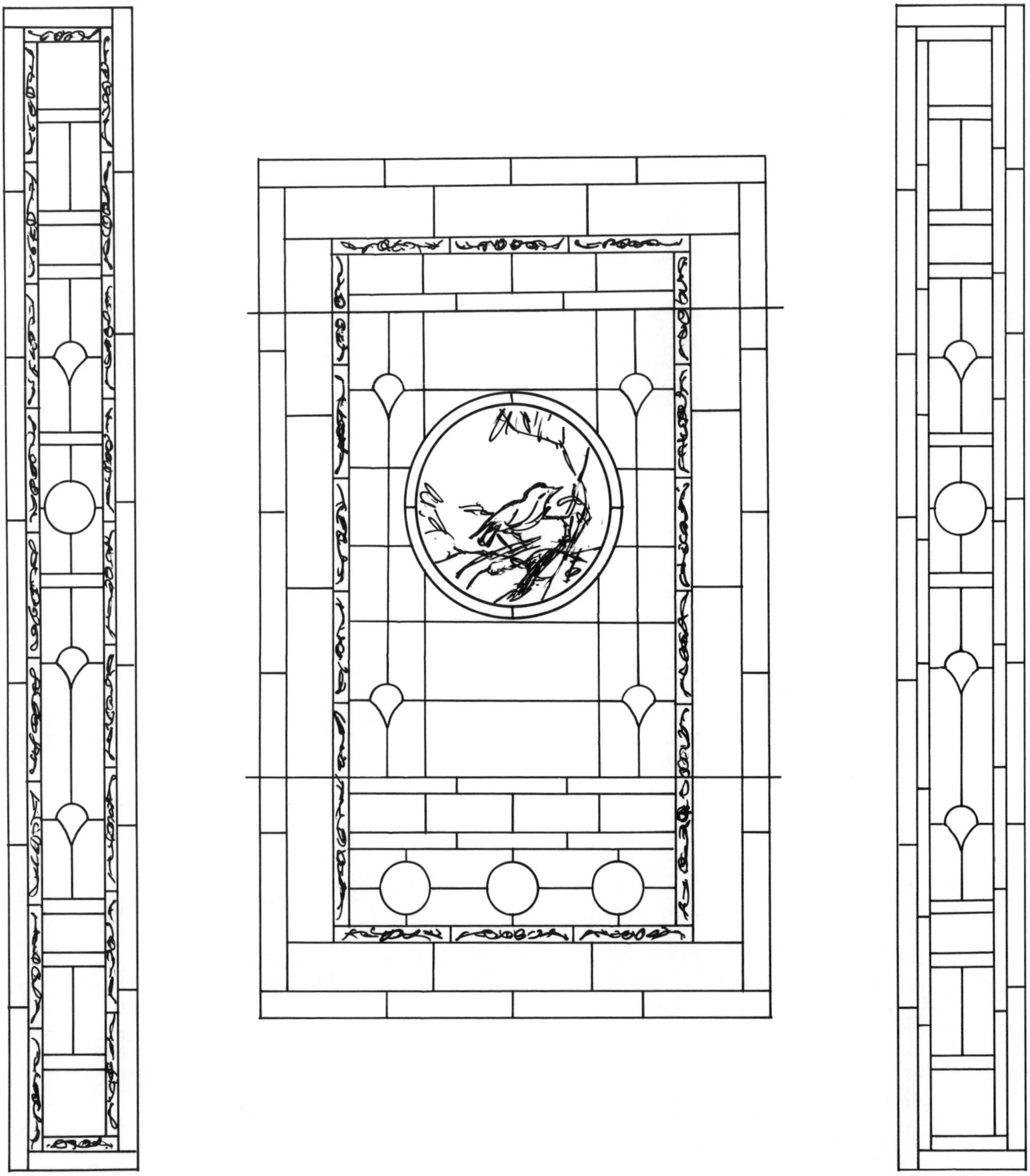

DOOR AND FRONT ENTRY PANELS USING STAINED GLASS BIRD AND BORDER

DOOR PANEL OR WINDOW USING STAINED GLASS BIRD AND BORDER

DOOR PANELS AND TRANSOM USING STAINED GLASS BIRD

DOUBLE HUNG WINDOW USING STAINED GLASS BIRD AND BORDER

FRONT ENTRY PANELS USING STAINED GLASS BIRD AND BORDER

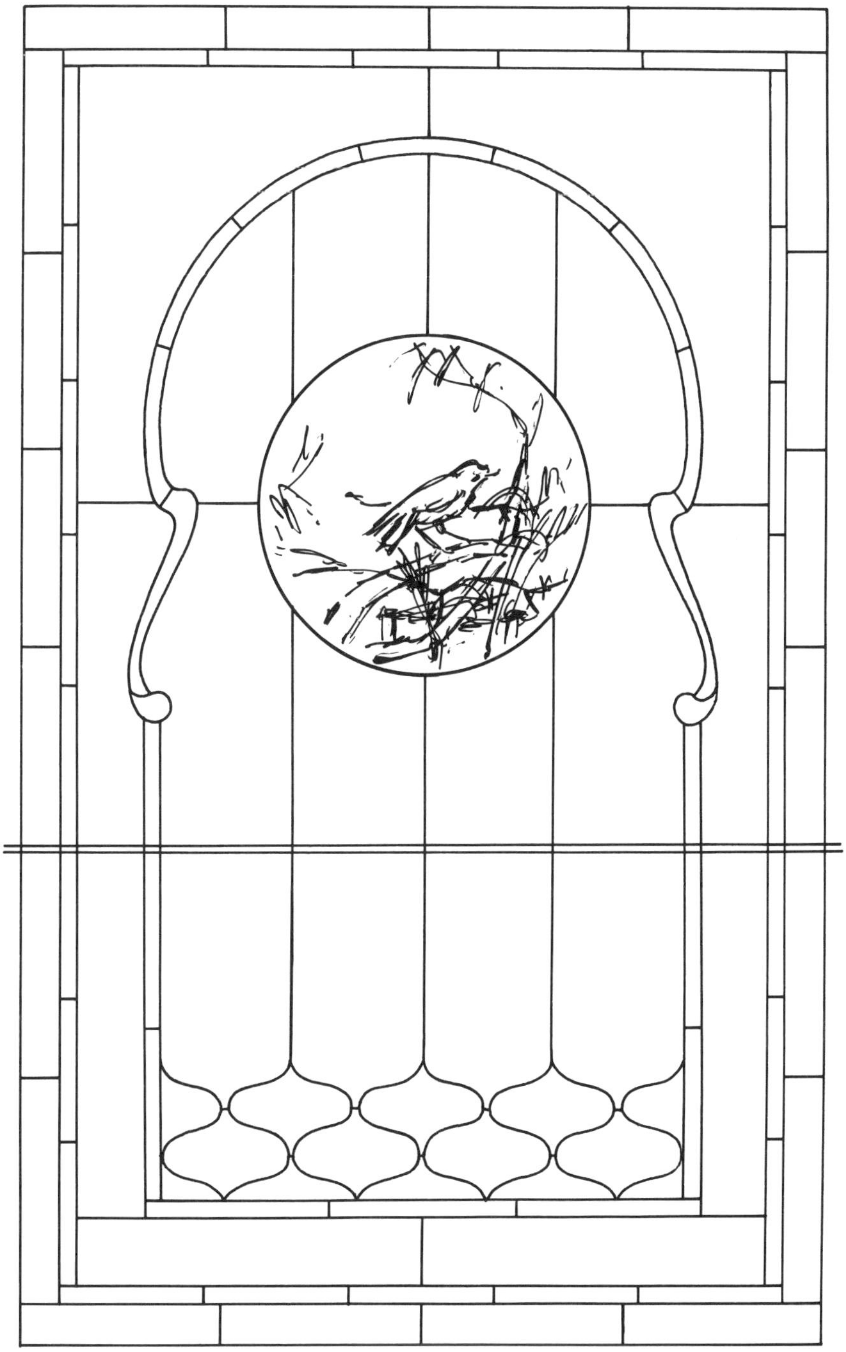

WINDOW OR PANEL USING STAINED GLASS BIRD

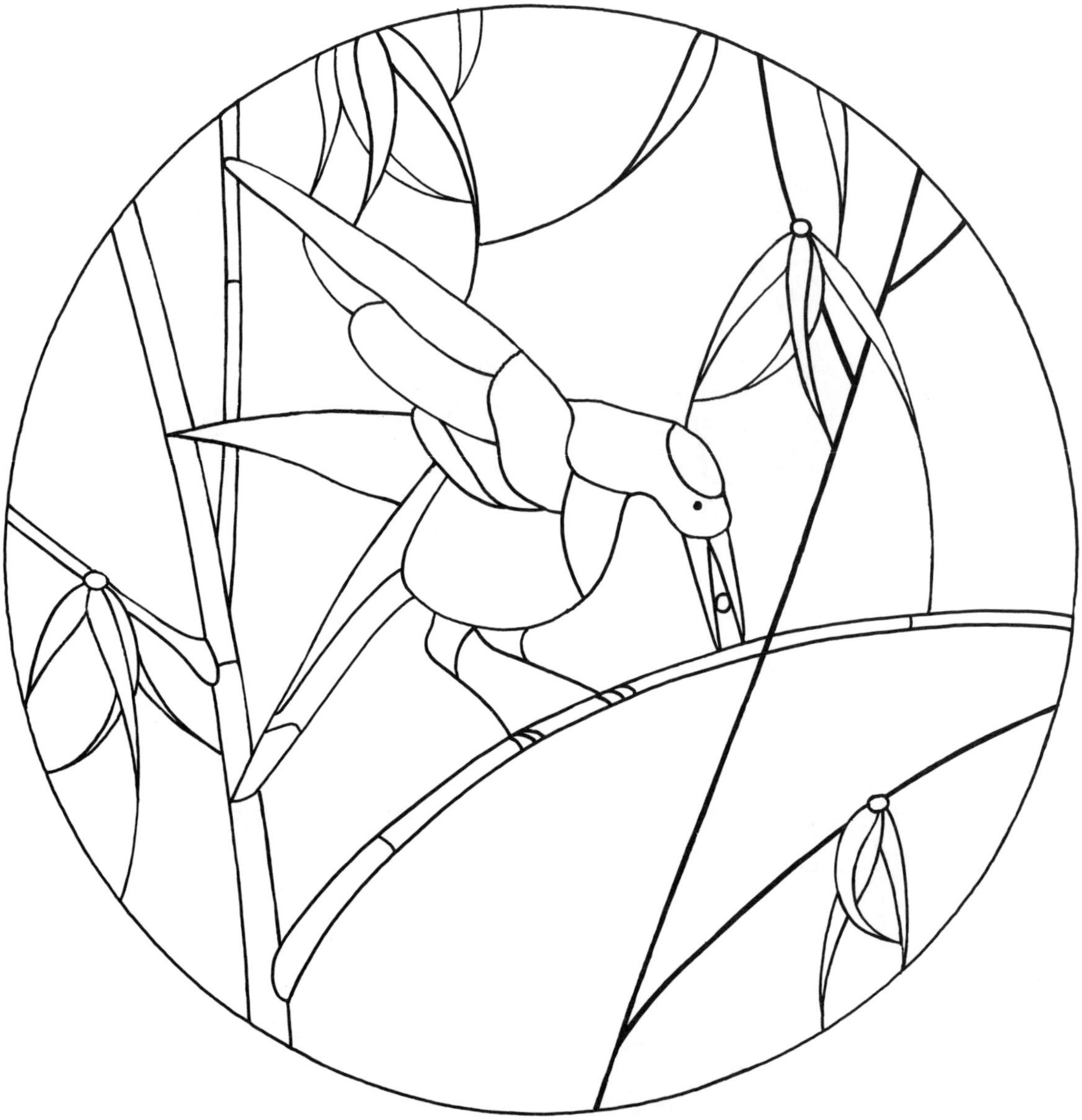

MAGPIE PORTHOLE WINDOW

PLATYPUS PANEL

ROSELLAS PANEL

AUSTRALIAN FINCHES PANEL

PENGUINS PANEL

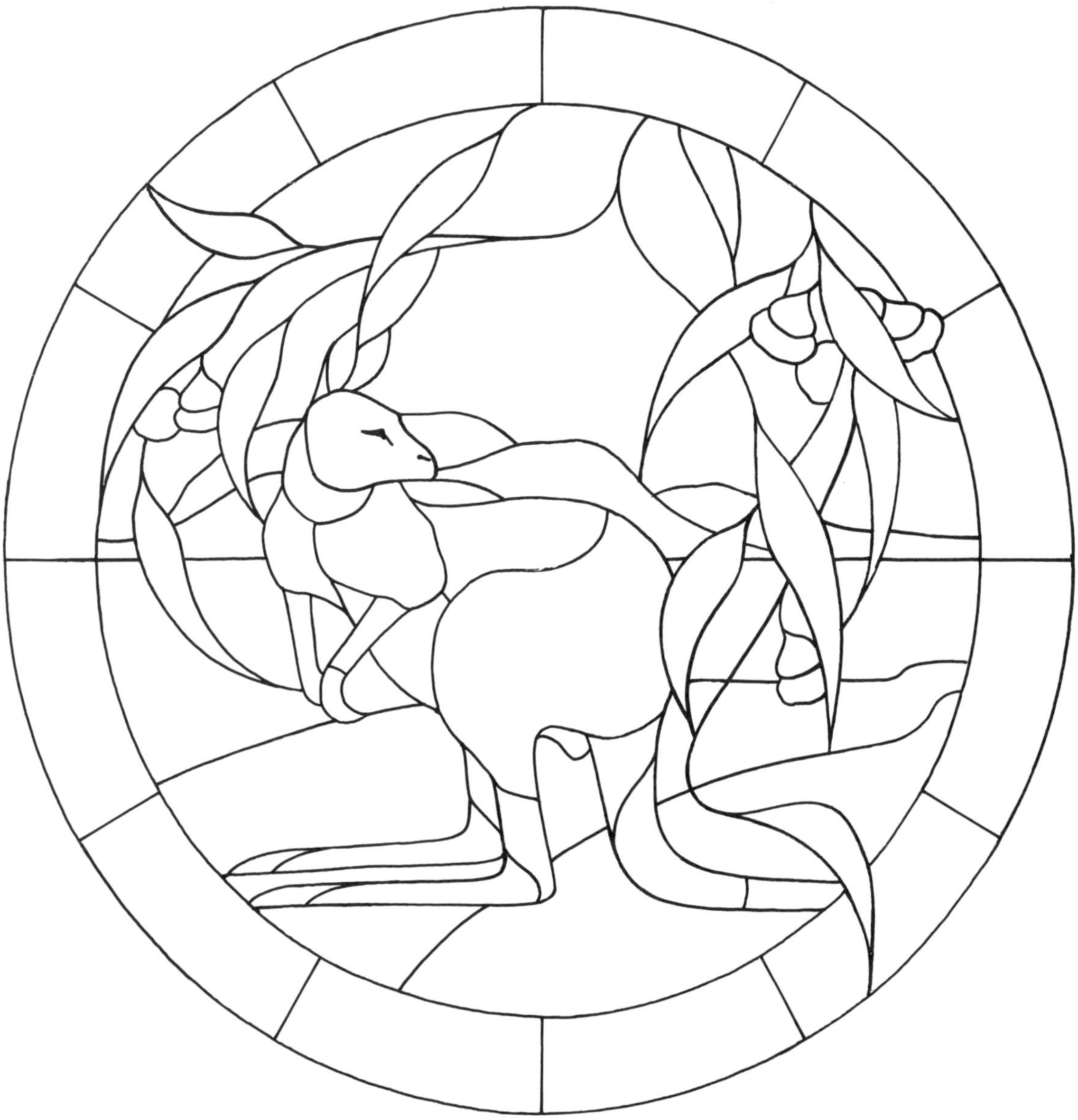

KANGAROO PANEL

GANG-GANG COCKATOOS

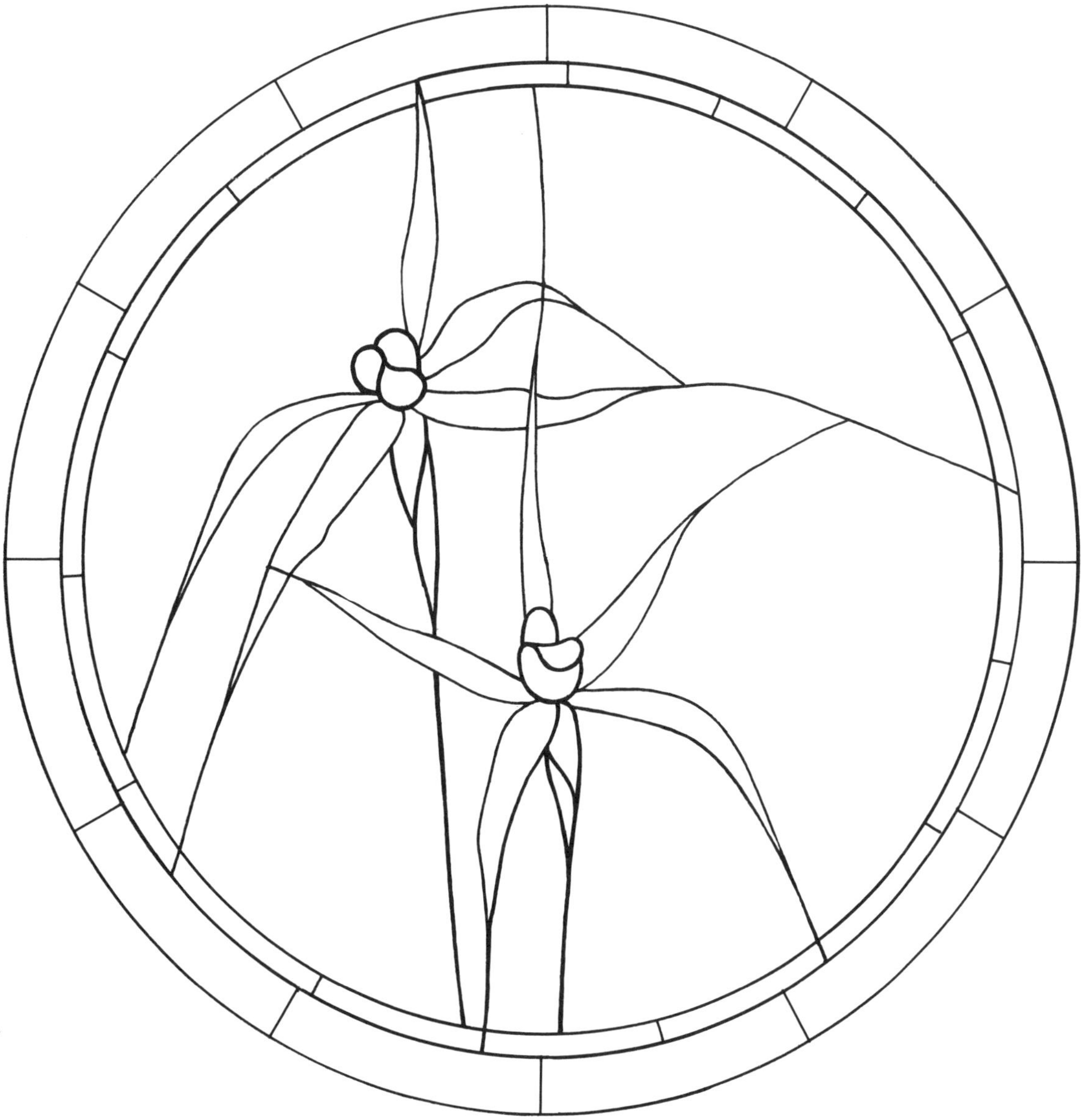

SPIDER ORCHID PORTHOLE WINDOW

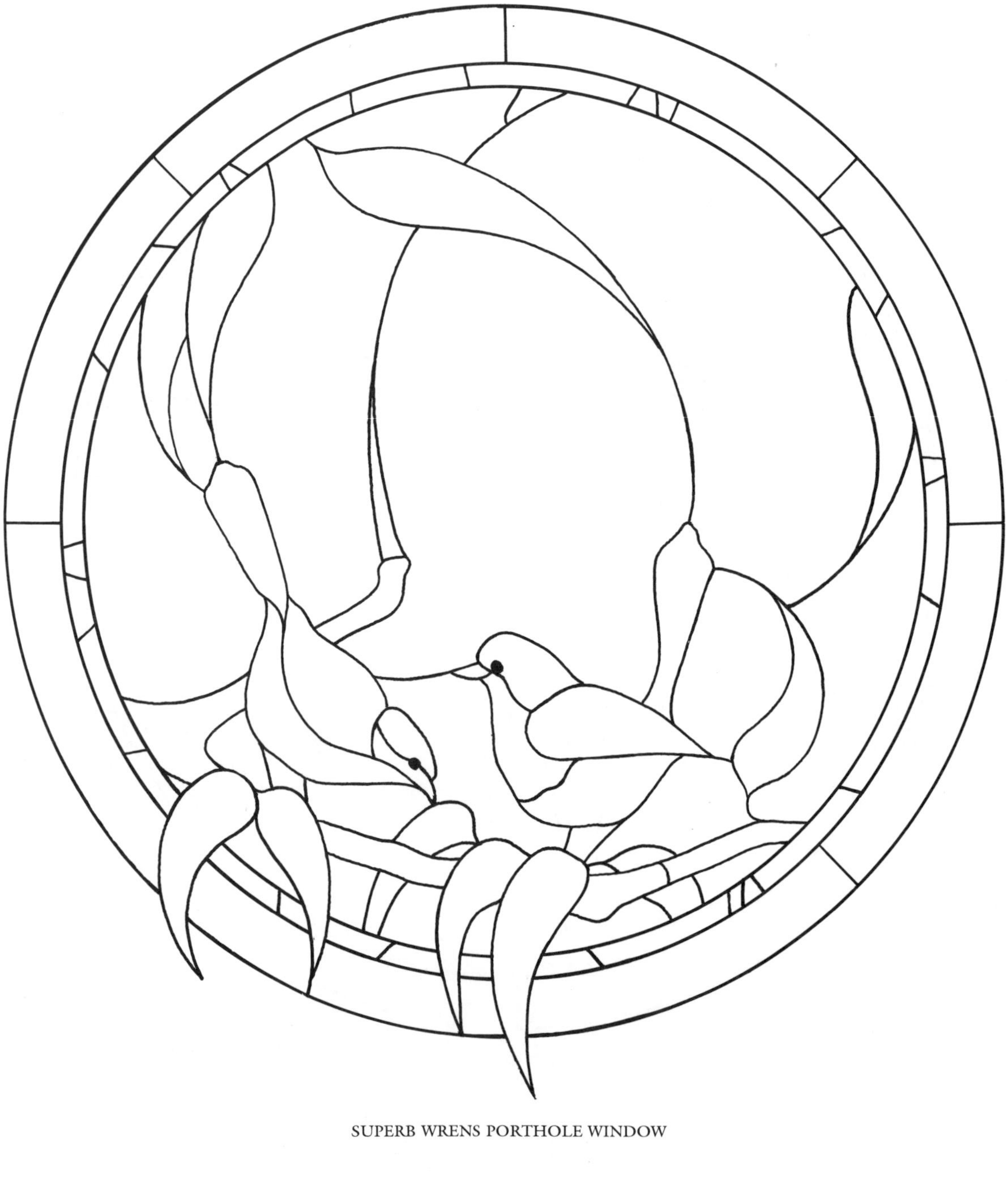

SUPERB WRENS PORTHOLE WINDOW

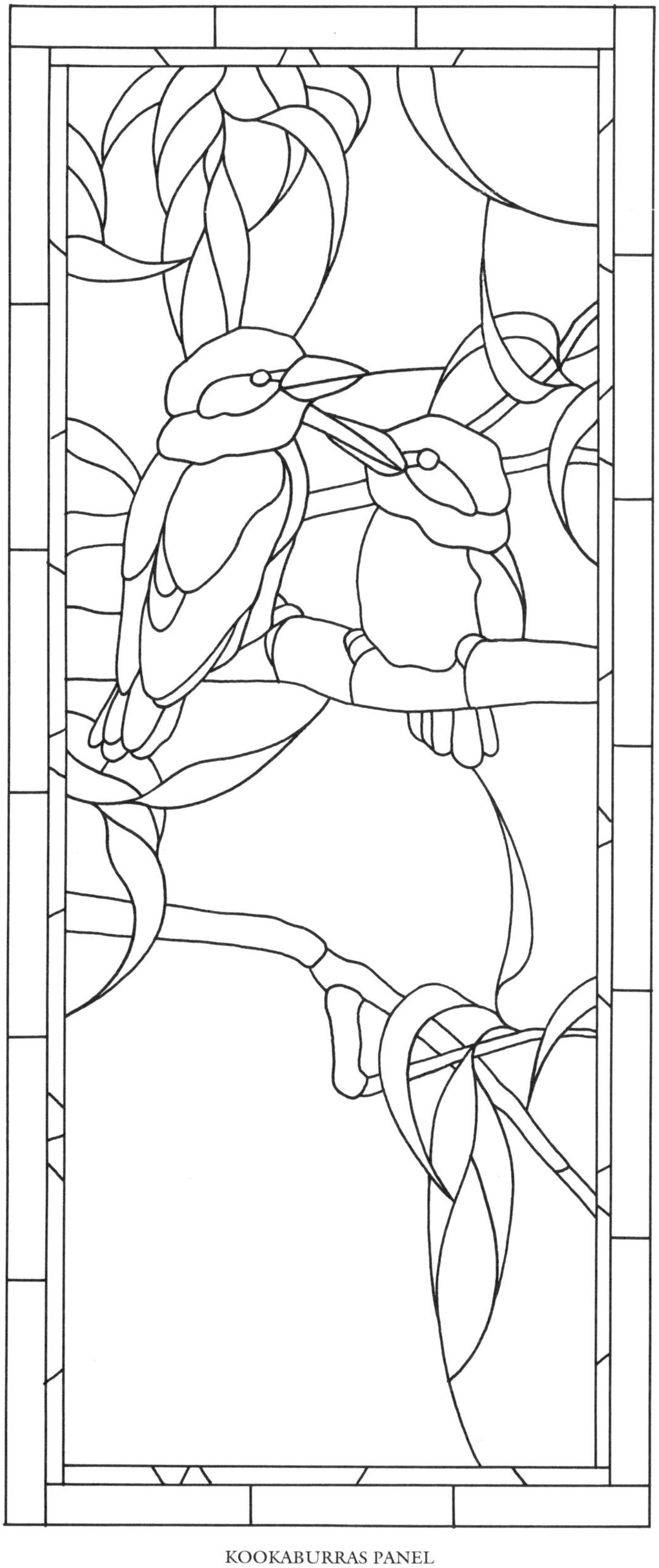

KOOKABURRAS PANEL

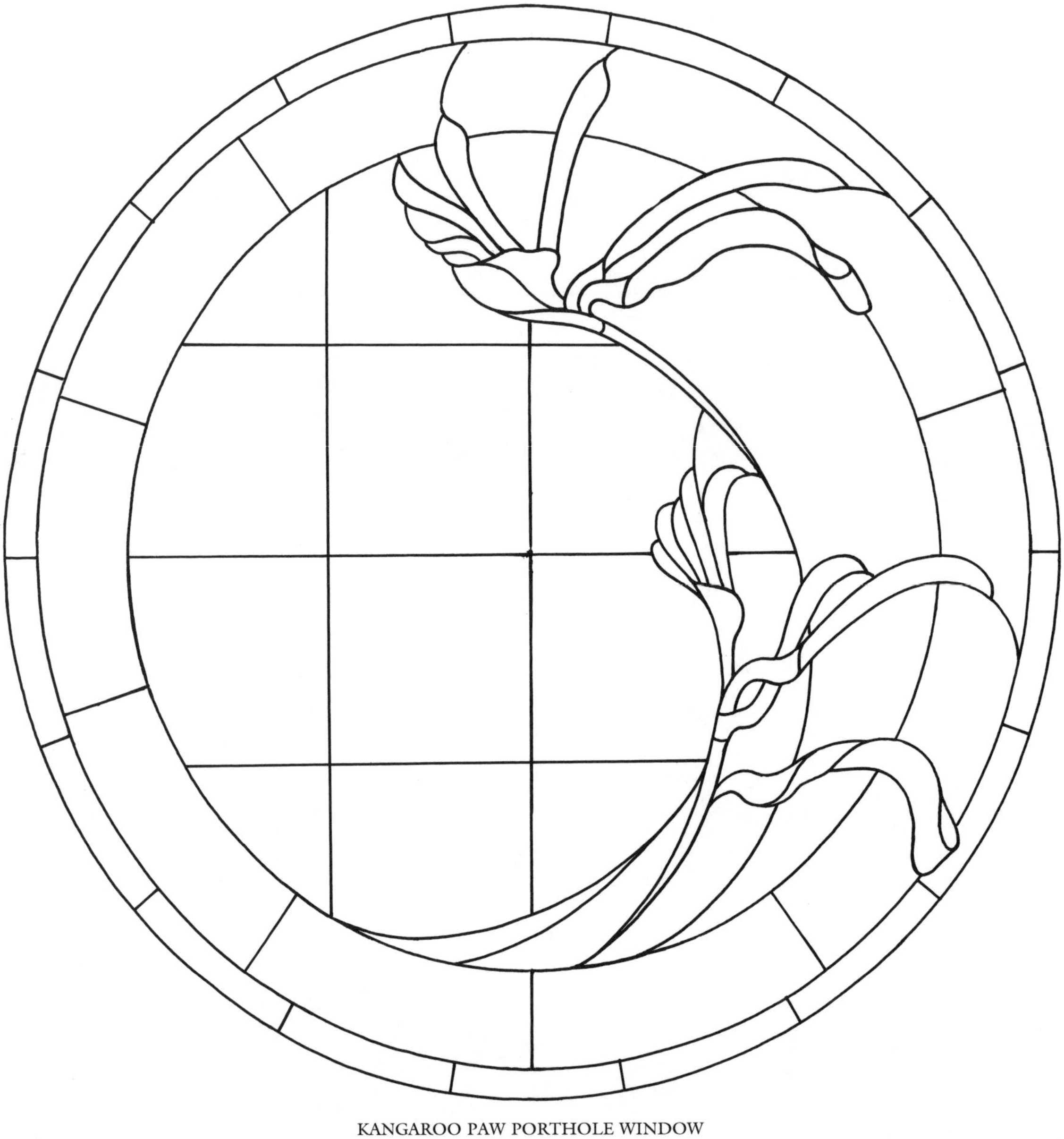

KANGAROO PAW PORTHOLE WINDOW

VICTORIAN DOOR ENTRY PANELS

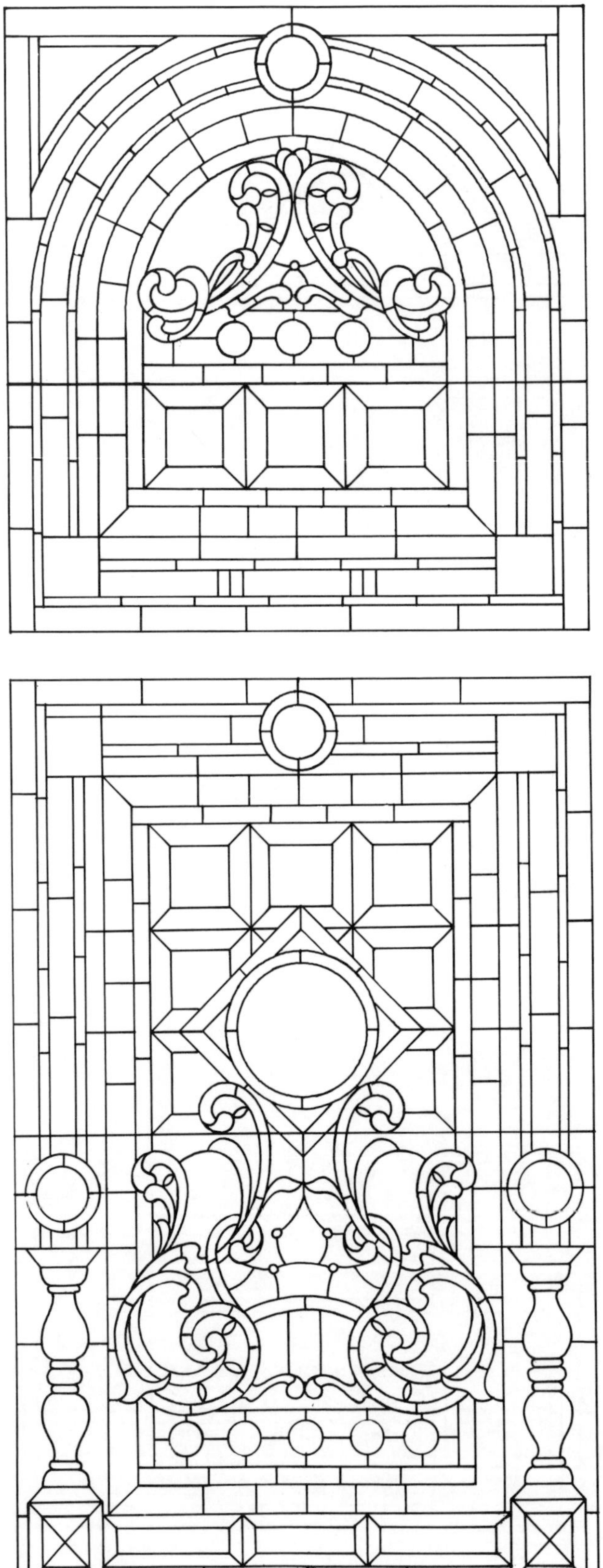

VICTORIAN WINDOW SET
(see colour plates)

VICTORIAN WINDOW
(see colour plates)

VICTORIAN FEATURE PANEL, SKYLIGHT OR MIRROR SURROUND

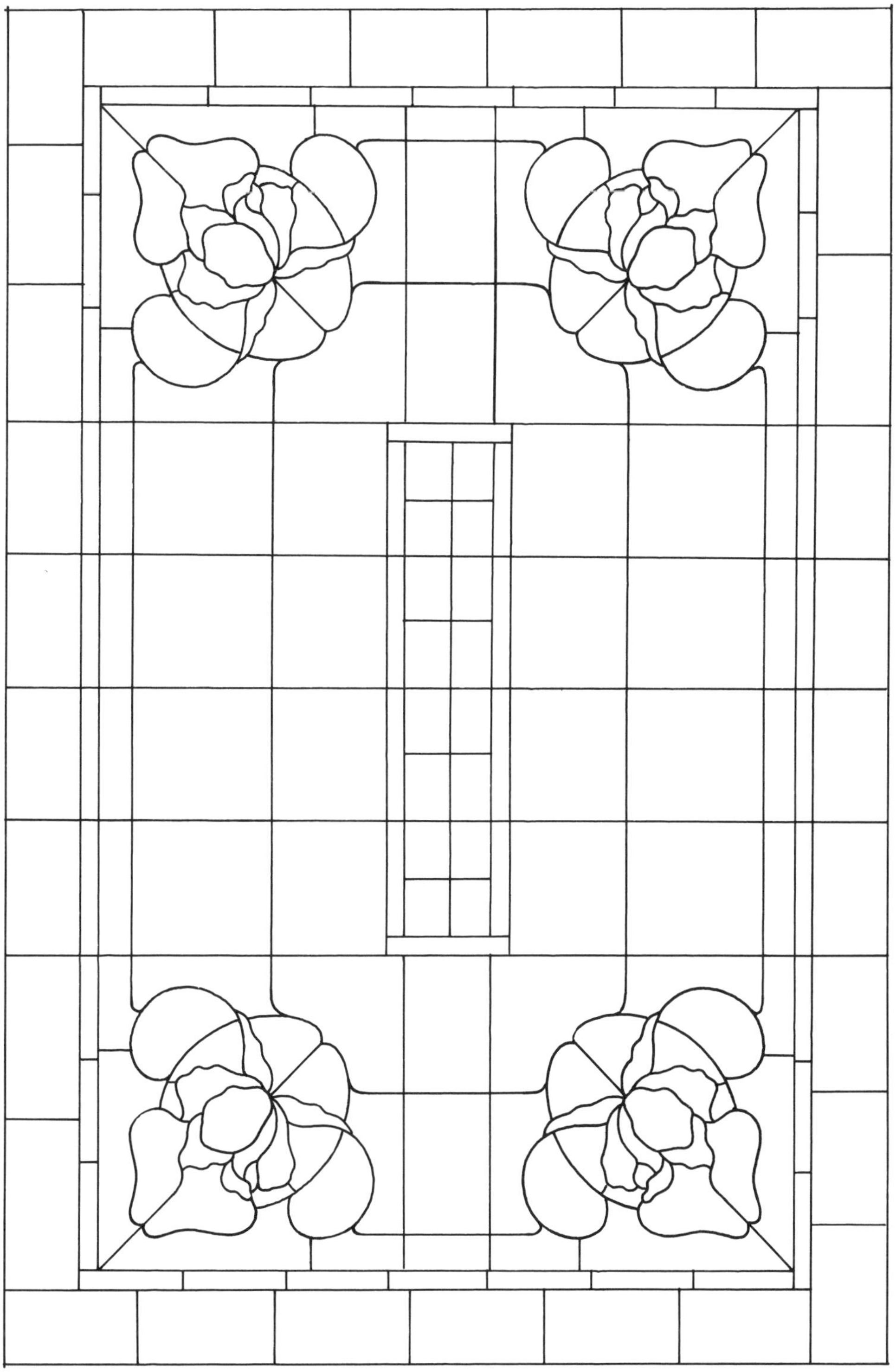

VICTORIAN WINDOW OR SKYLIGHT

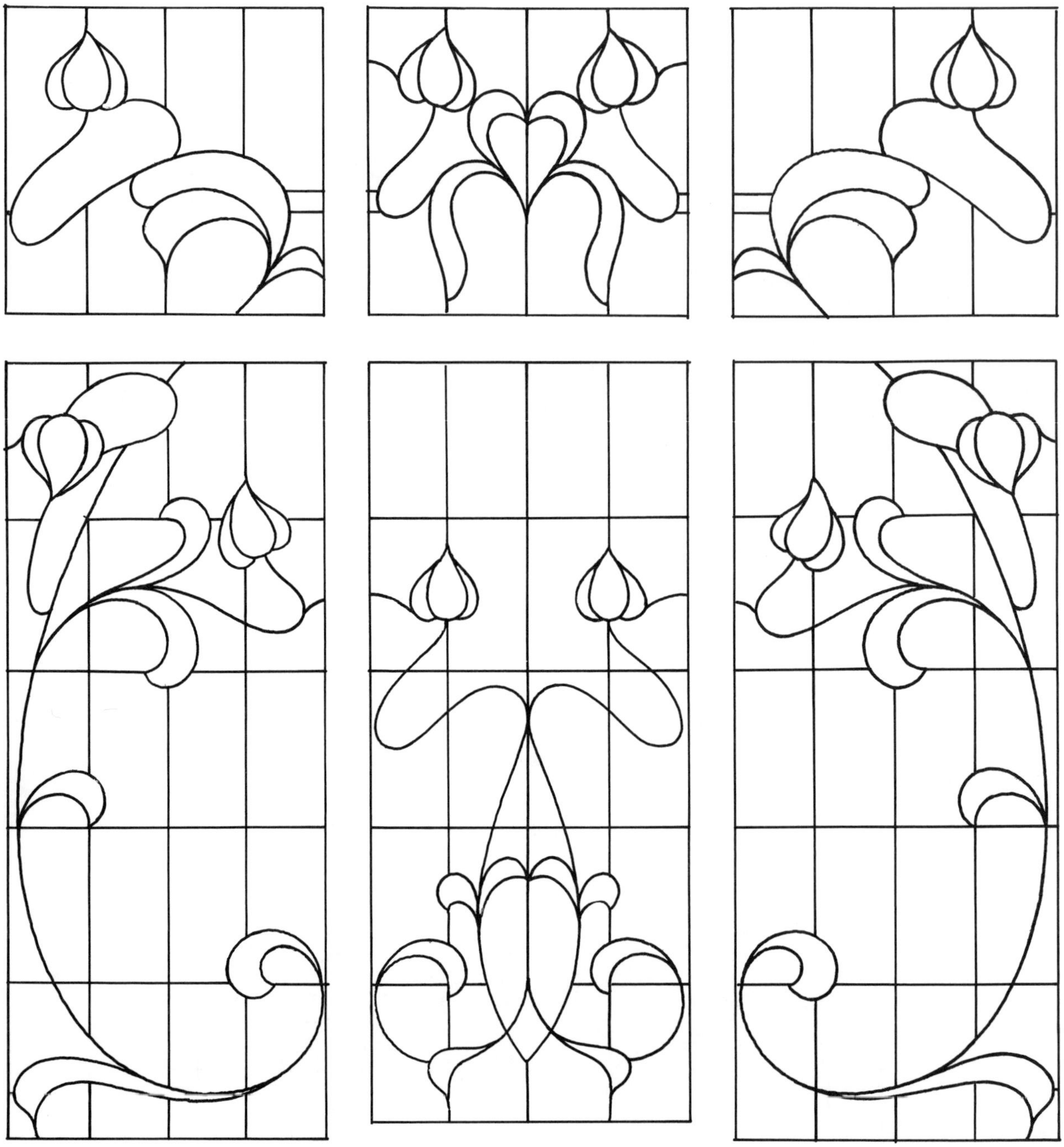

ART NOUVEAU WINDOW SET

ART NOUVEAU WINDOW

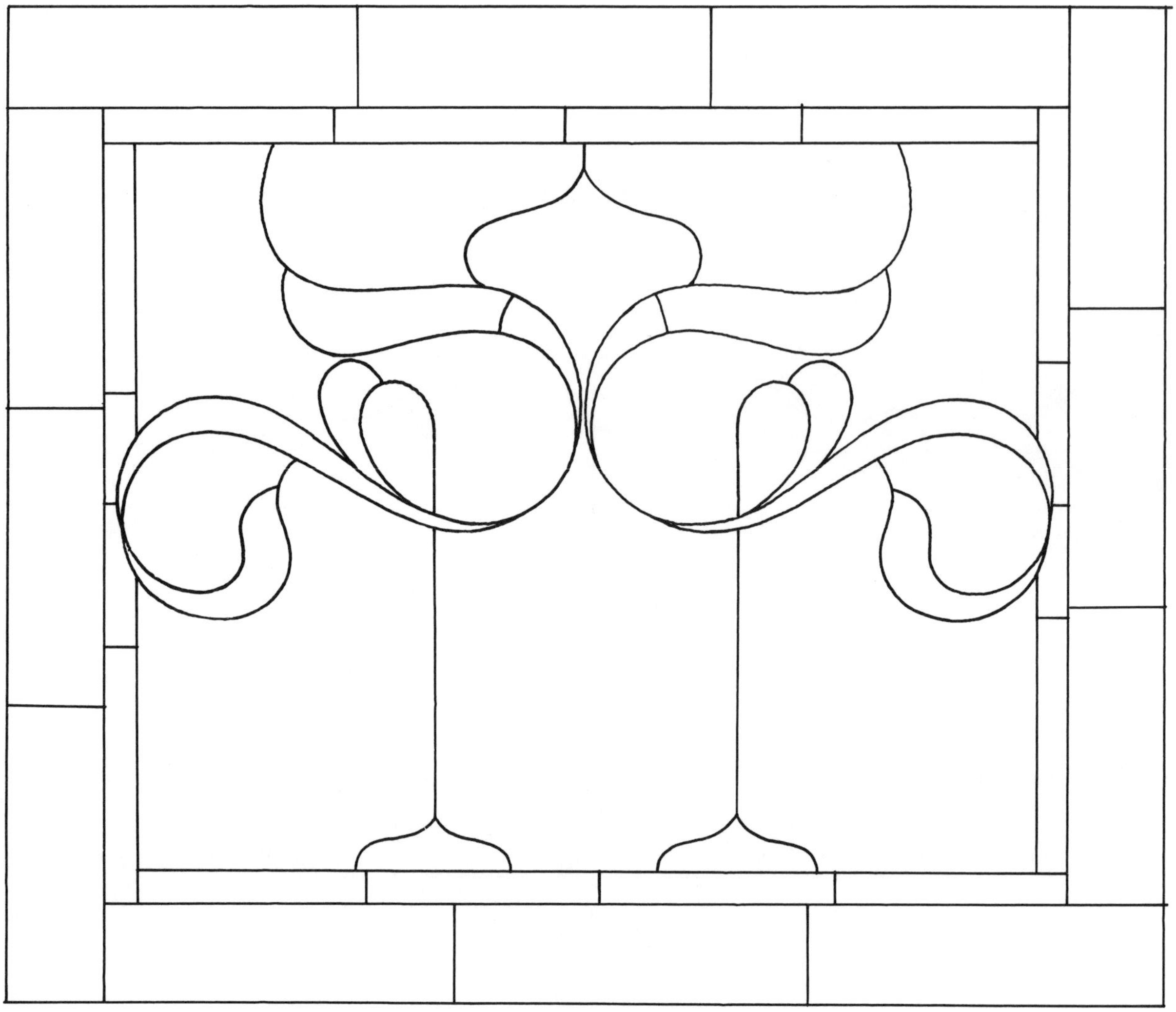

ART NOUVEAU WINDOW OR PANEL

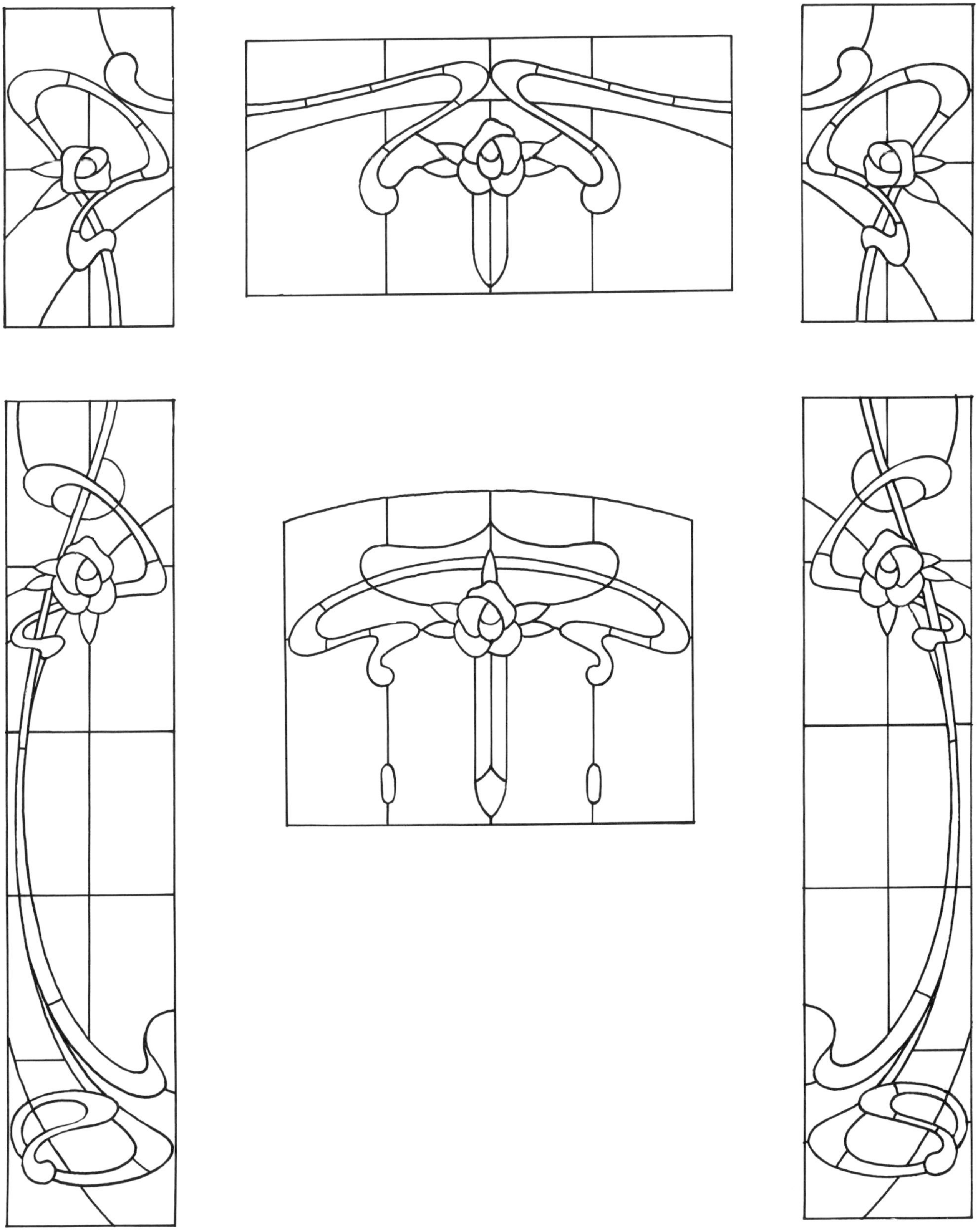

ART NOUVEAU DOOR AND FRONT ENTRY PANELS

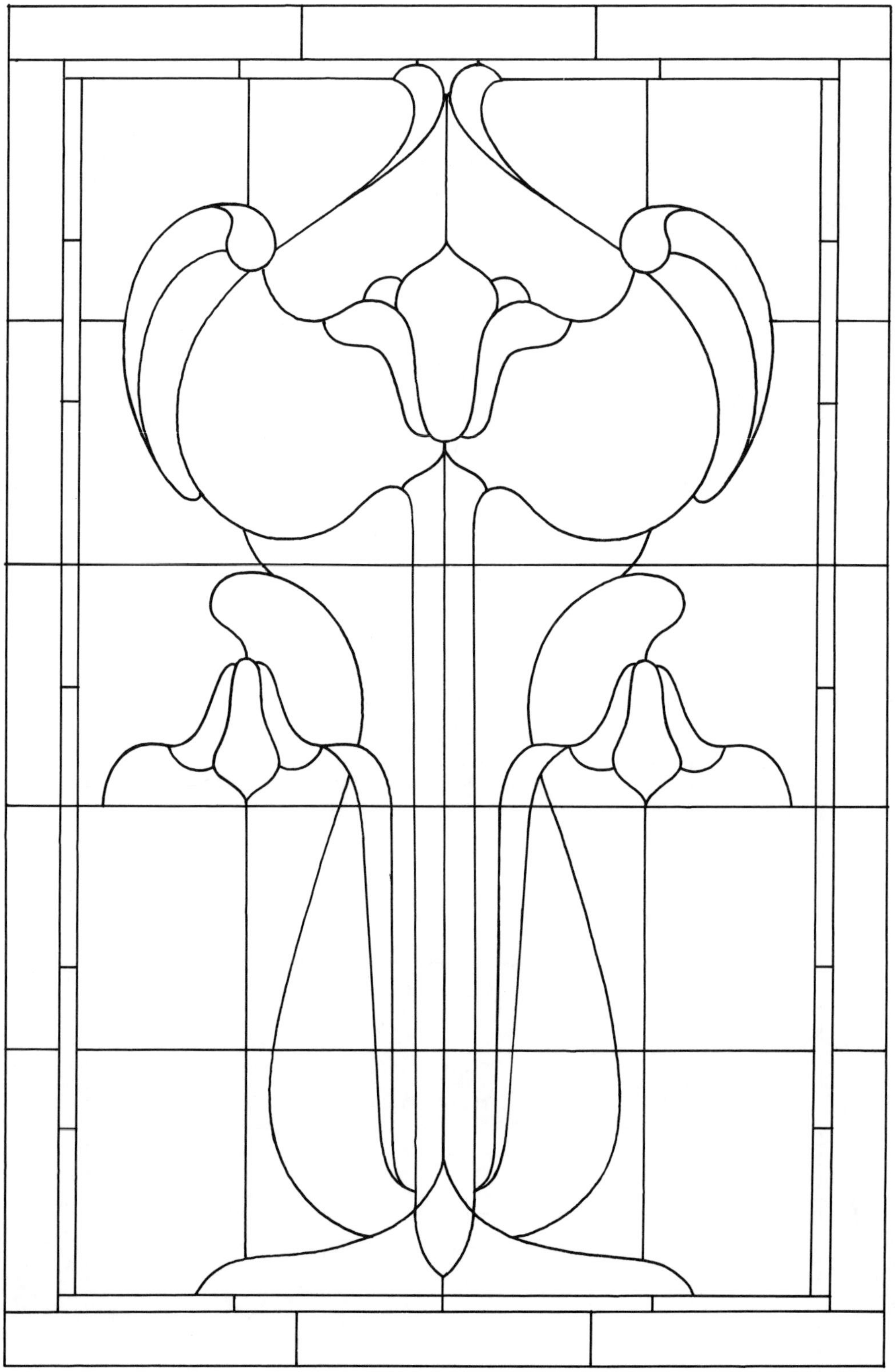

ART NOUVEAU WINDOW

ART NOUVEAU WINDOW

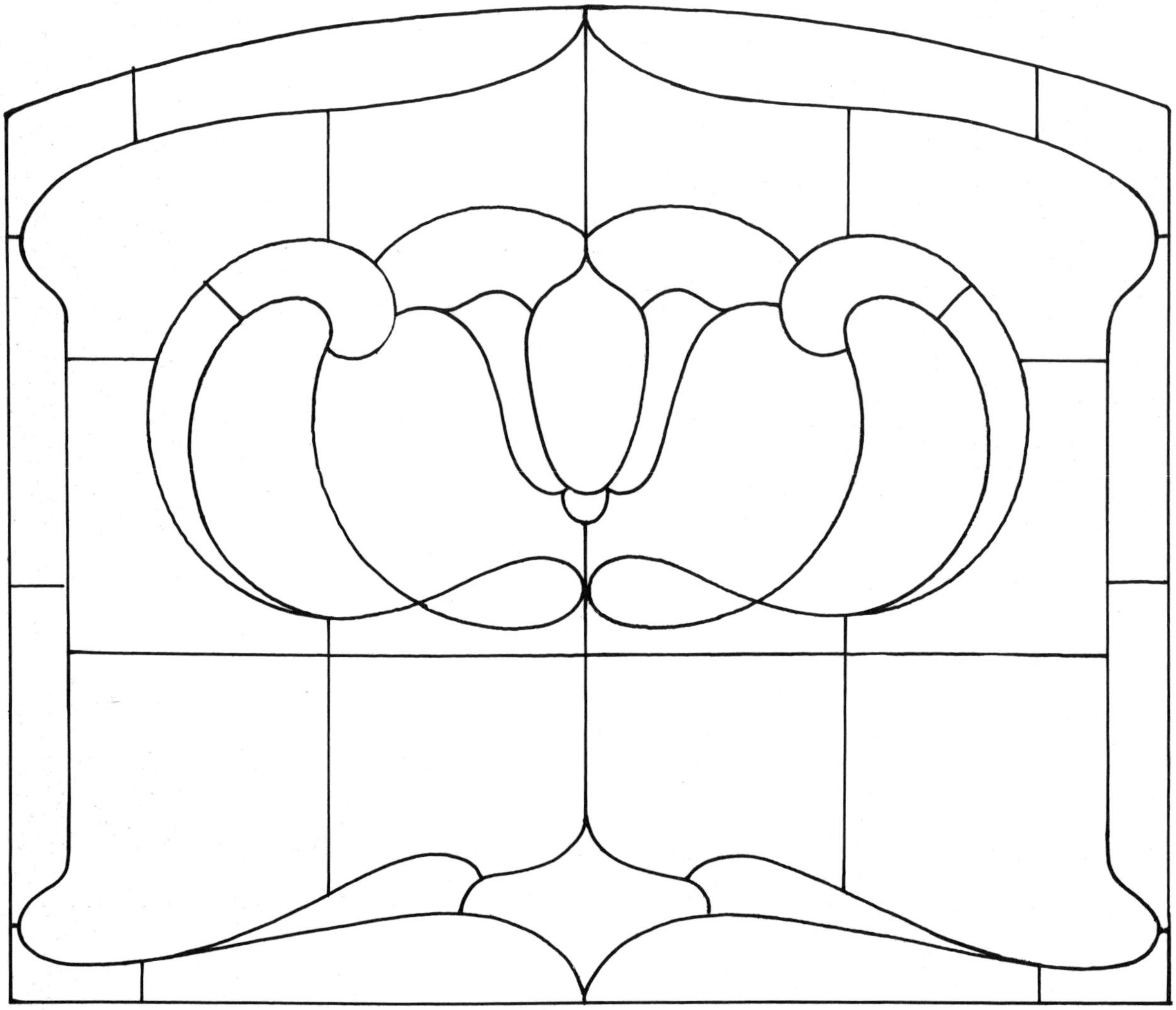

FEDERATION WINDOW OR DOOR PANEL

Superb bluewren

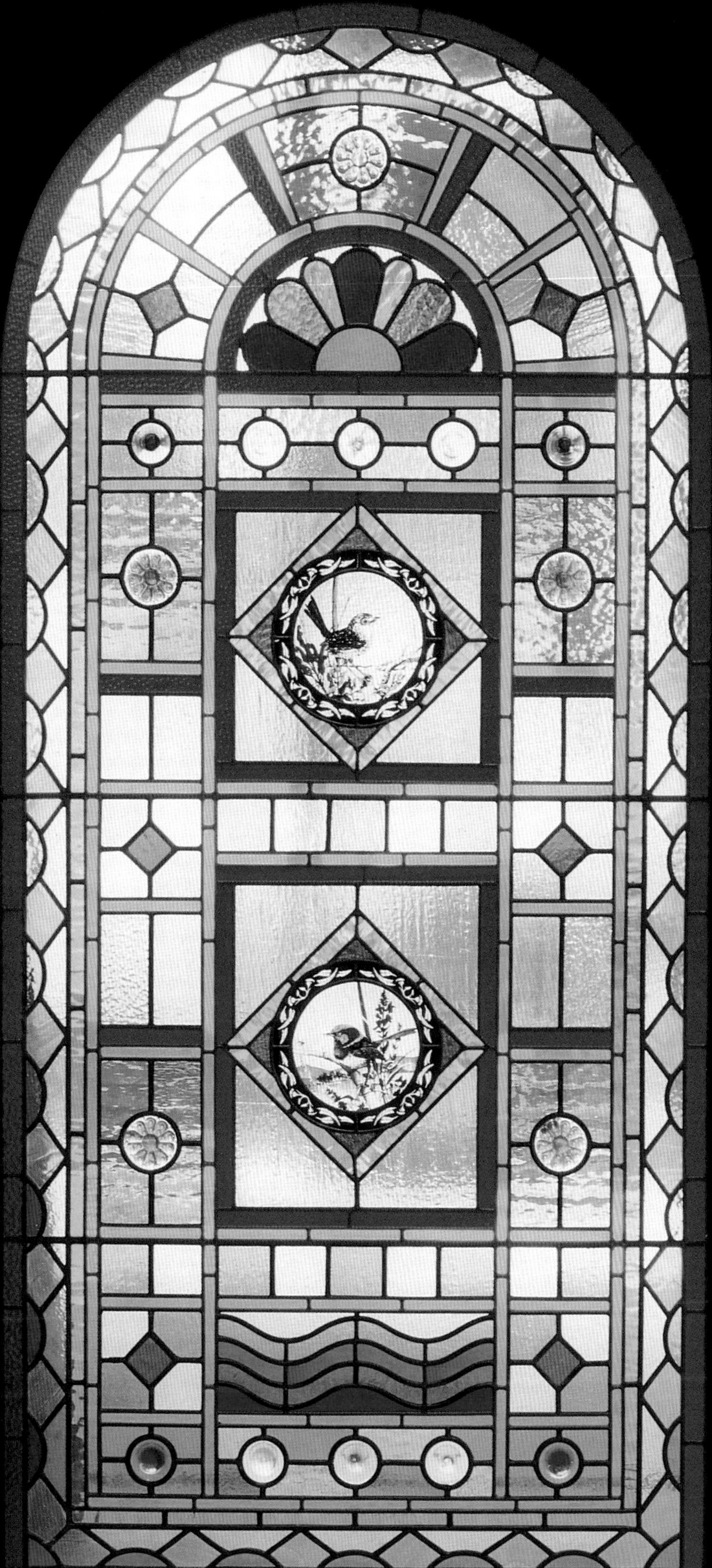

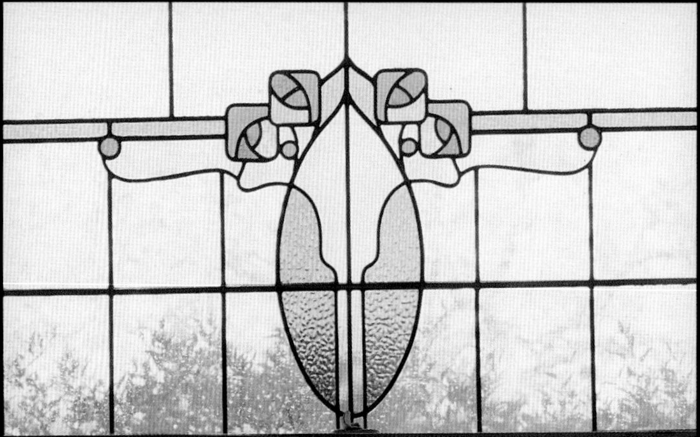

FEDERATION DOOR AND FRONT ENTRY PANELS

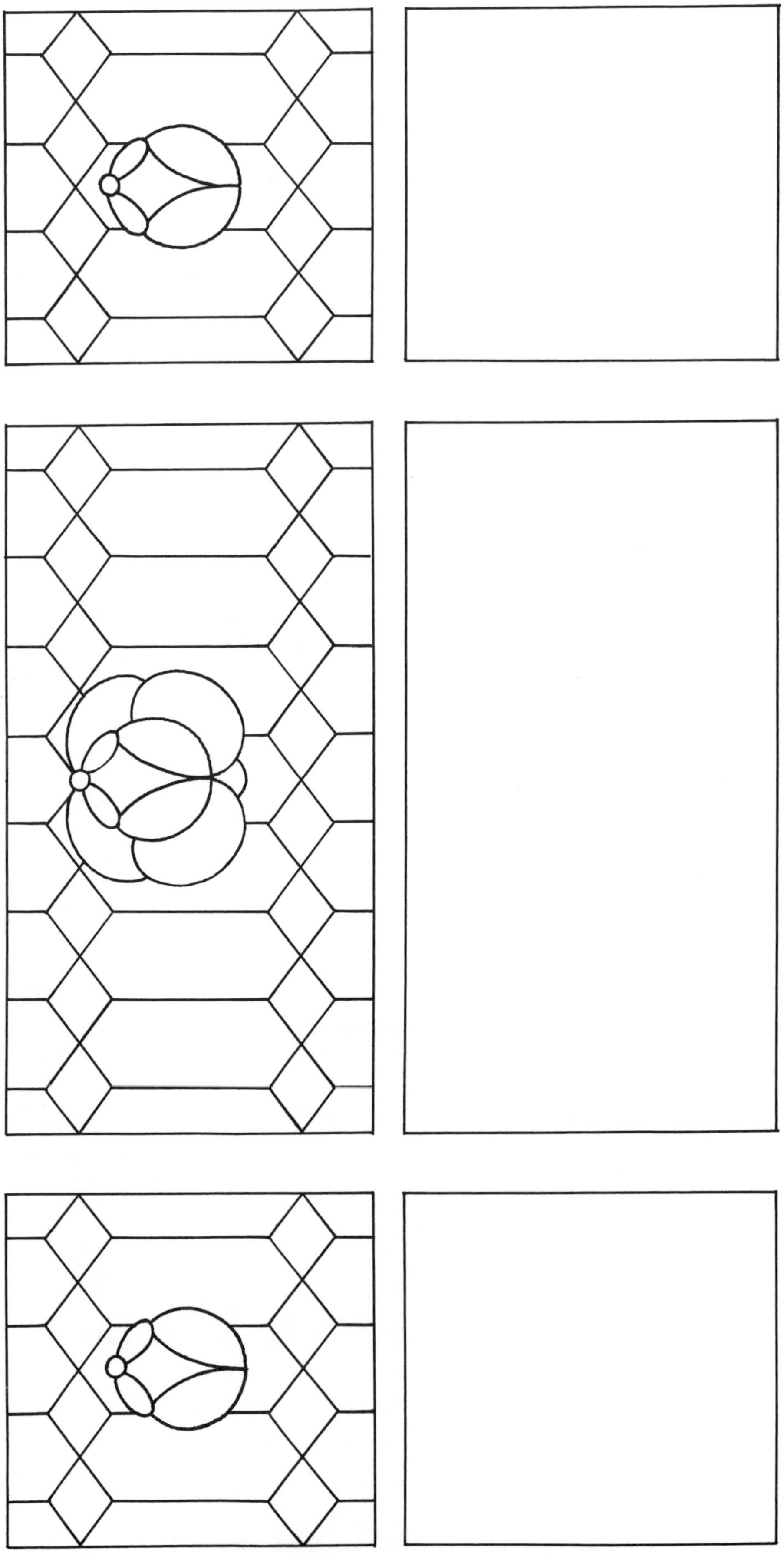

(top)

FEDERATION WINDOW SET

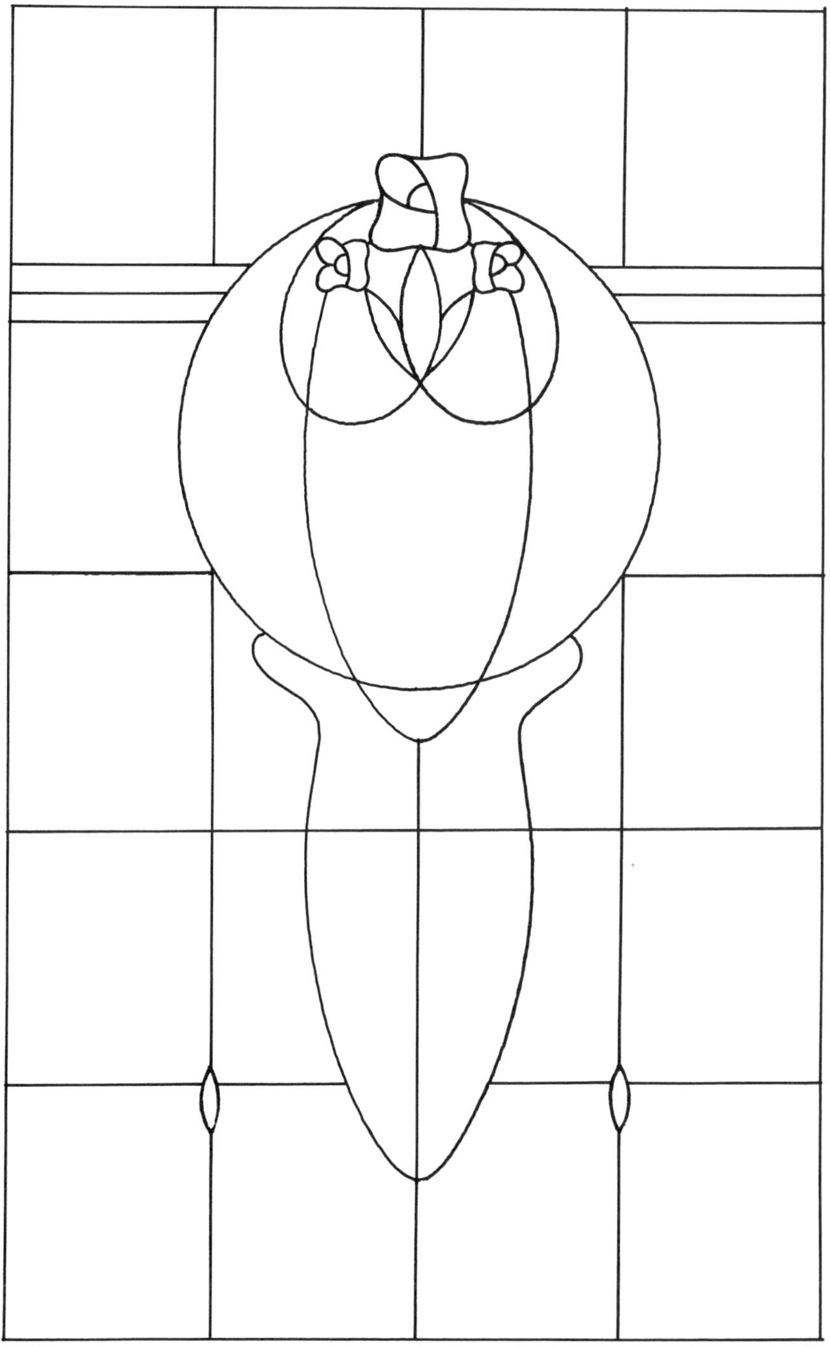

FEDERATION WINDOW OR DOOR PANEL

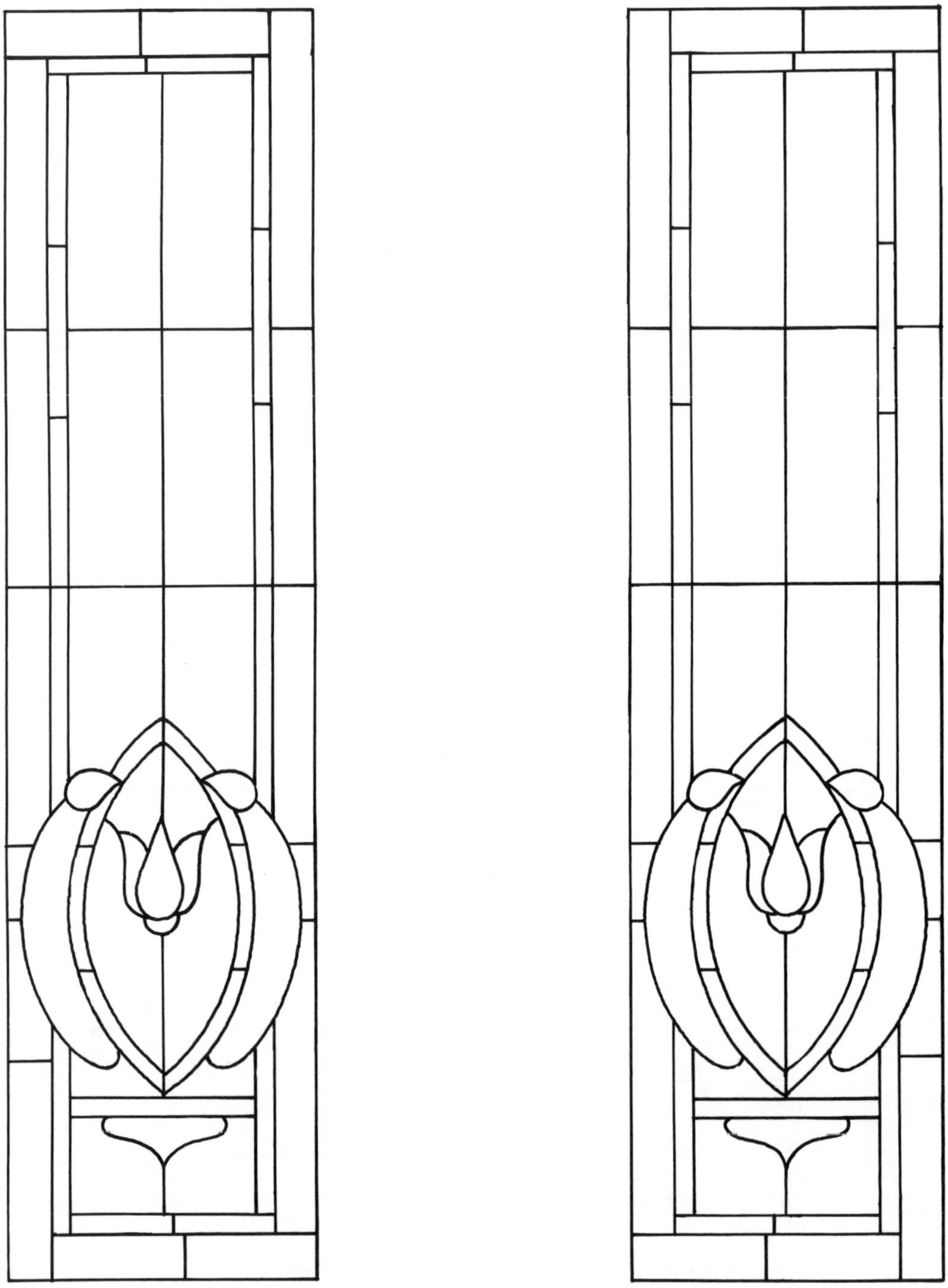

FEDERATION WINDOWS OR FRONT ENTRY PANELS

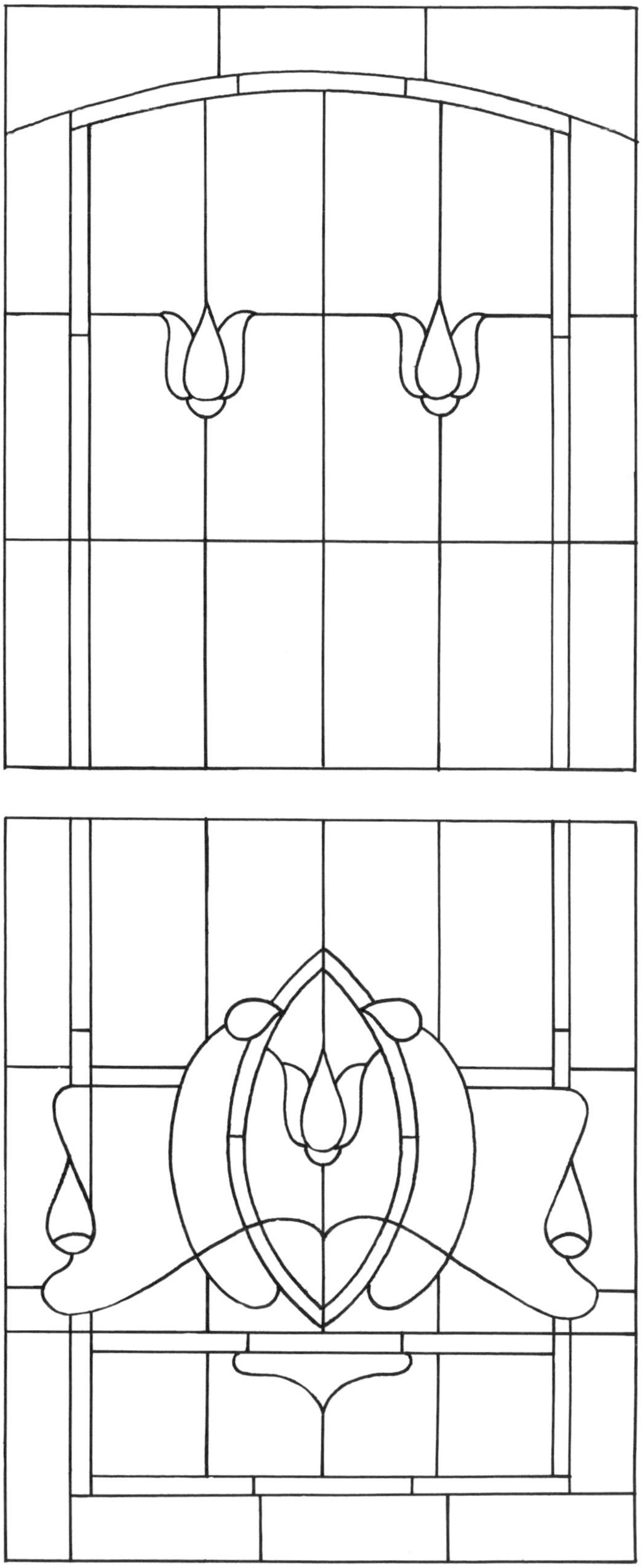

FEDERATION DOUBLE HUNG WINDOW

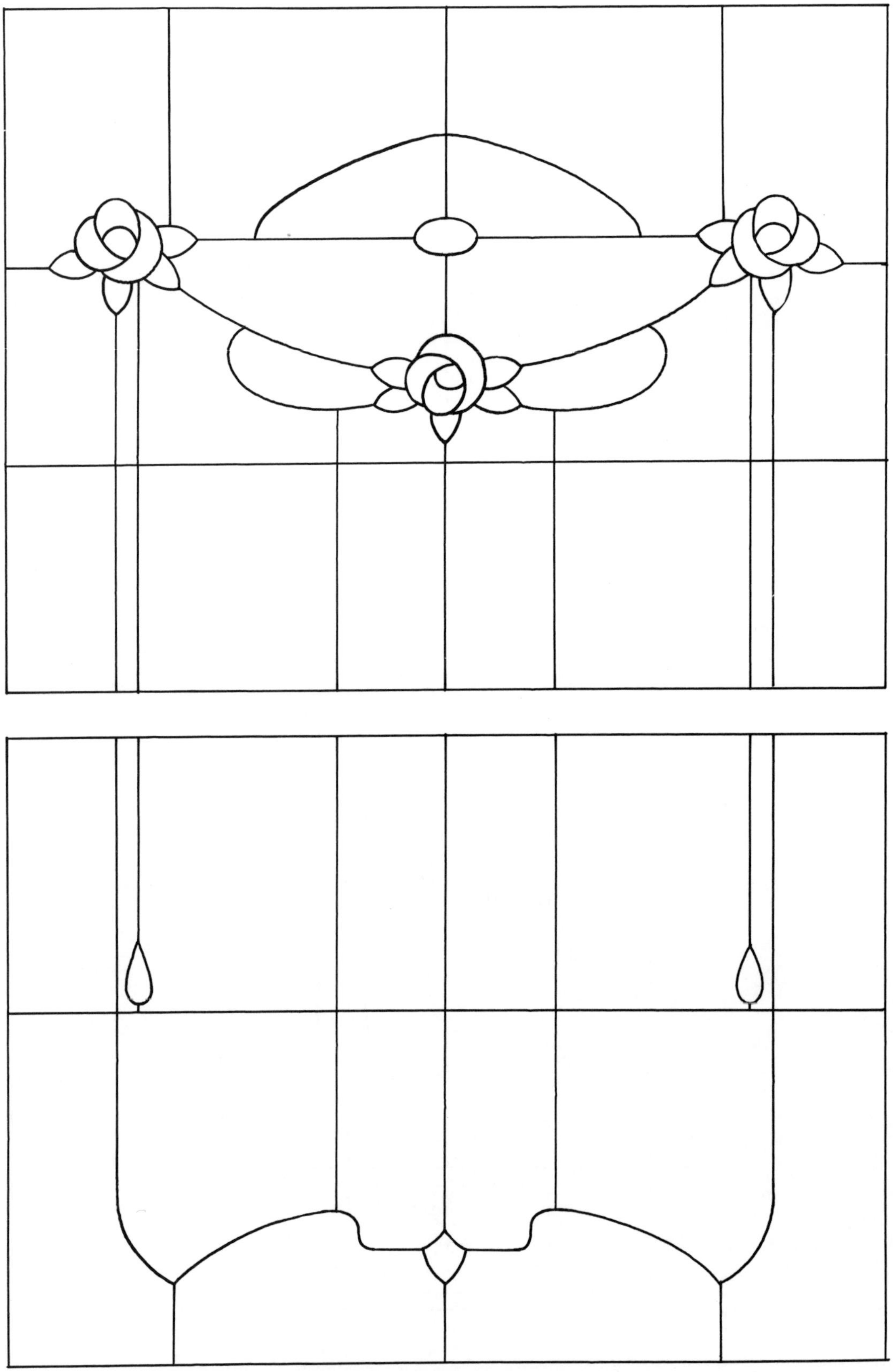

FEDERATION DOUBLE HUNG WINDOW
(see colour plates)

(top)

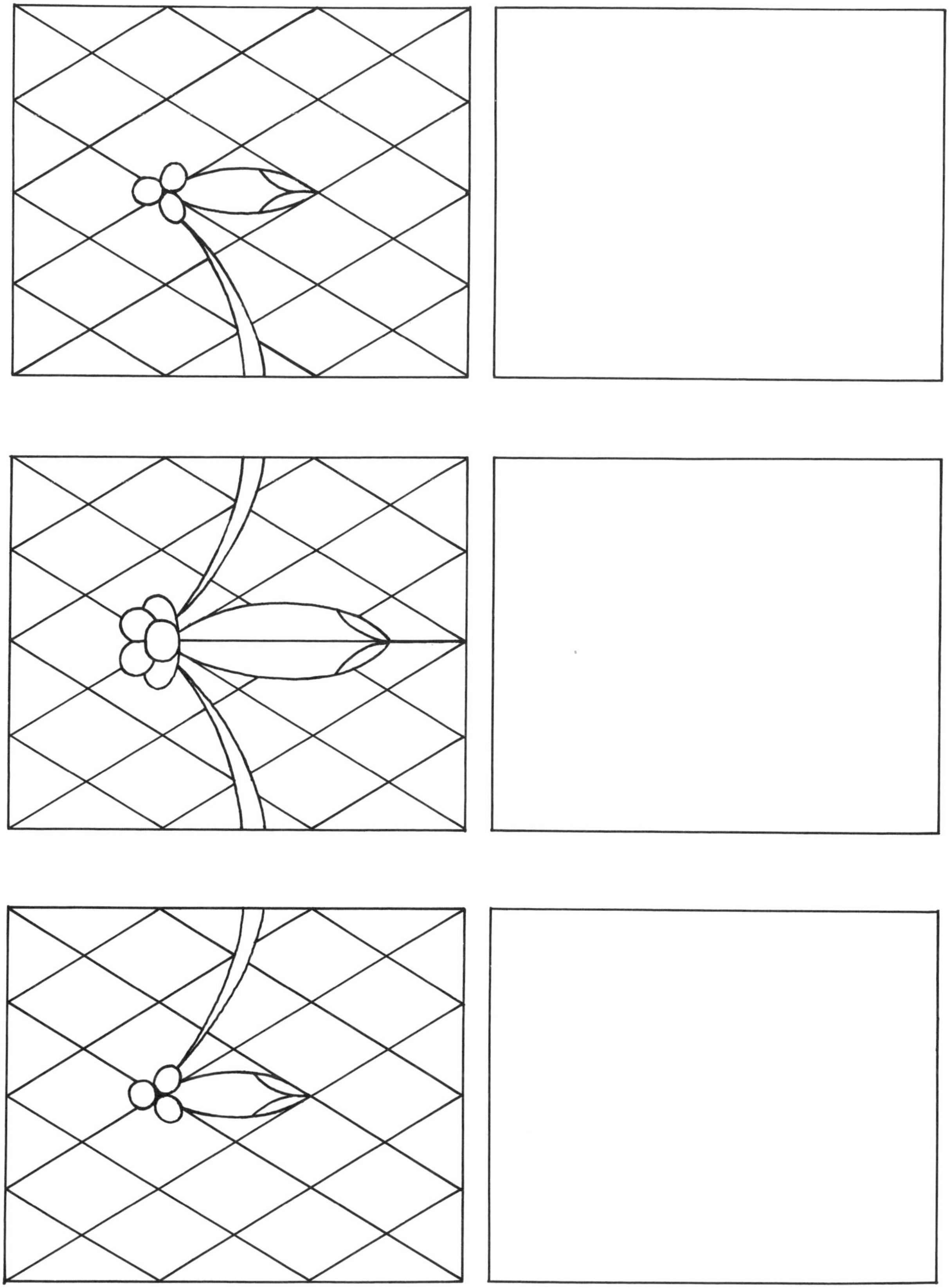

FEDERATION WINDOW SET

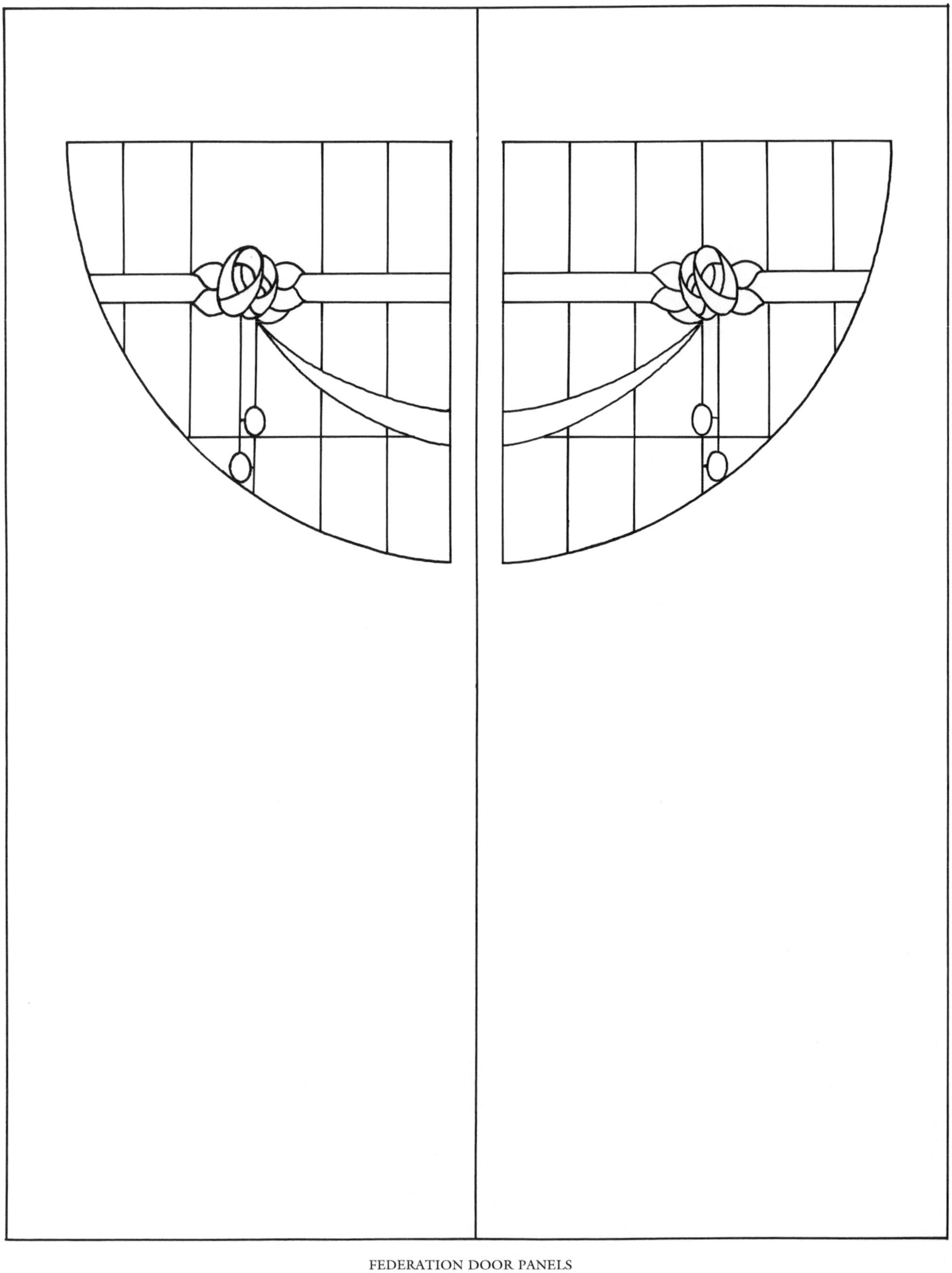

FEDERATION DOOR PANELS

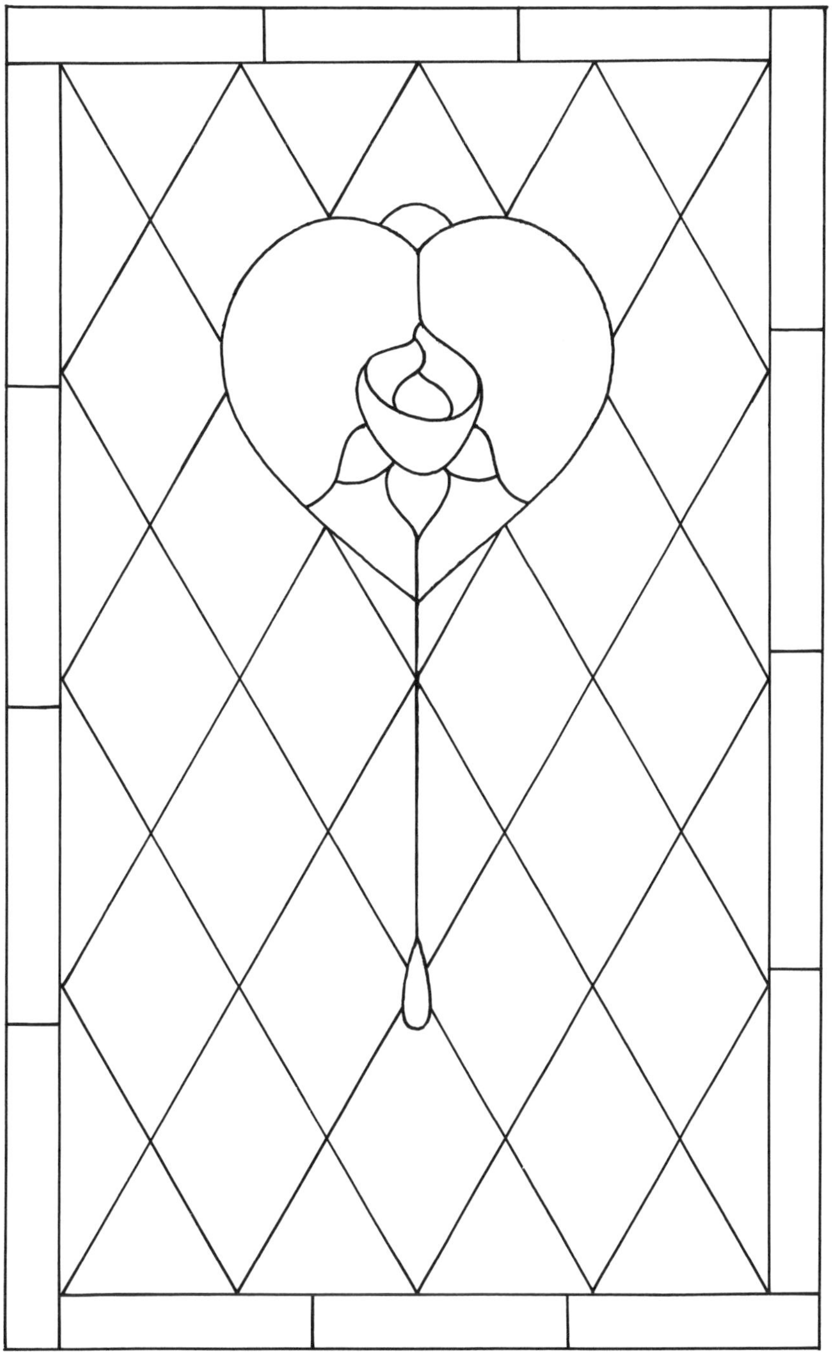

FEDERATION WINDOW

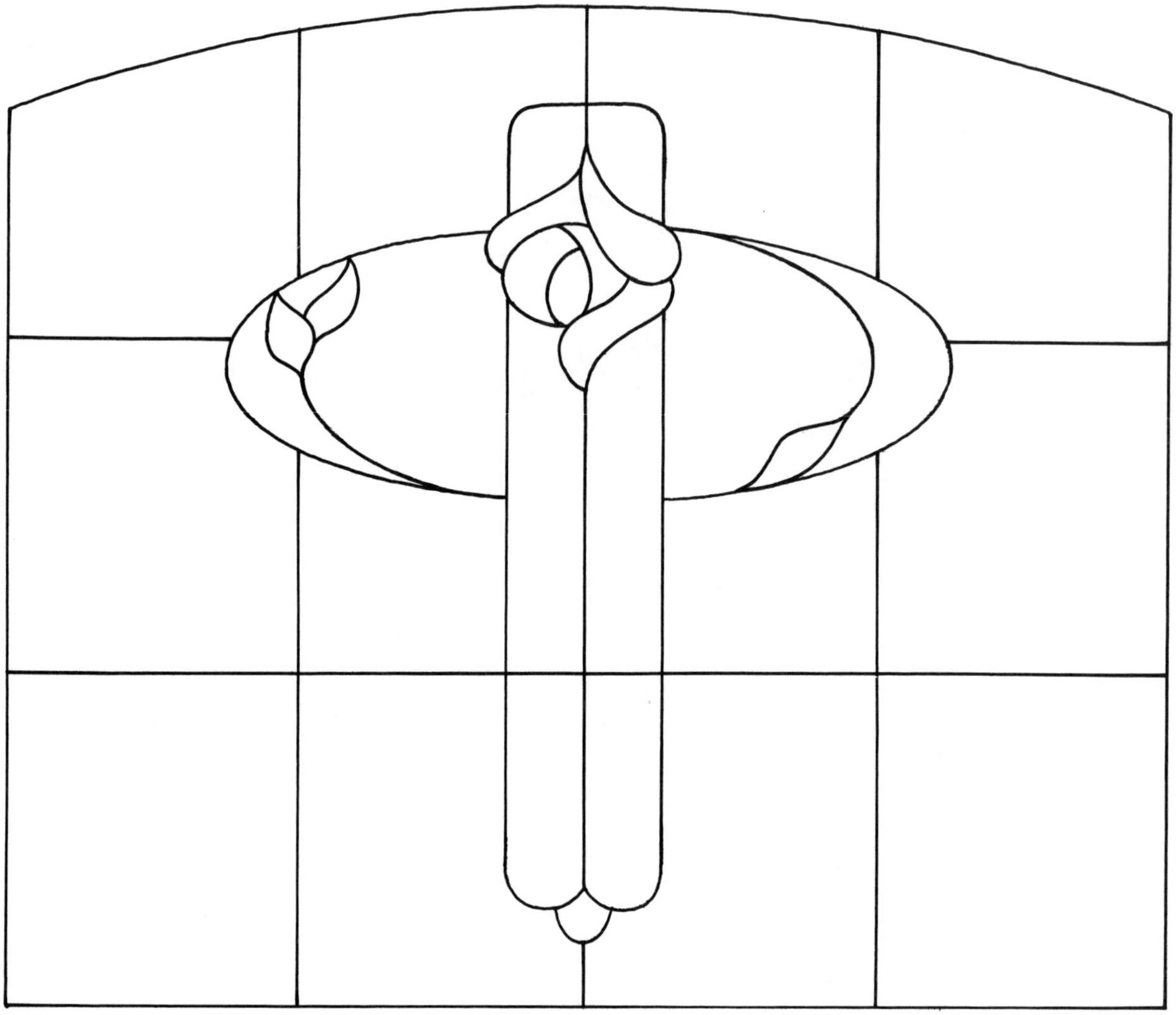

EDWARDIAN WINDOW OR DOOR PANEL

EDWARDIAN WINDOWS

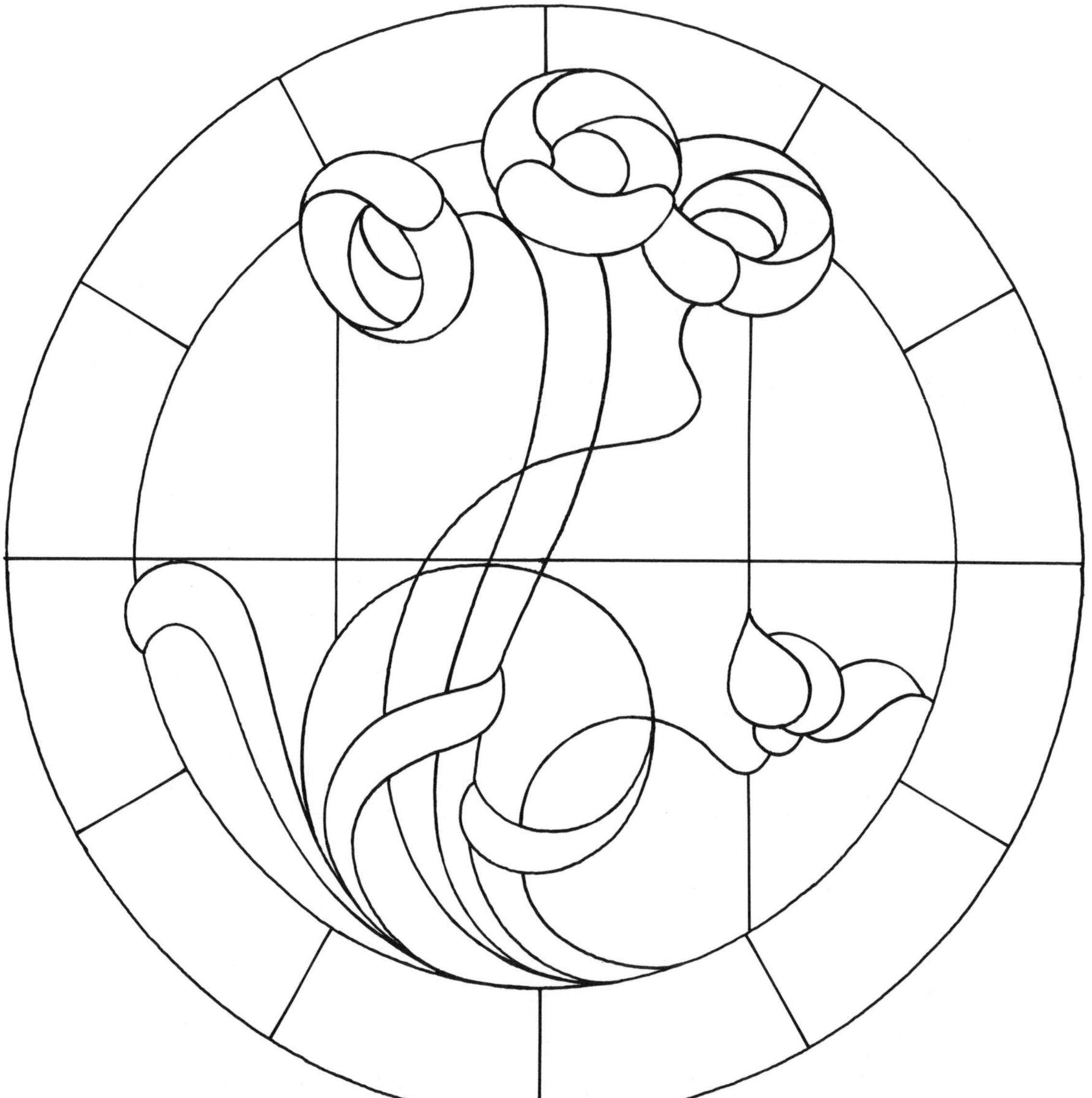

EDWARDIAN PORTHOLE WINDOW

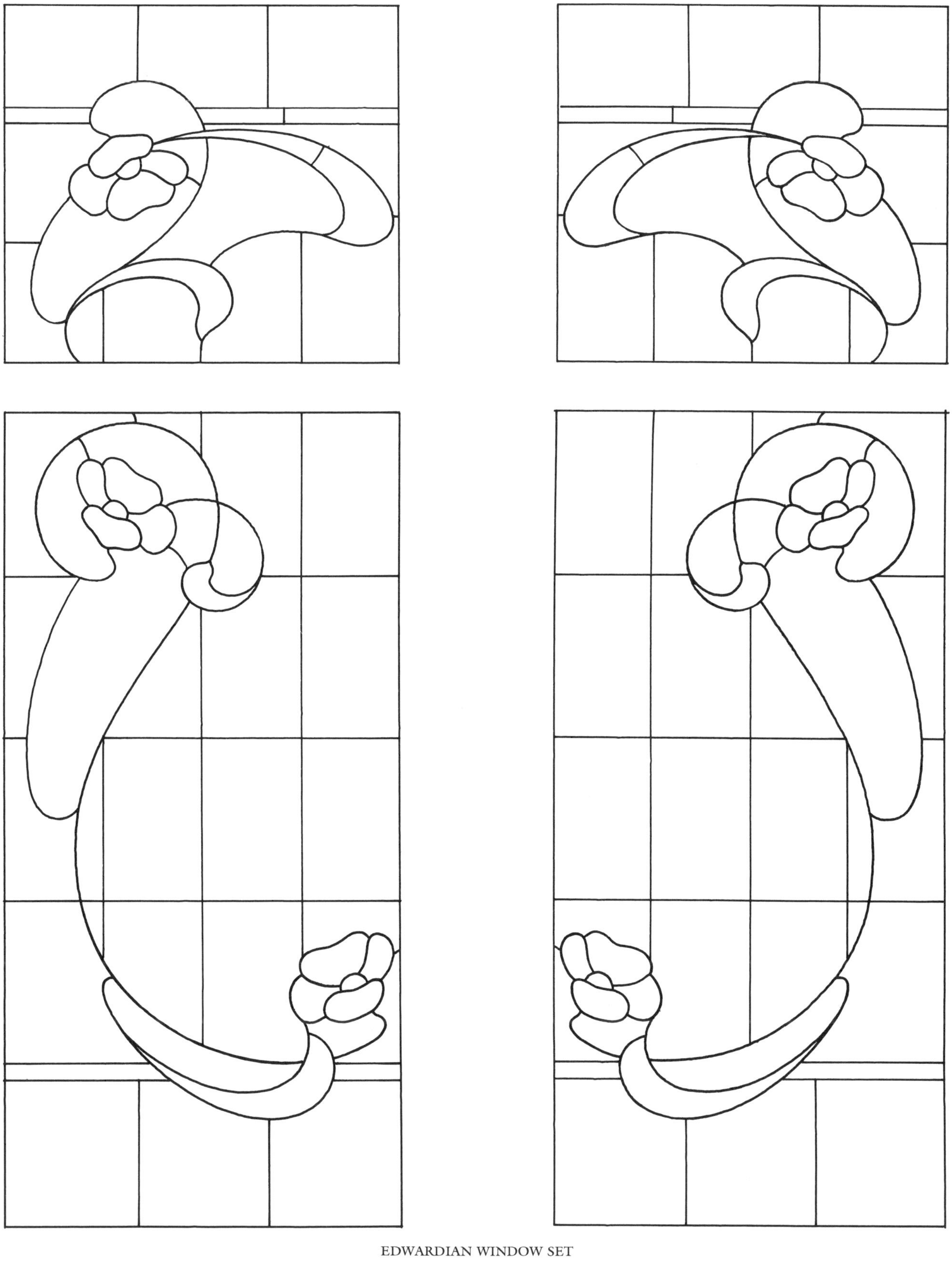

EDWARDIAN WINDOW SET

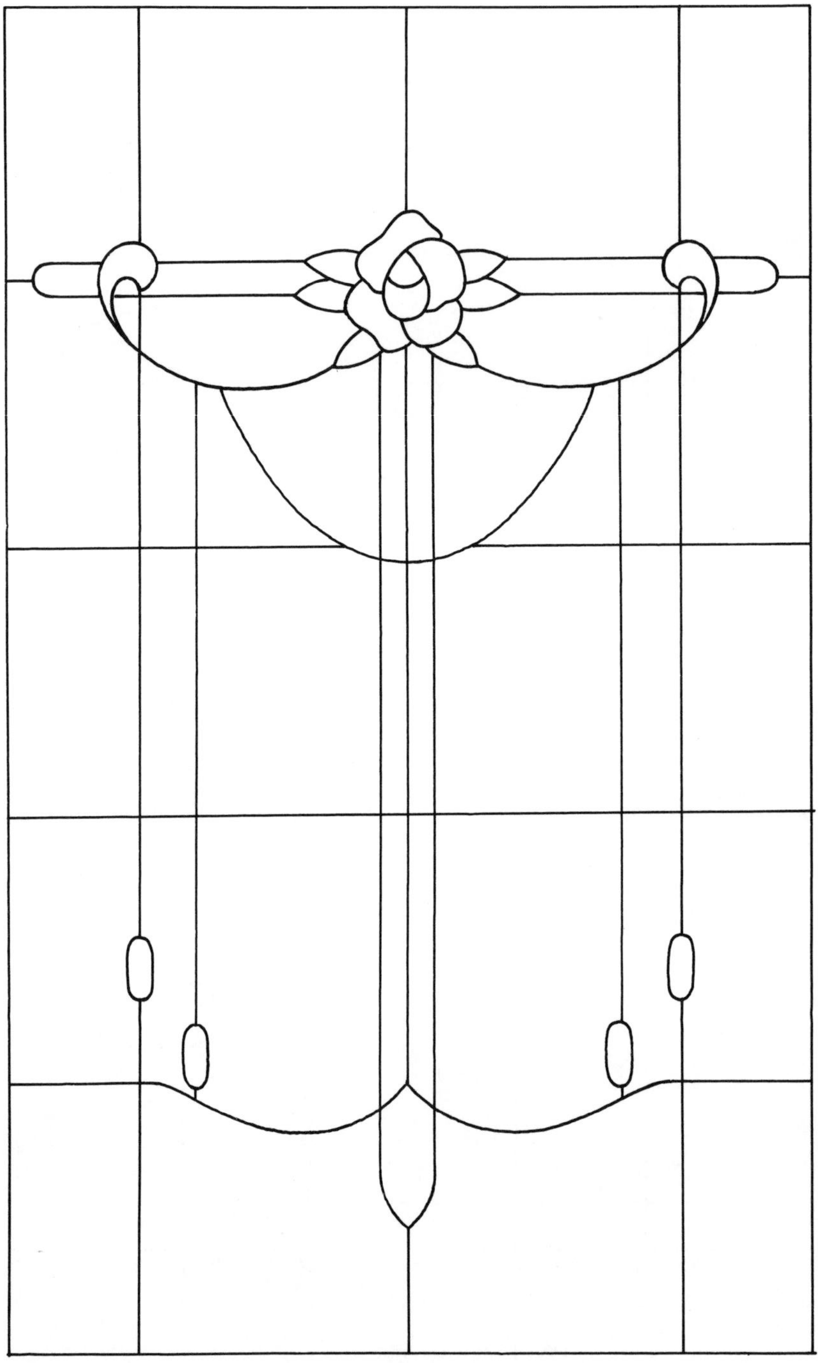

EDWARDIAN WINDOW
(see colour plates)

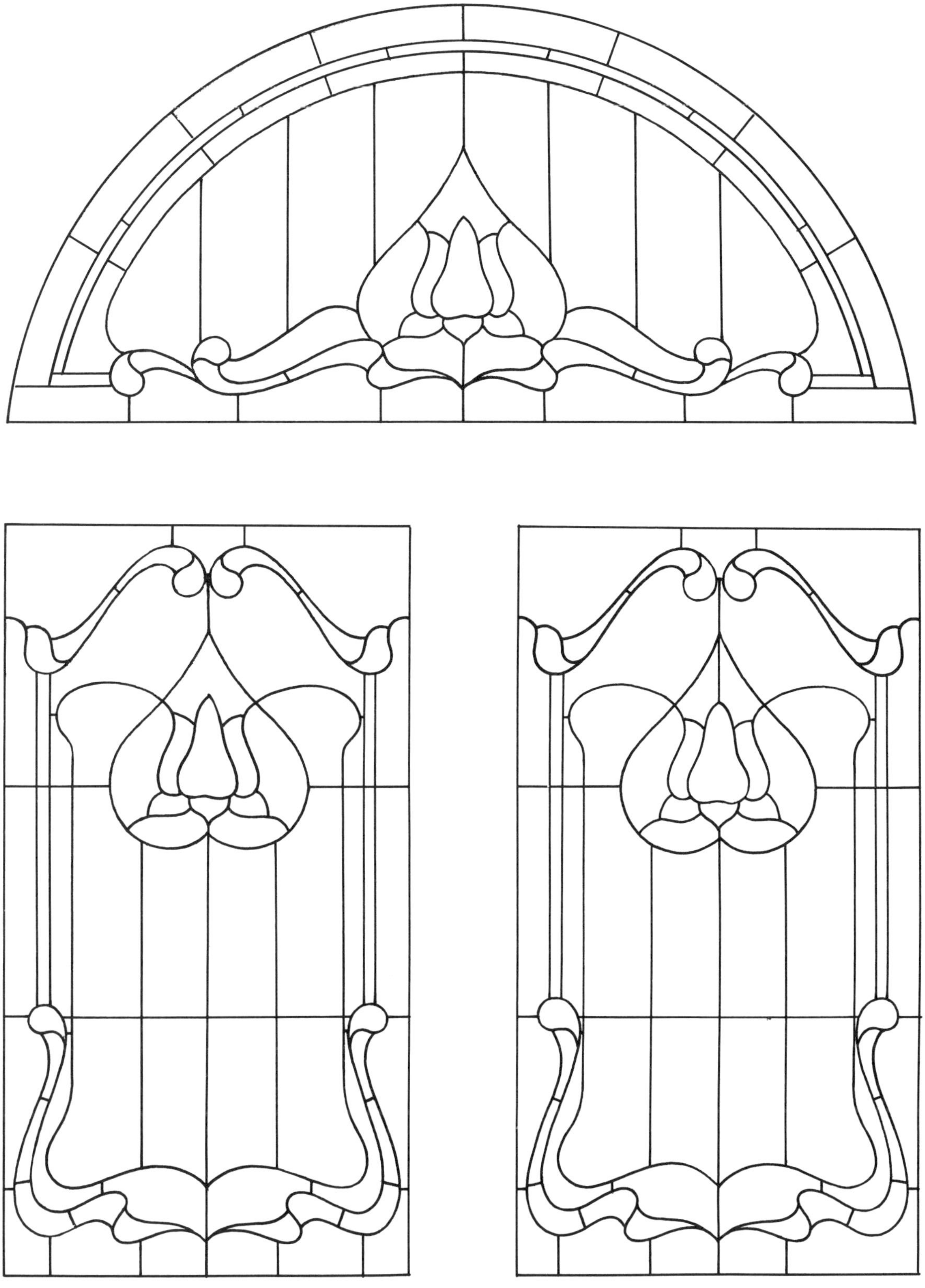

EDWARDIAN DOOR PANELS AND TRANSOM

EDWARDIAN WINDOW SET

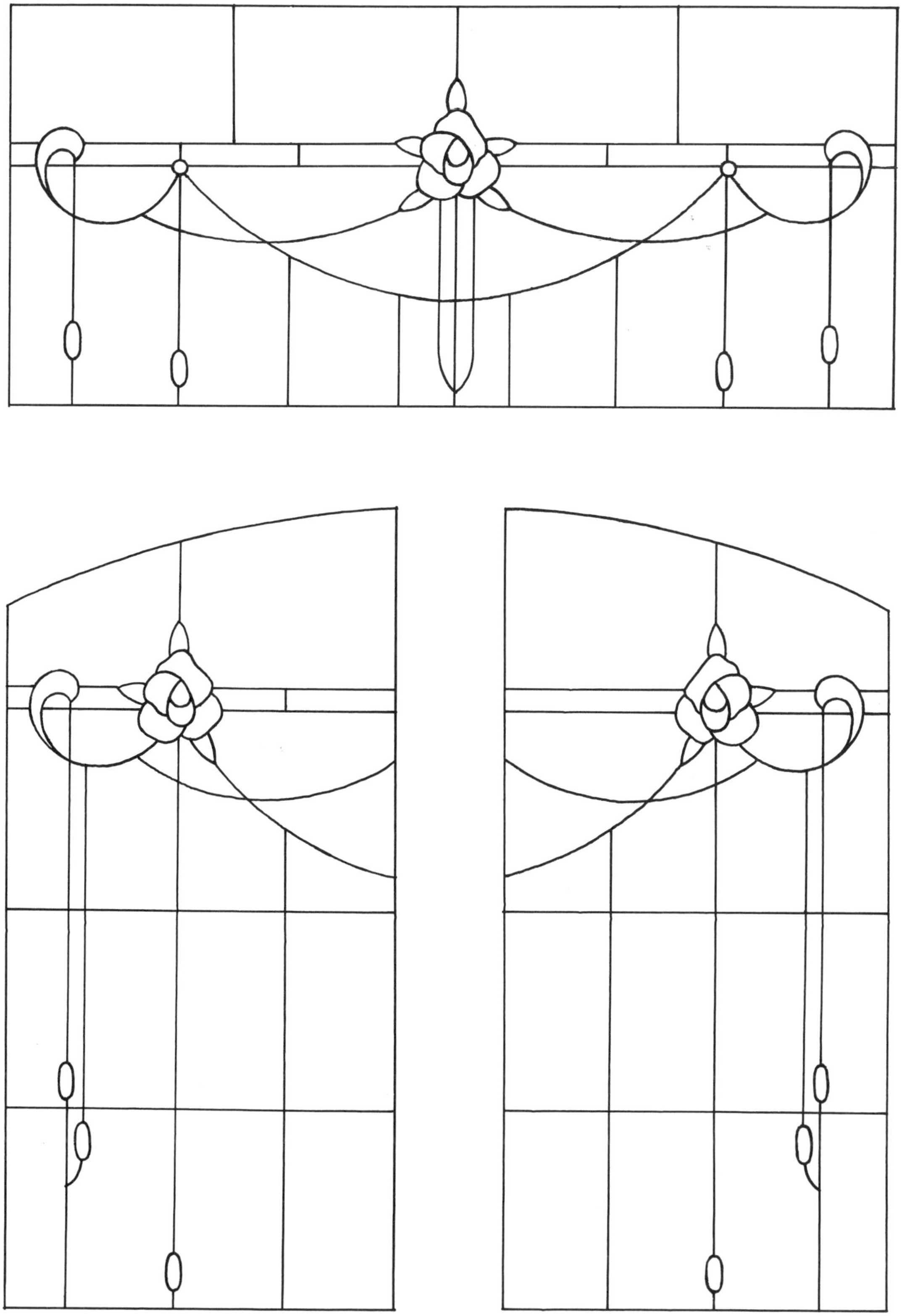

EDWARDIAN DOUBLE DOOR PANELS AND TRANSOM

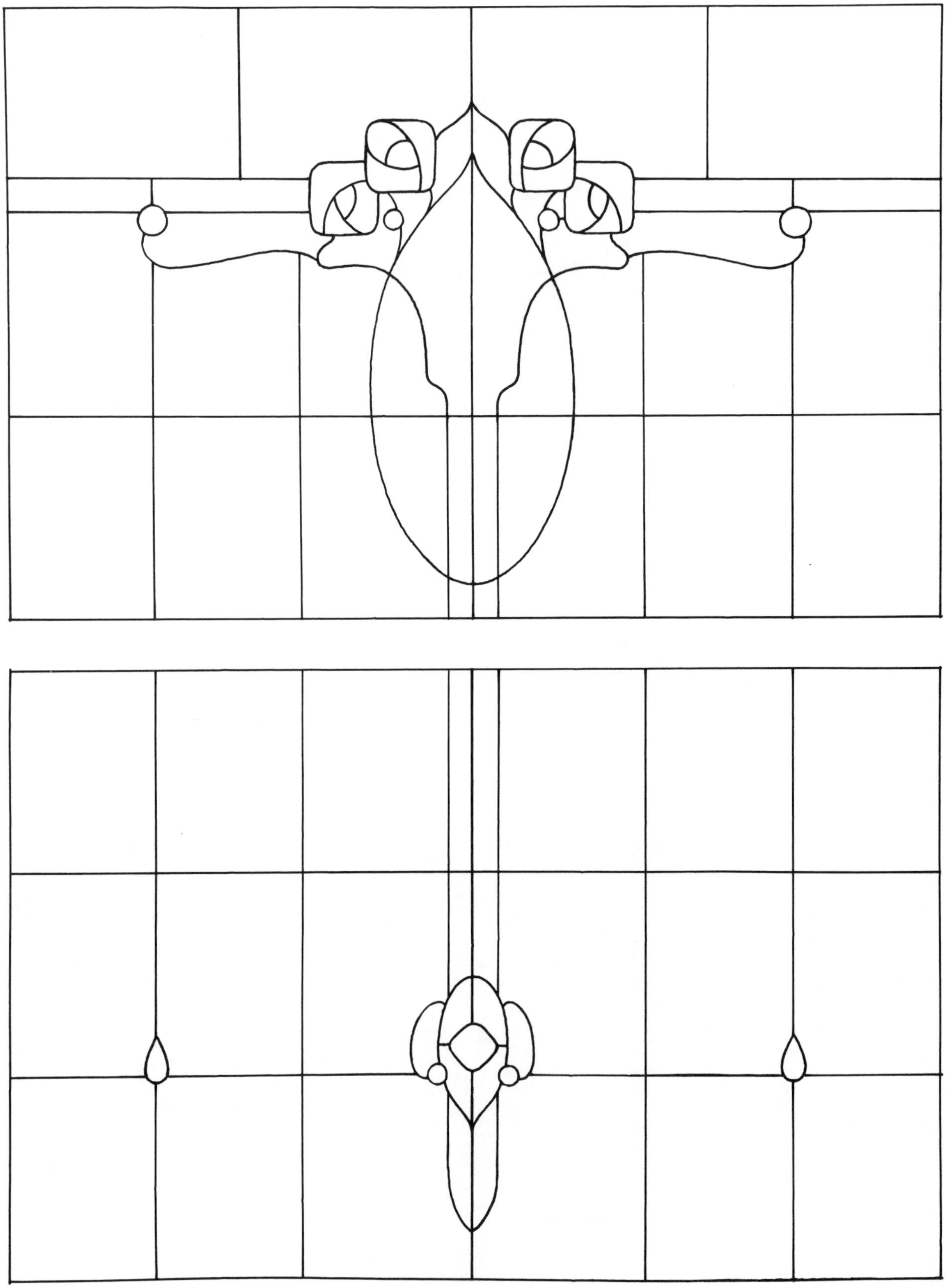

EDWARDIAN DOUBLE HUNG WINDOW
(see colour plates)

(top)

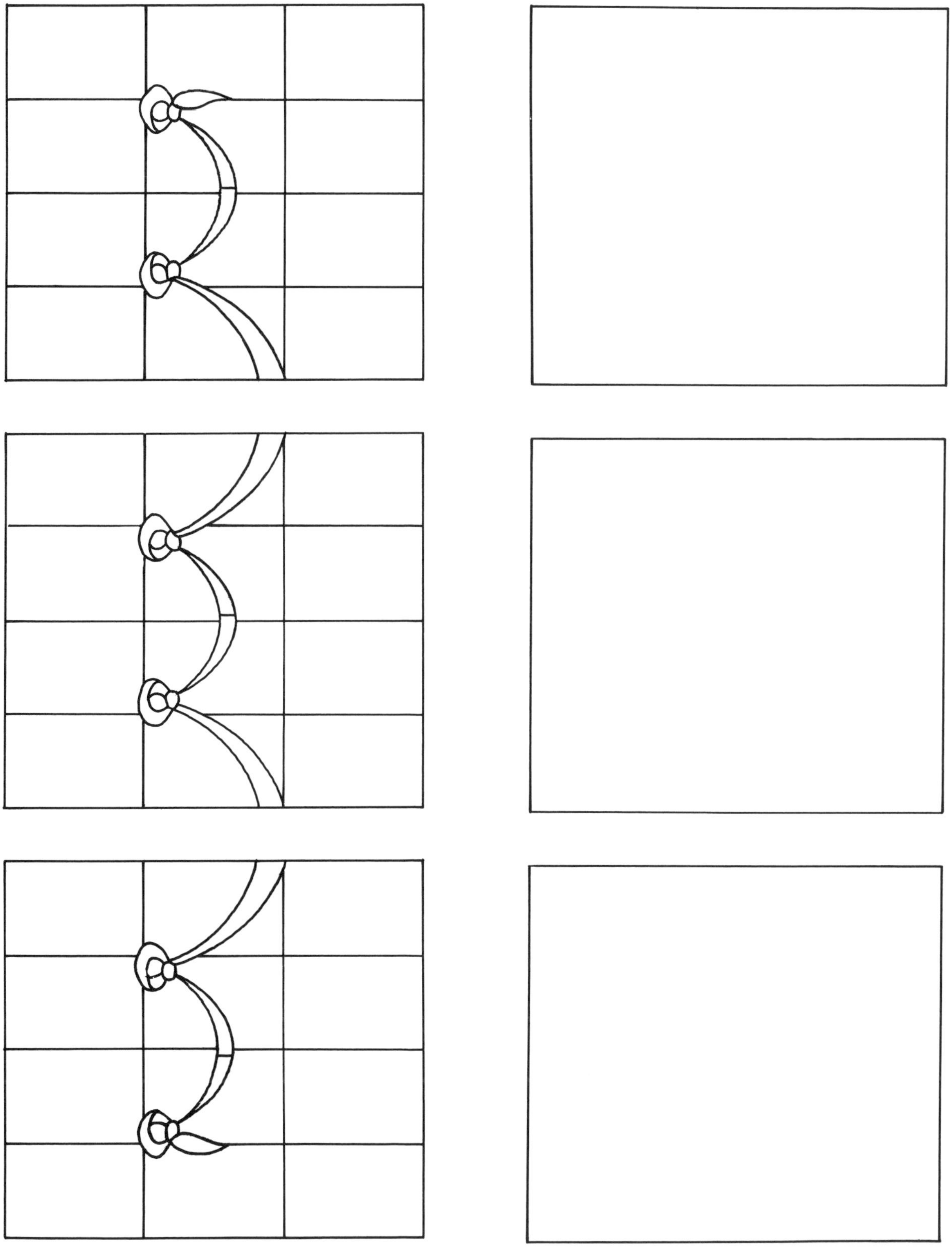

EDWARDIAN WINDOW SET

(top)

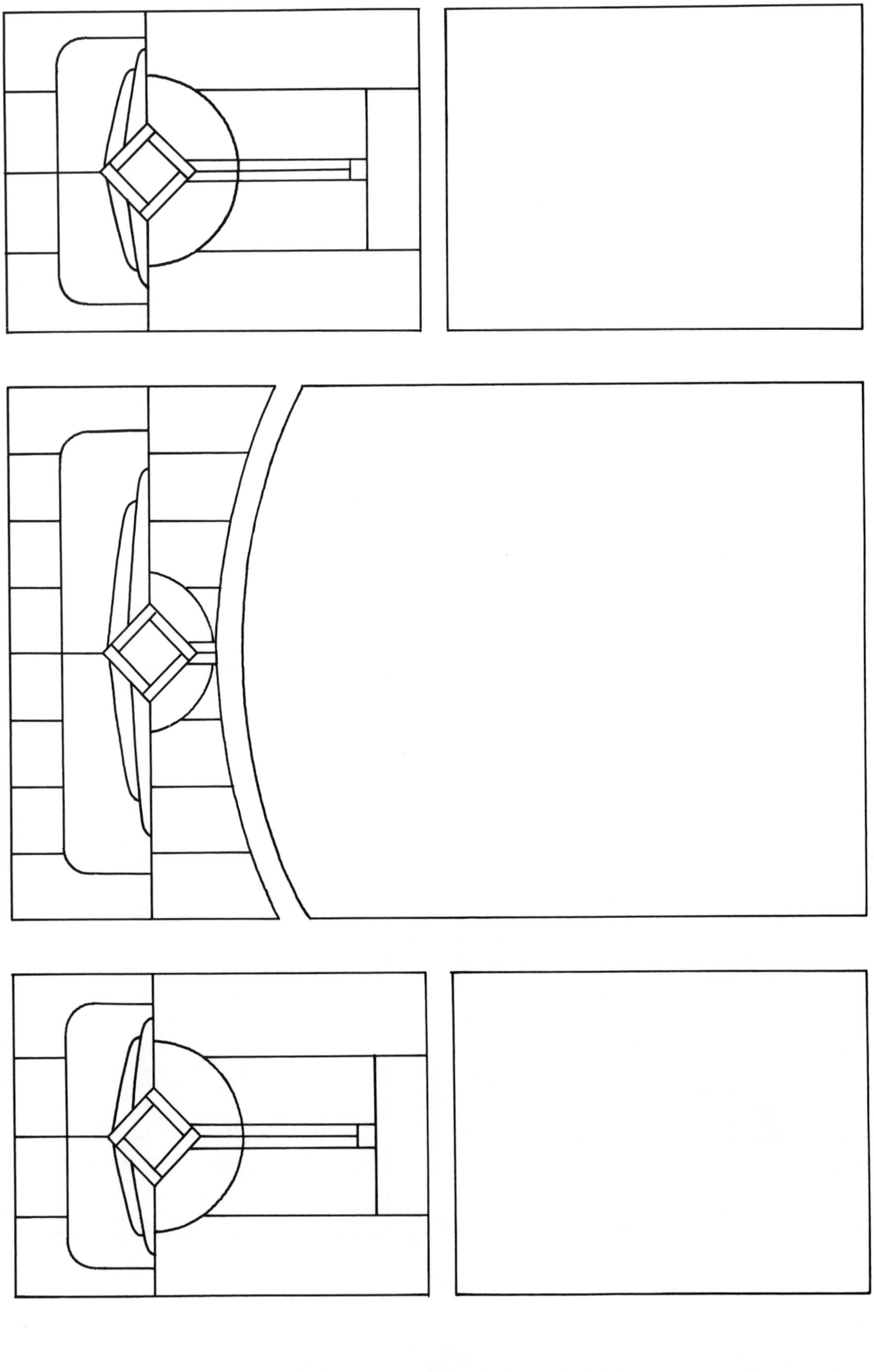

ART DECO WINDOW SET

ART DECO WINDOW OR DOOR PANEL

TWO VARIATIONS OF AN ART DECO WINDOW OR DOOR PANEL

(top)

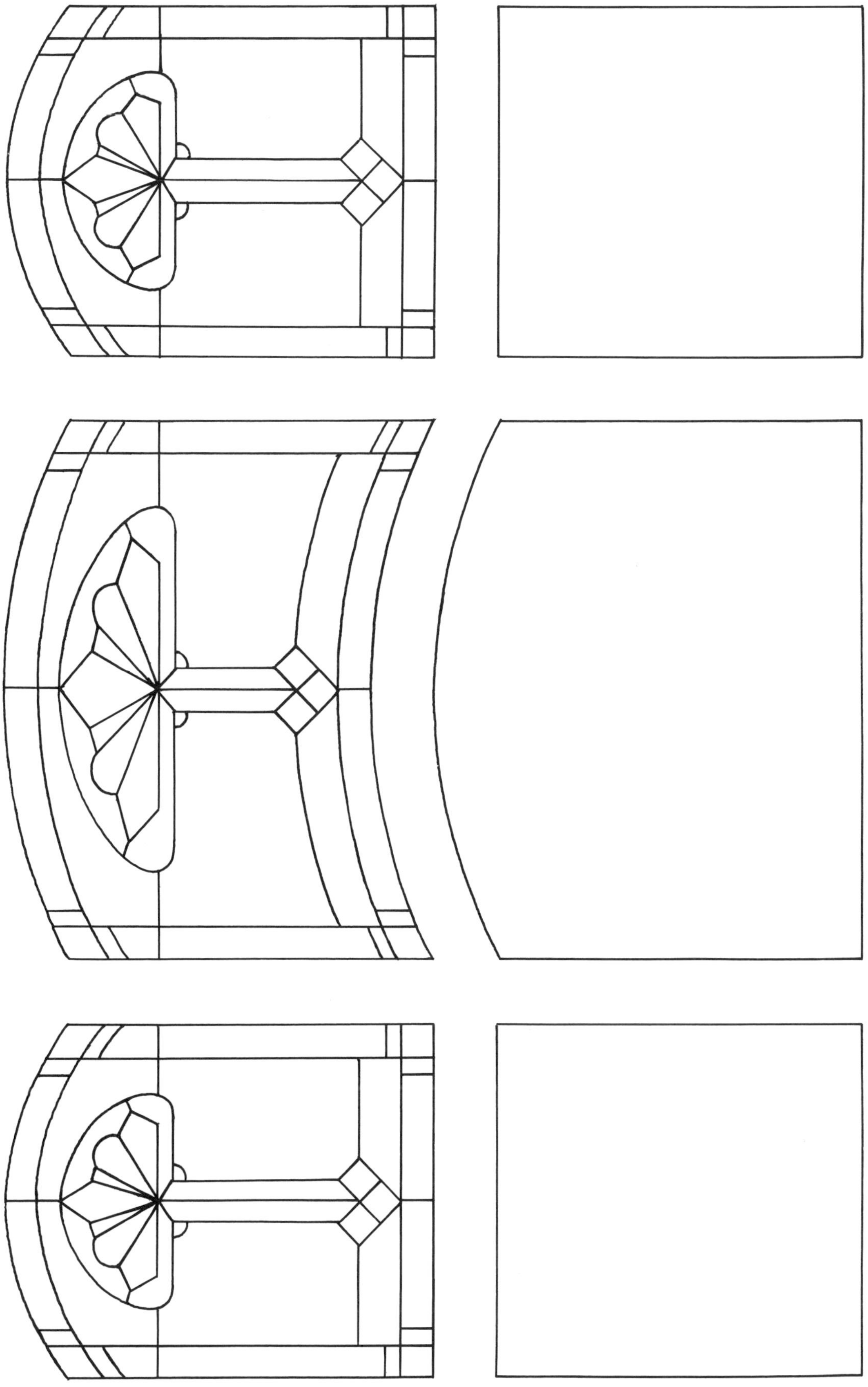

ART DECO WINDOW SET

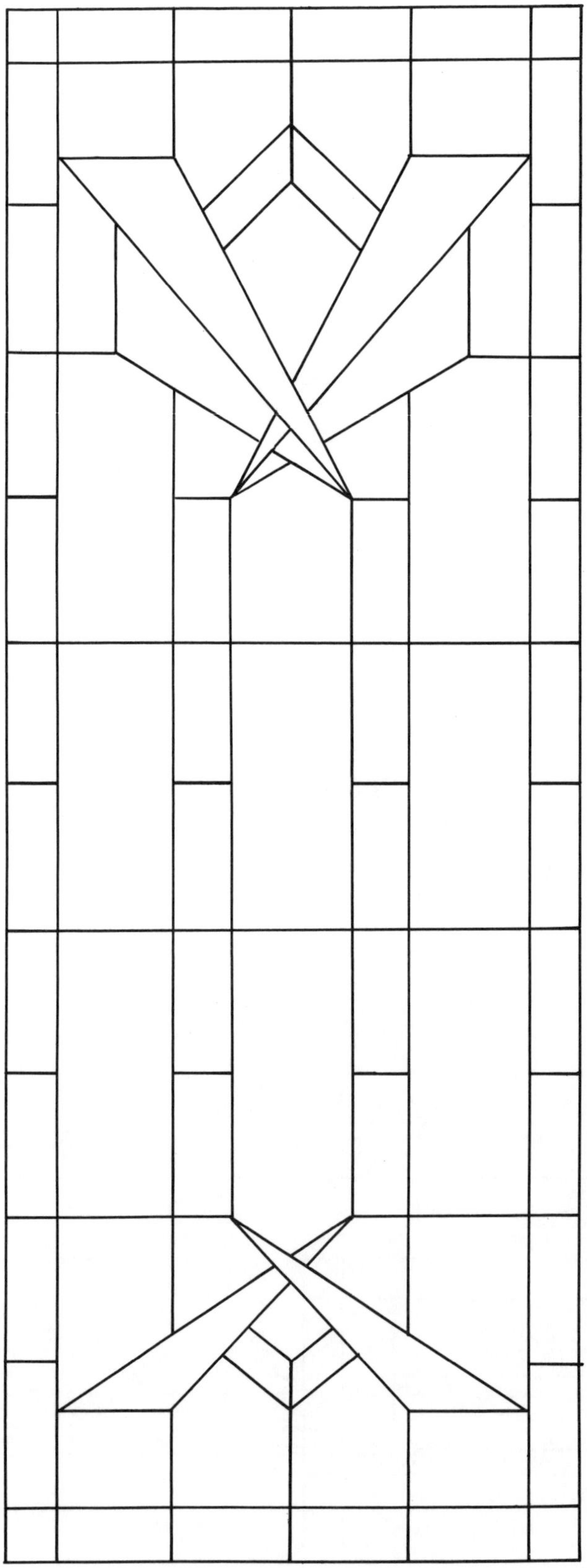

ART DECO WINDOW OR DOOR PANEL

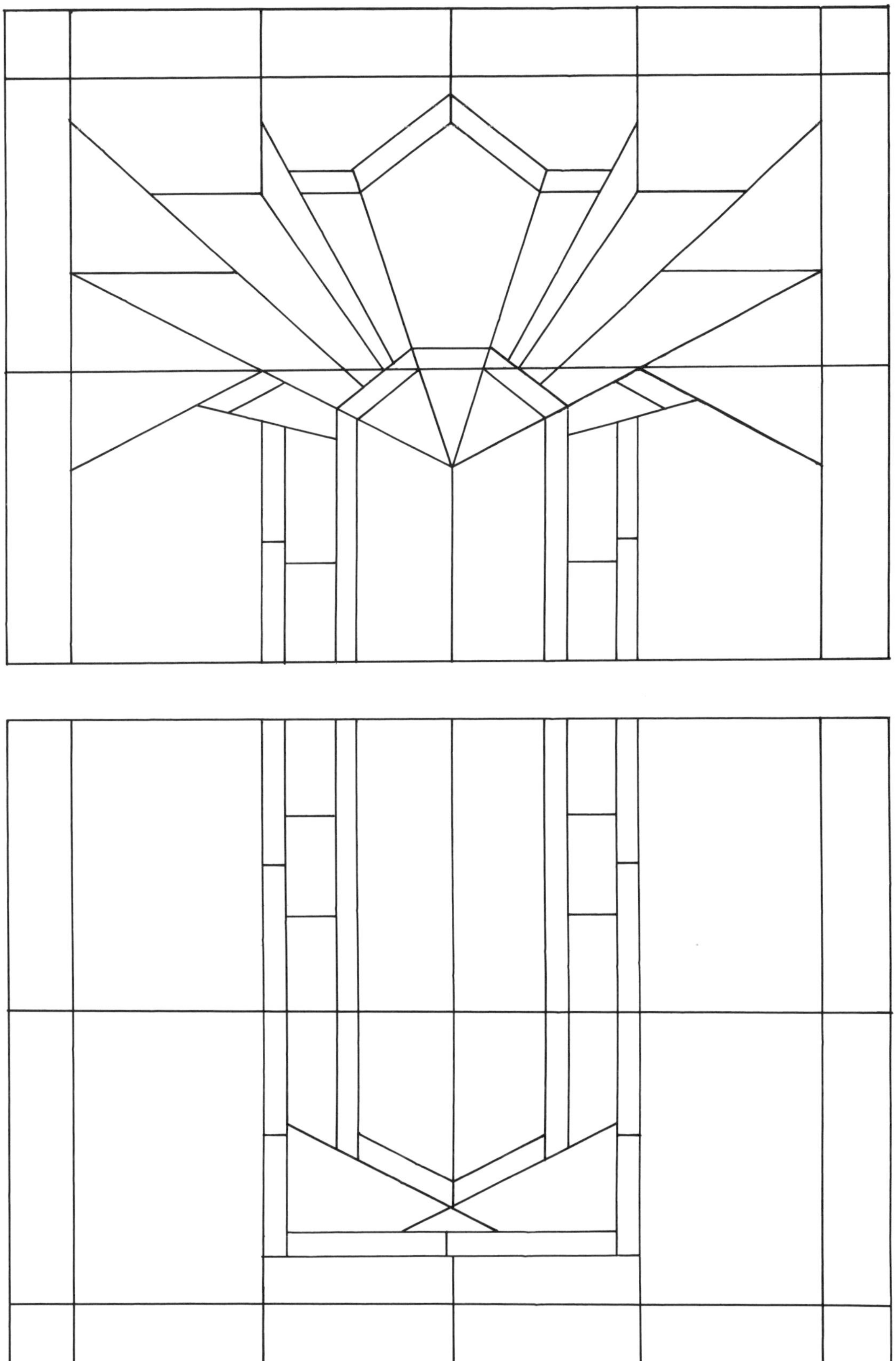

ART DECO DOUBLE HUNG WINDOW

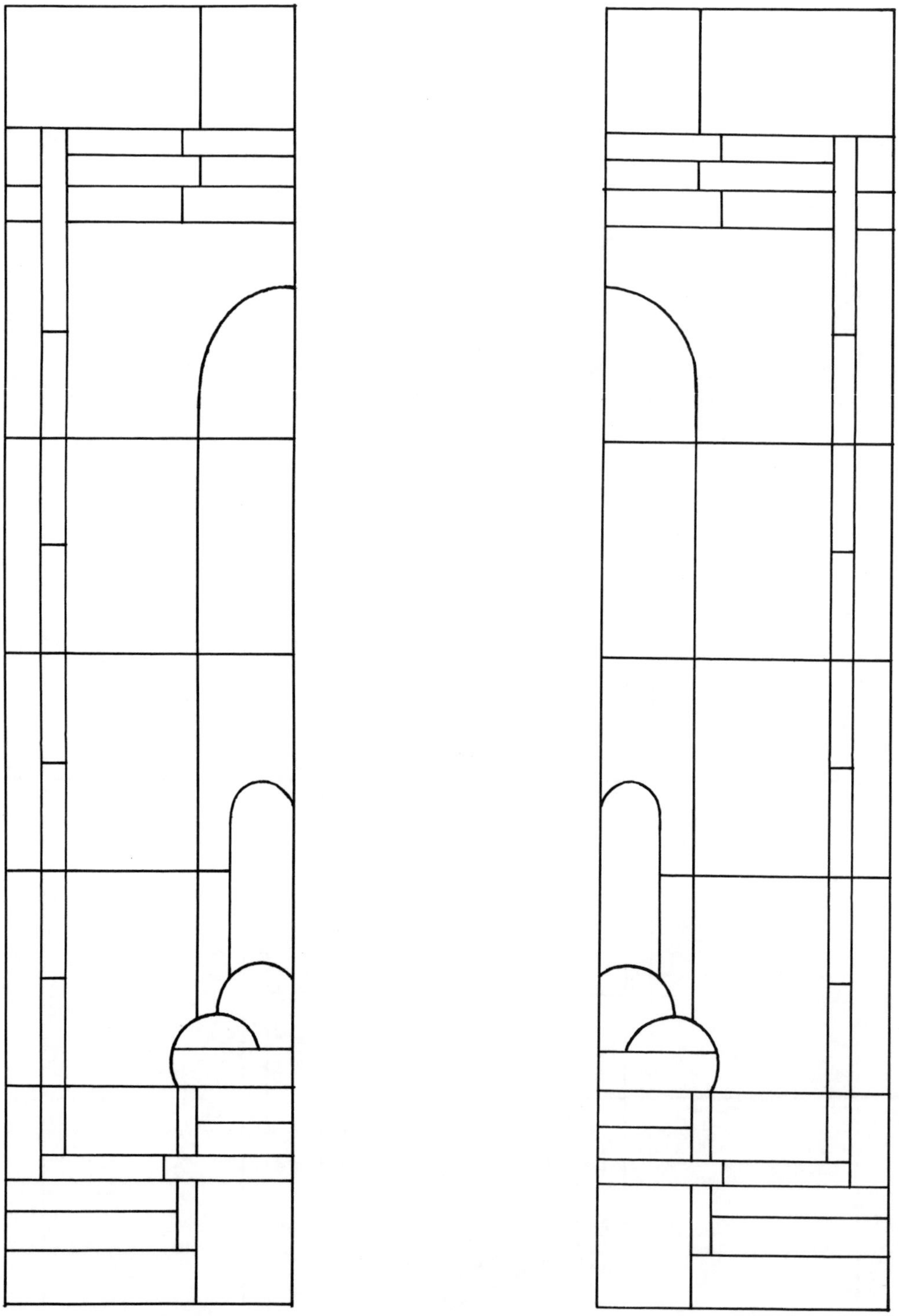

ART DECO DOOR ENTRY PANELS

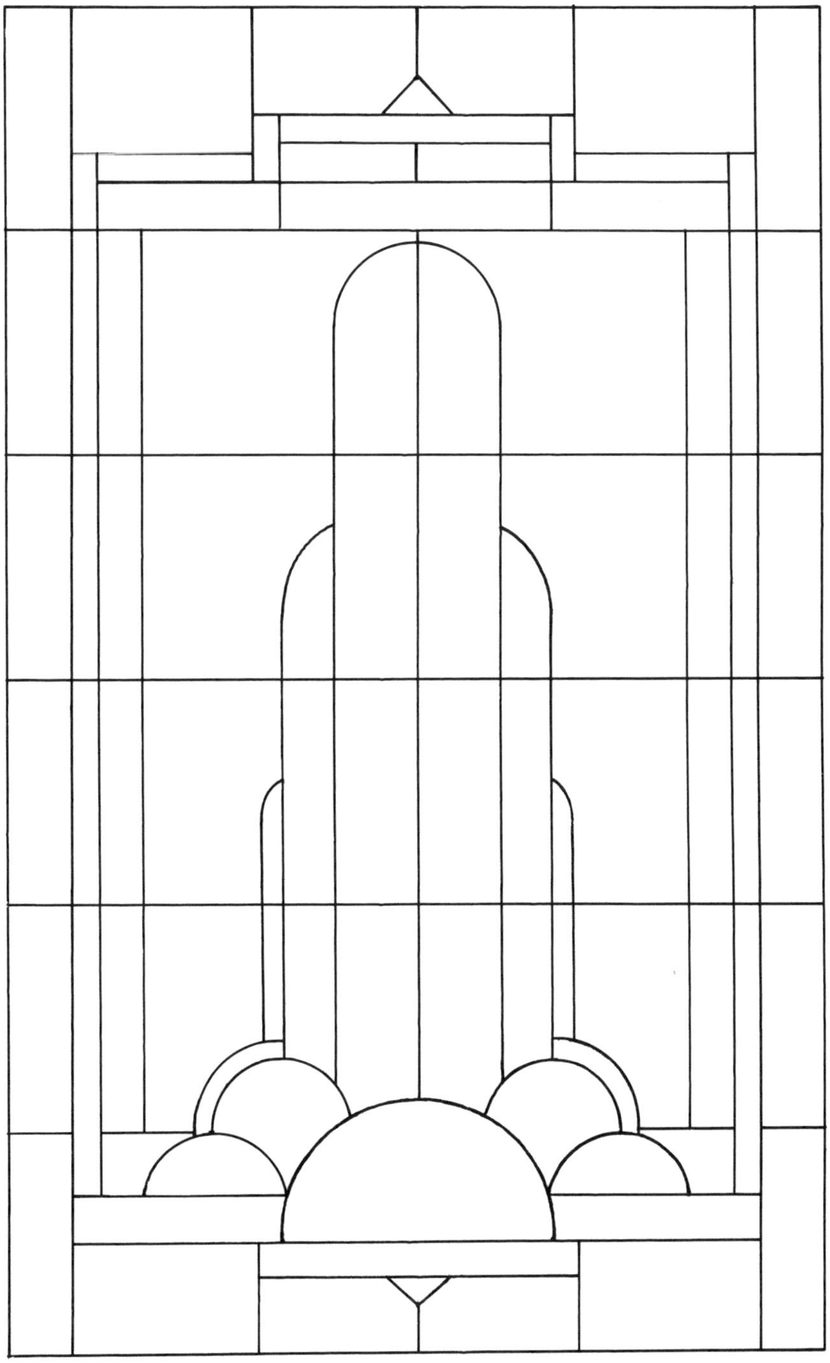

ART DECO WINDOW

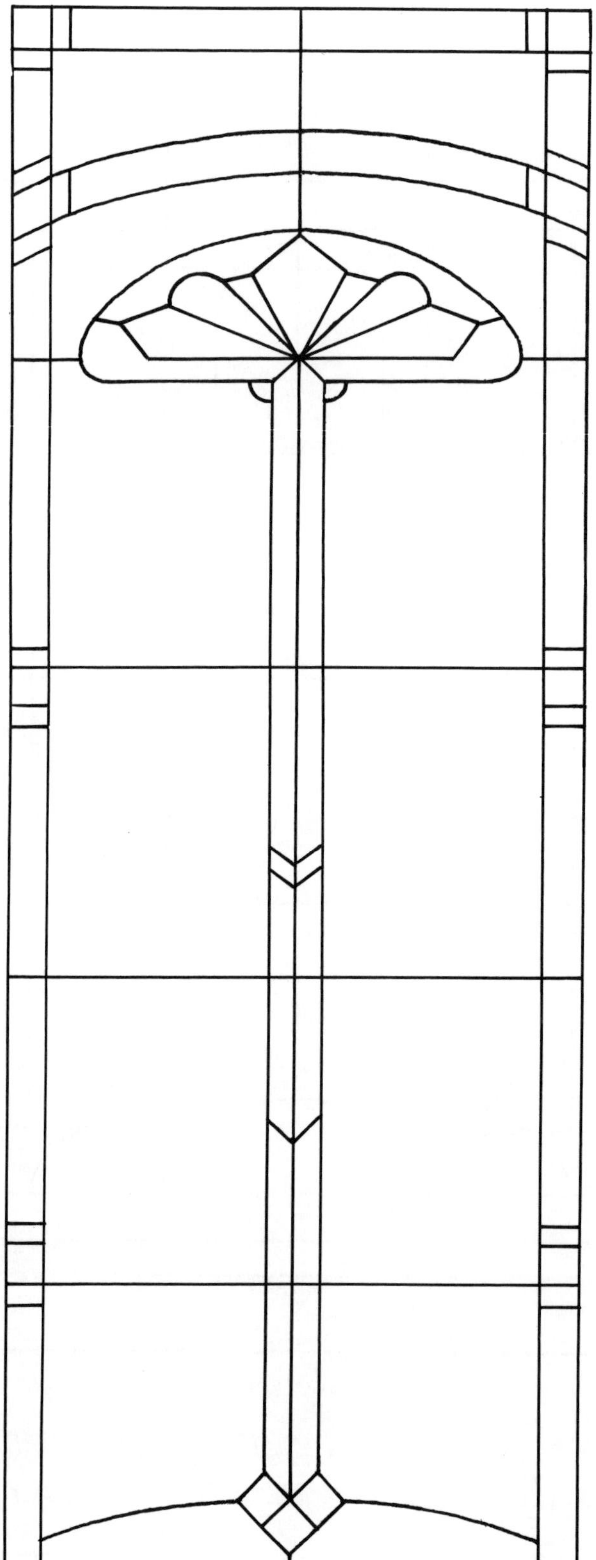

ART DECO WINDOW OR DOOR PANEL

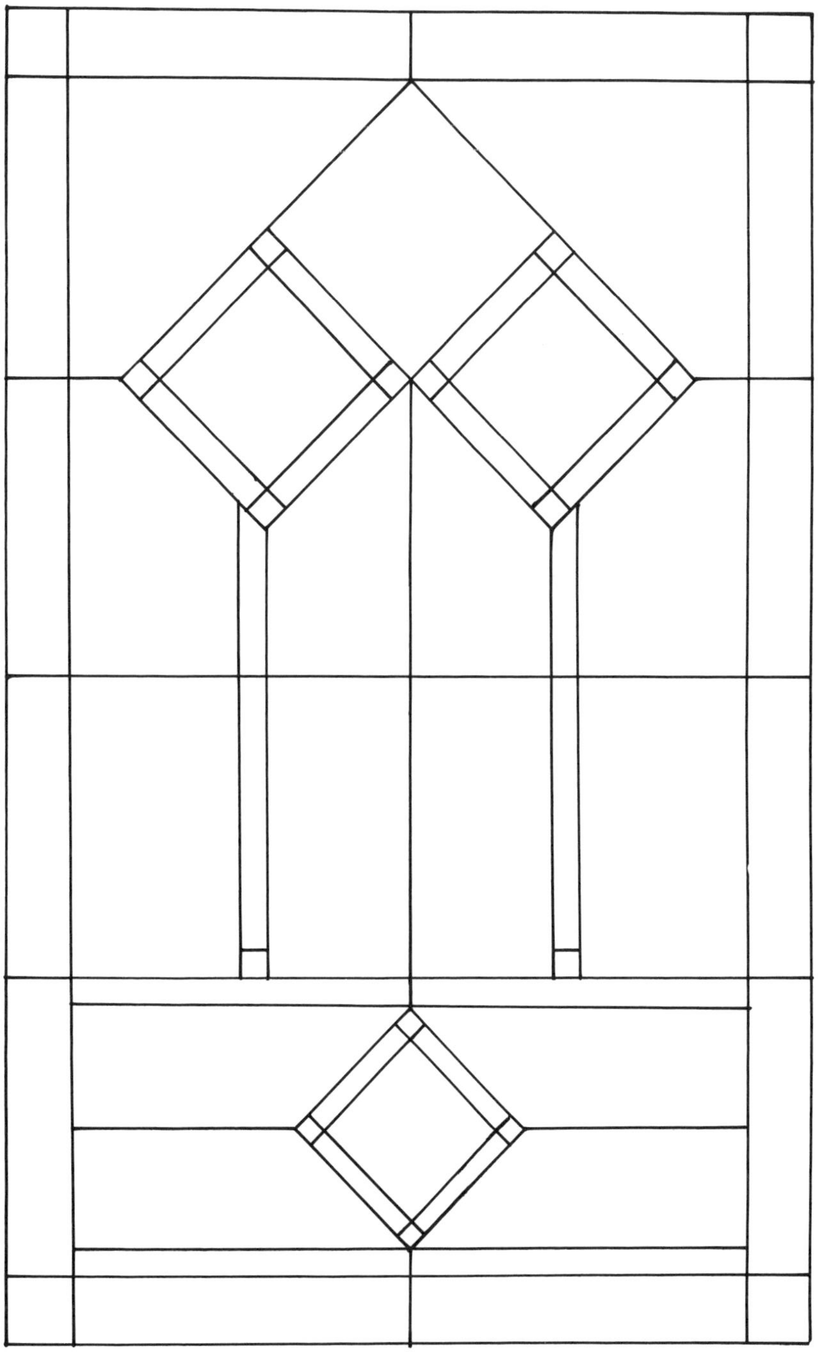

ART DECO WINDOW
(see colour plates)

ART DECO WINDOW

(top)

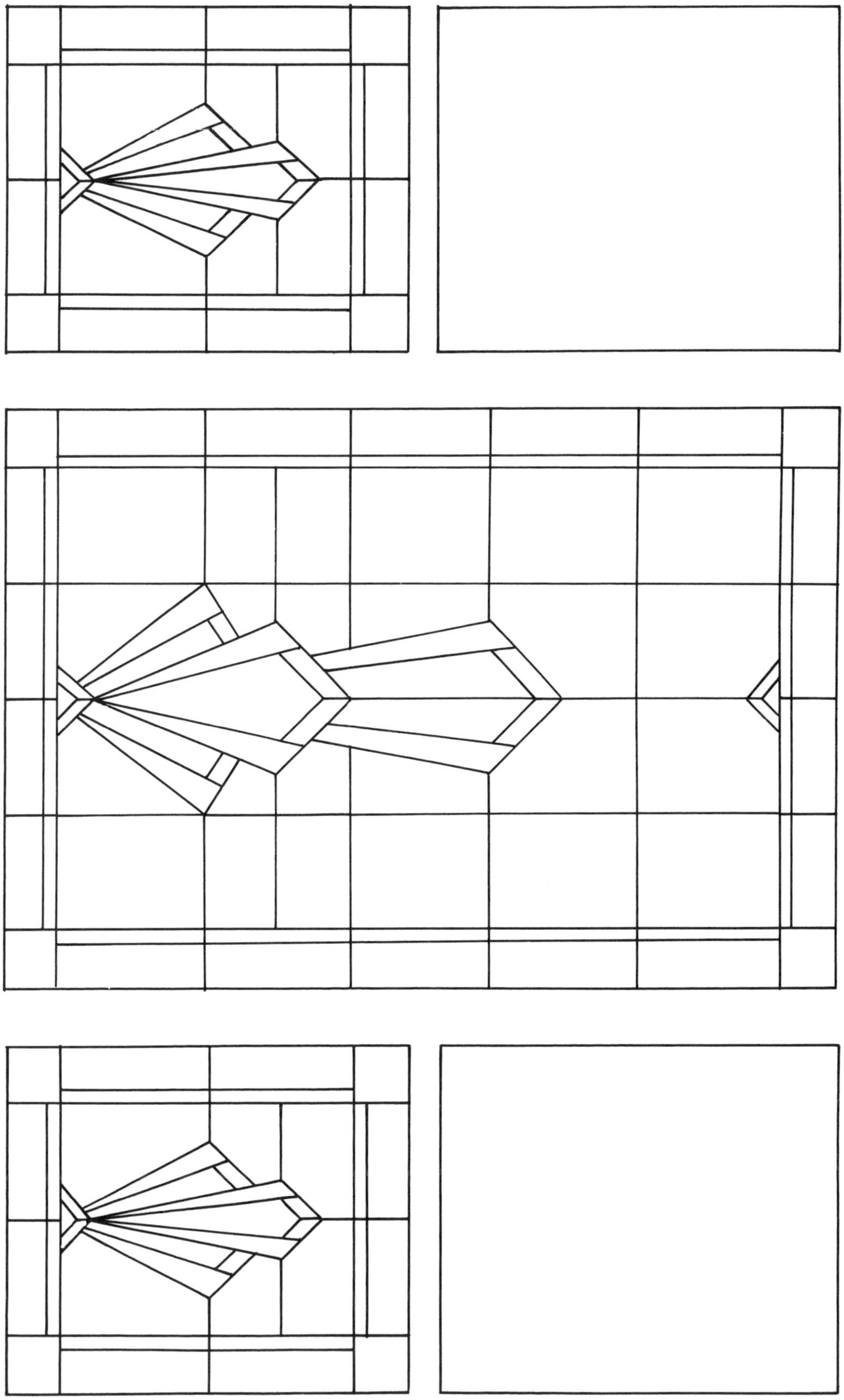

ART DECO WINDOW SET

(top)

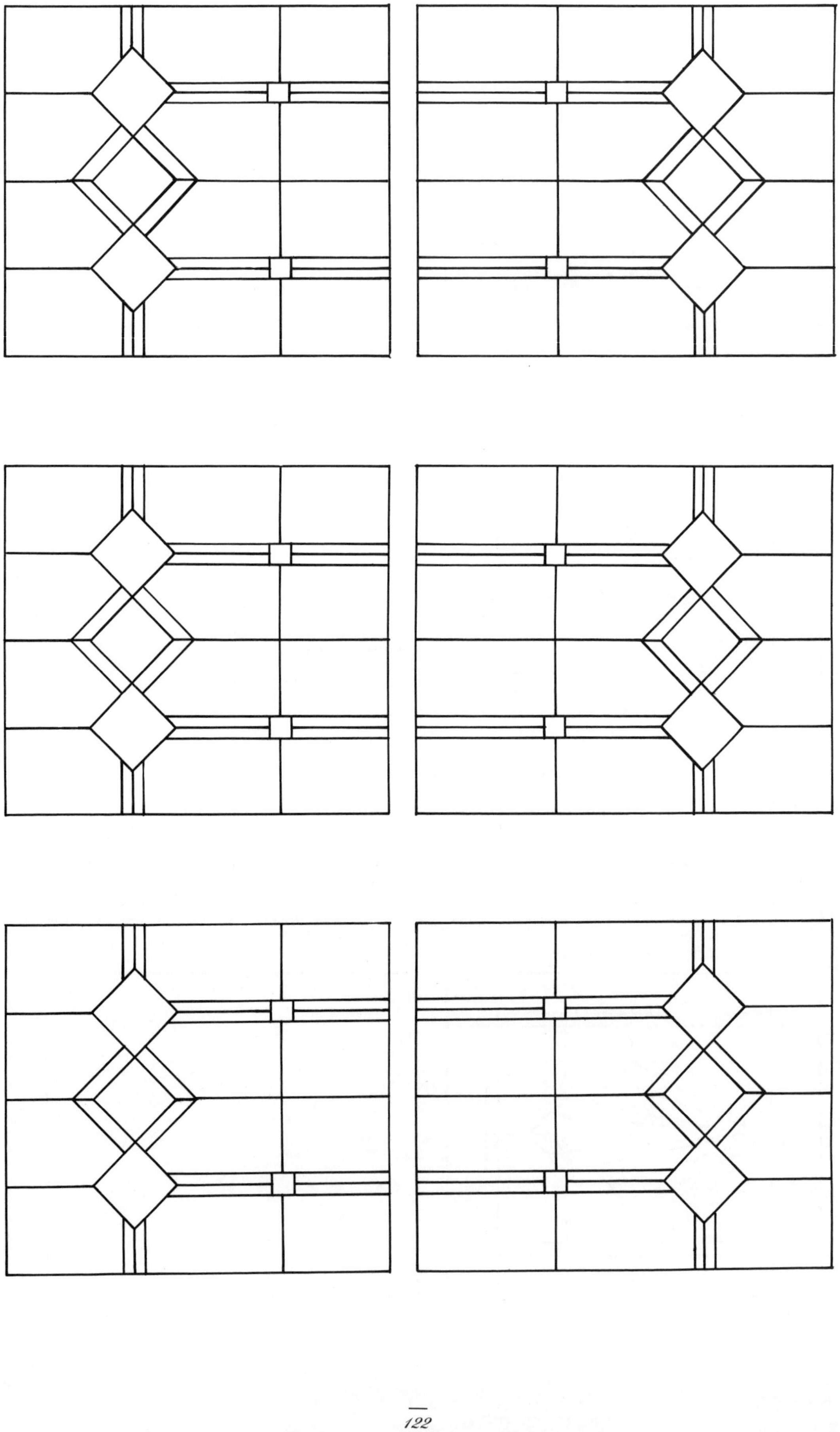

ART DECO DOUBLE HUNG WINDOW SET

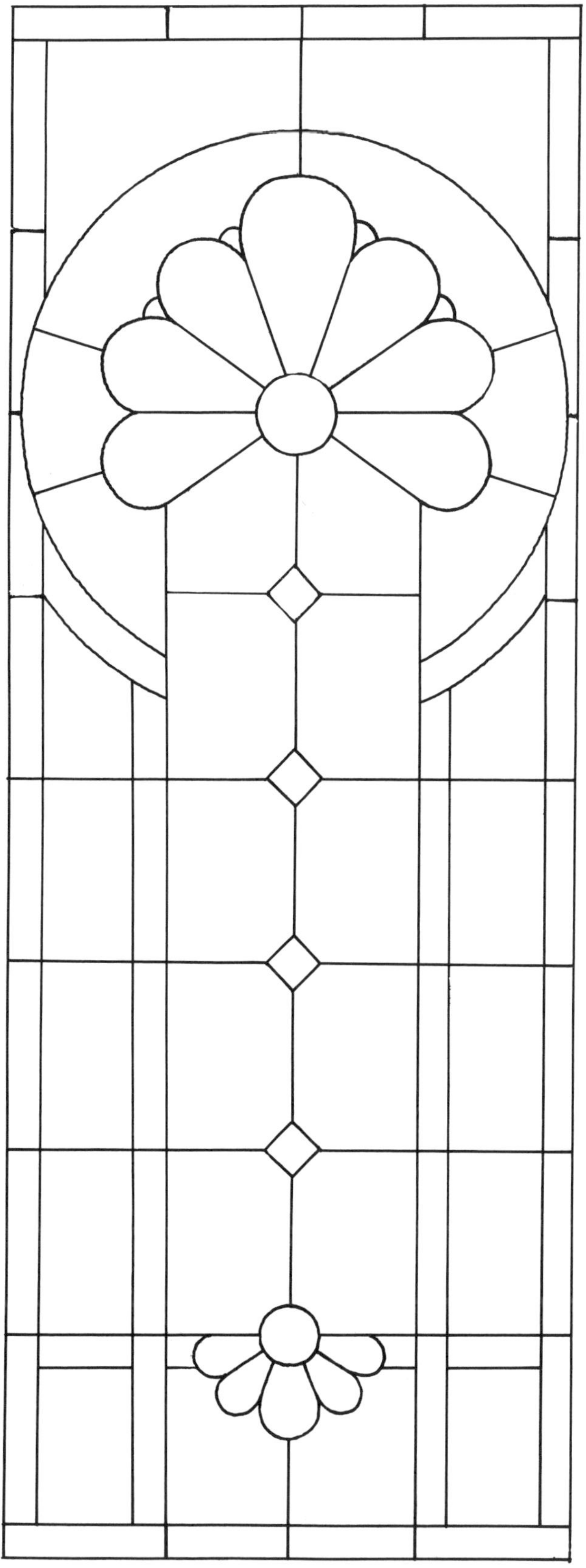

ART DECO WINDOW OR DOOR PANEL

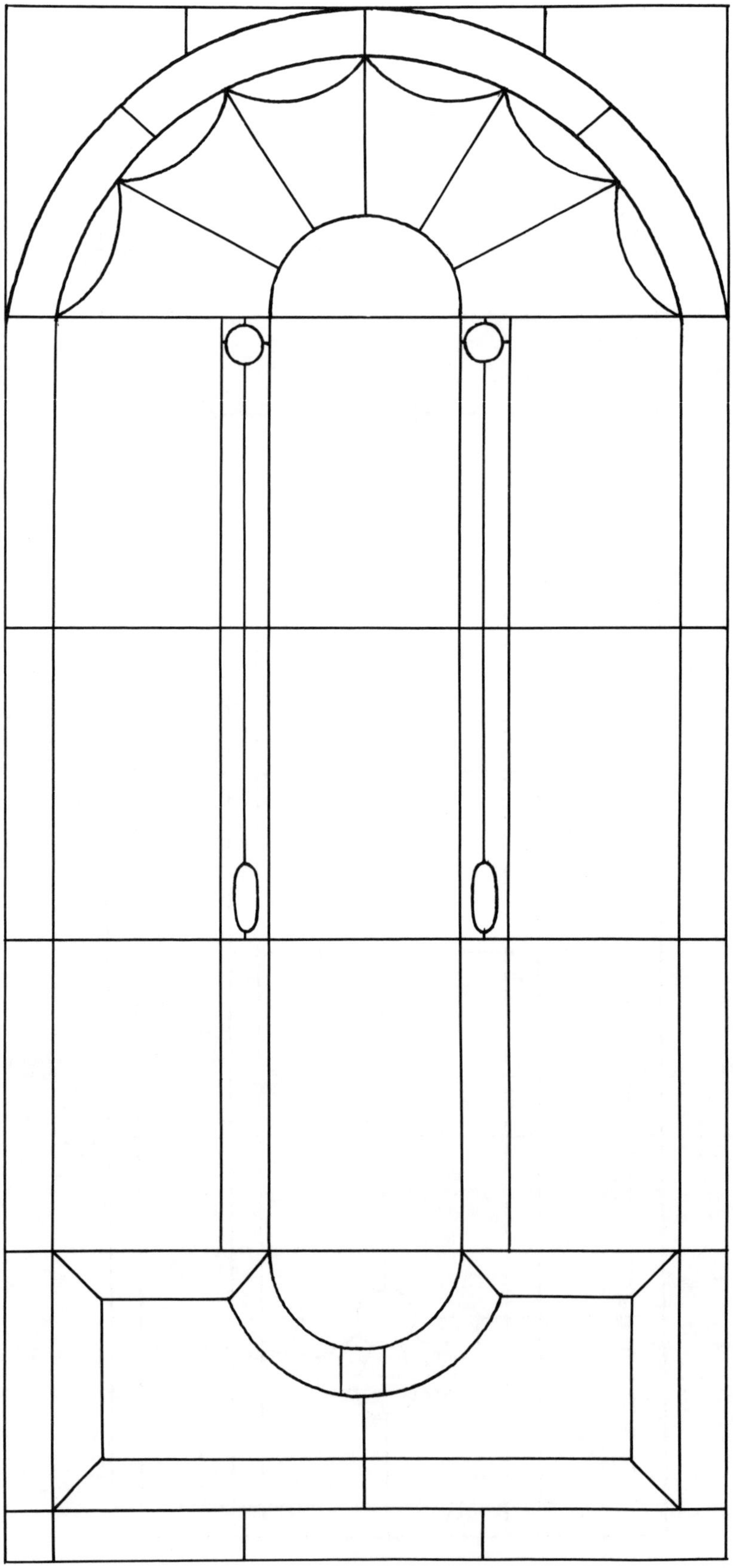

ART DECO WINDOW

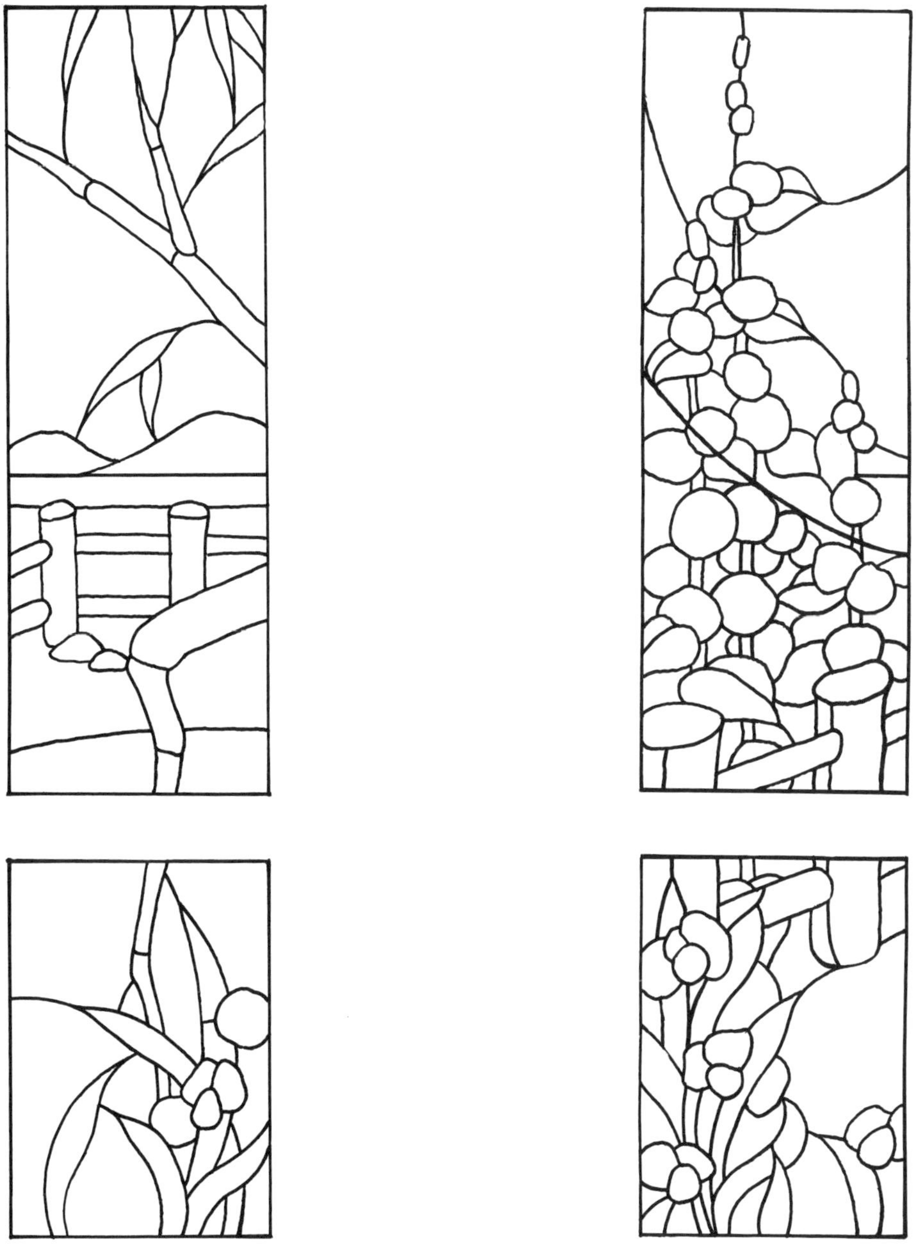

TIFFANY-STYLE FRONT ENTRY PANELS

TIFFANY-STYLE FRONT ENTRY PANELS

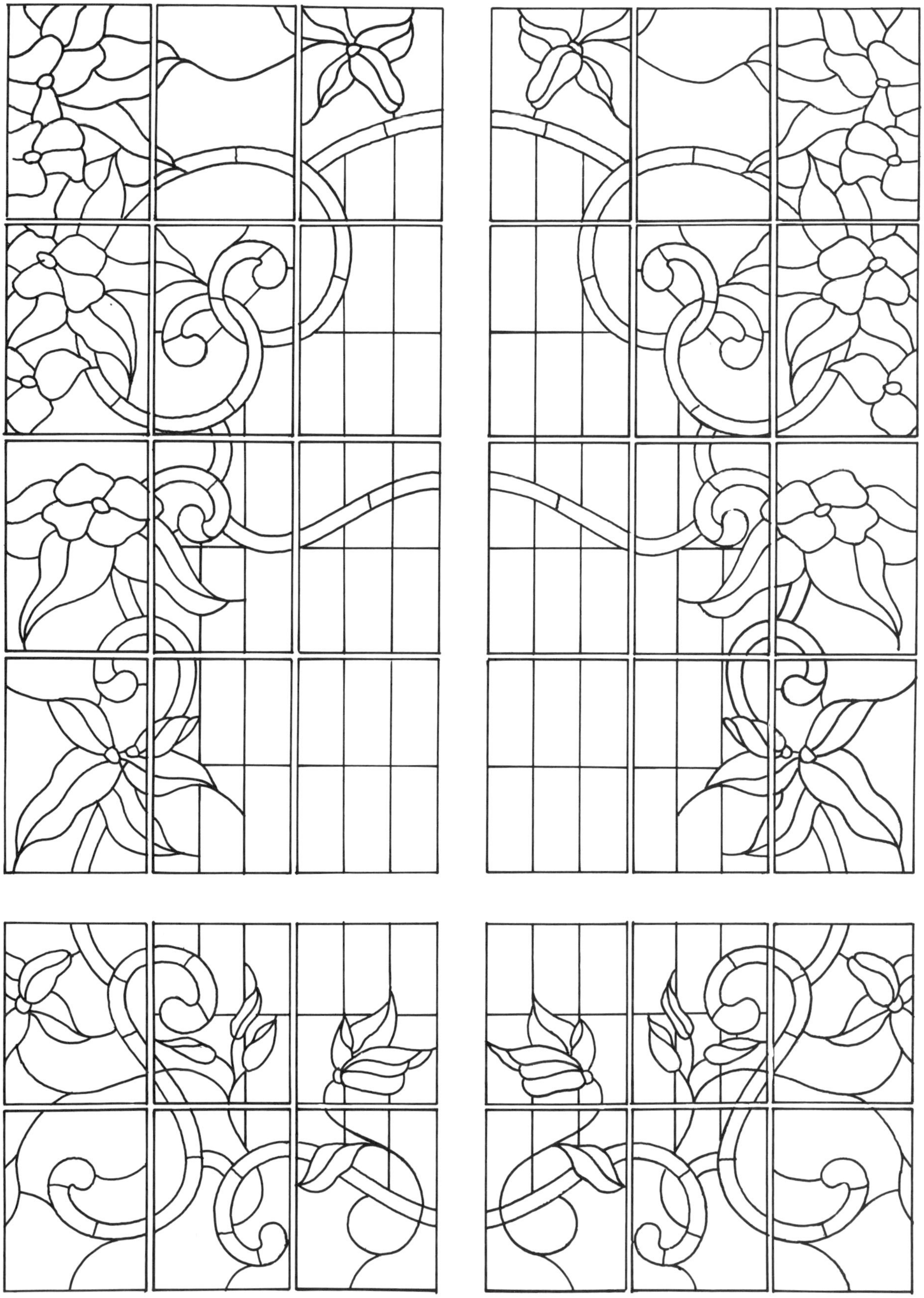

CONTEMPORARY WINDOW
(see front cover)

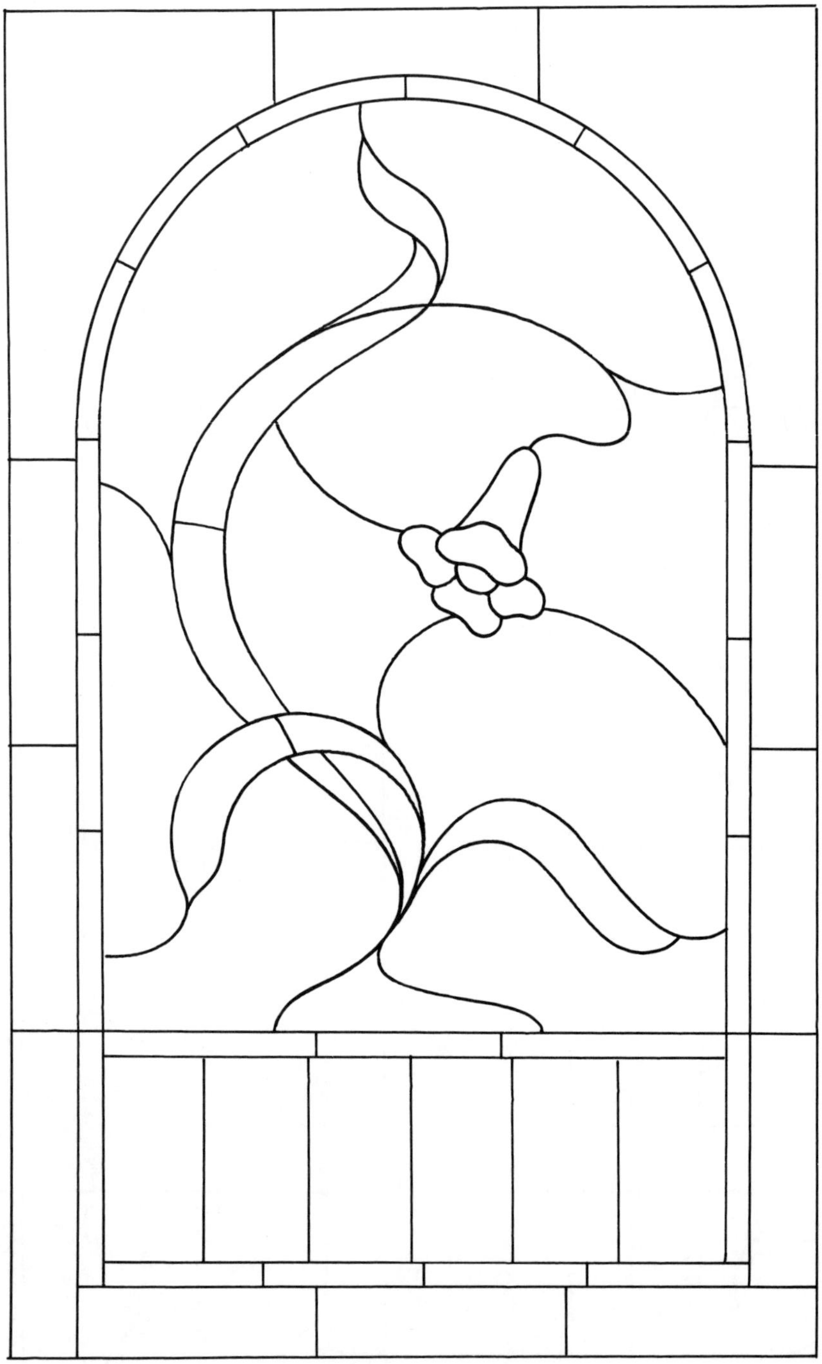

CONTEMPORARY WINDOW

CONTEMPORARY FRONT ENTRY PANELS

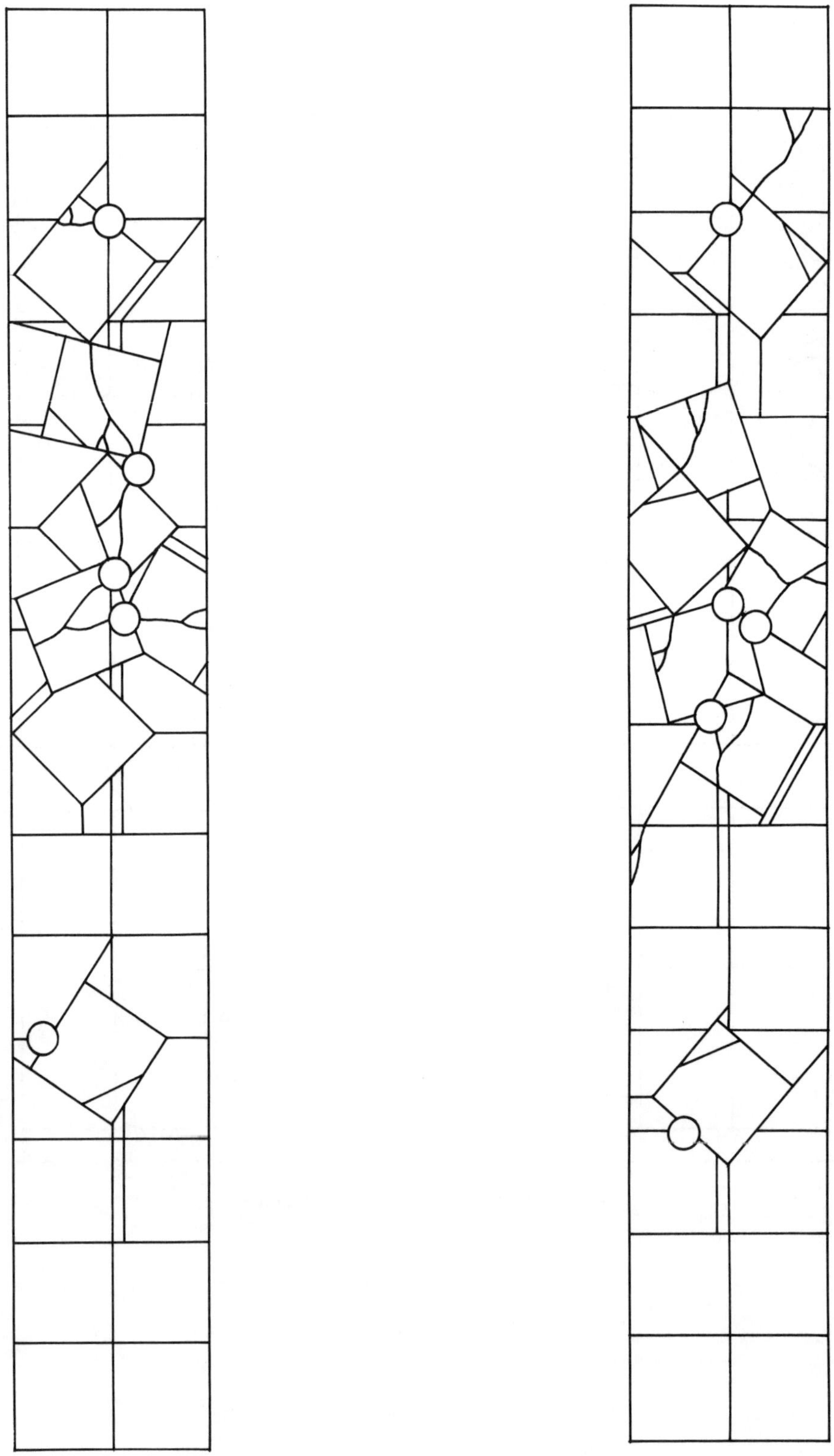

CONTEMPORARY FRONT ENTRY PANELS

CONTEMPORARY PORTHOLE WINDOW

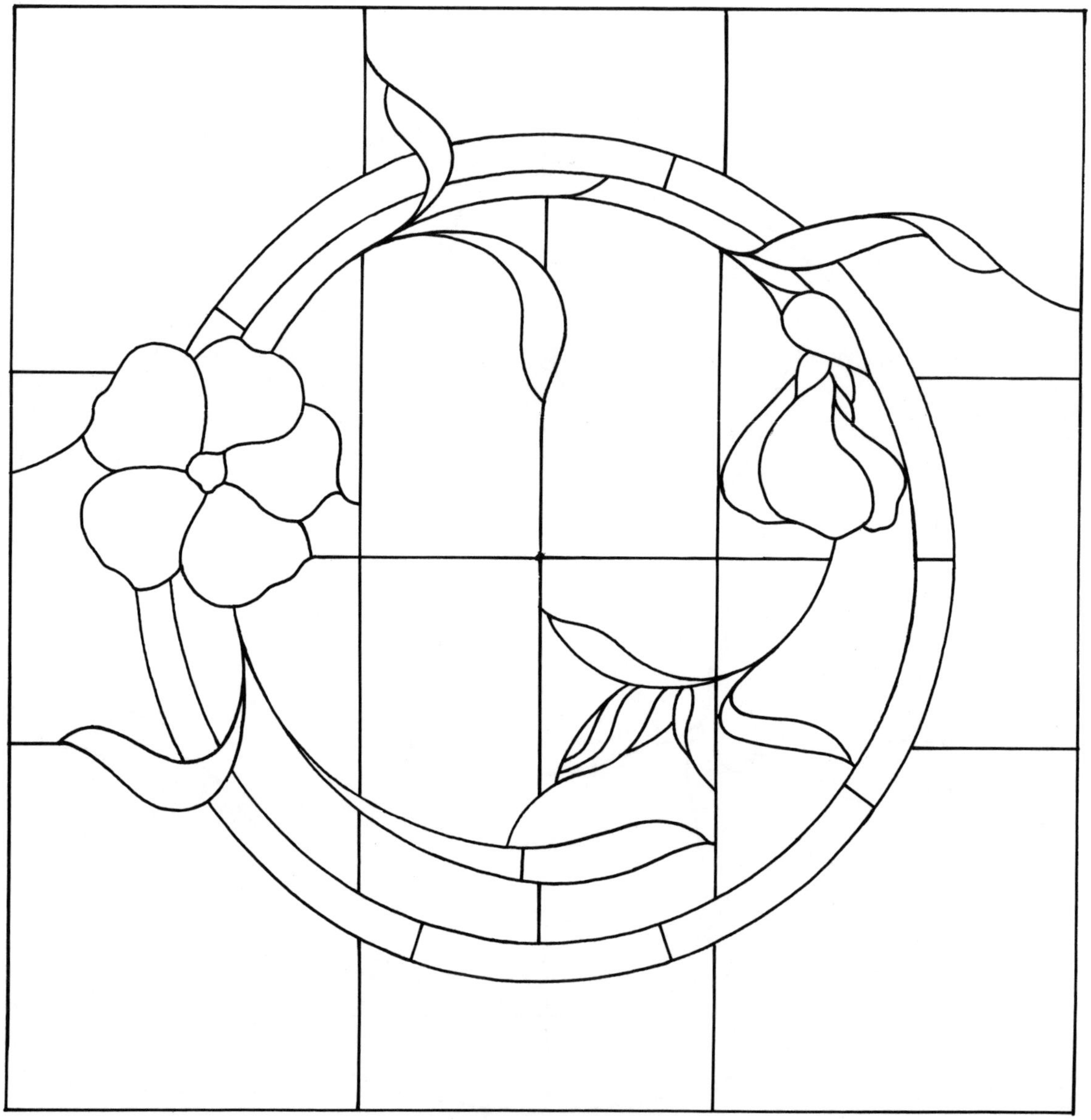

CONTEMPORARY WINDOW

(top)

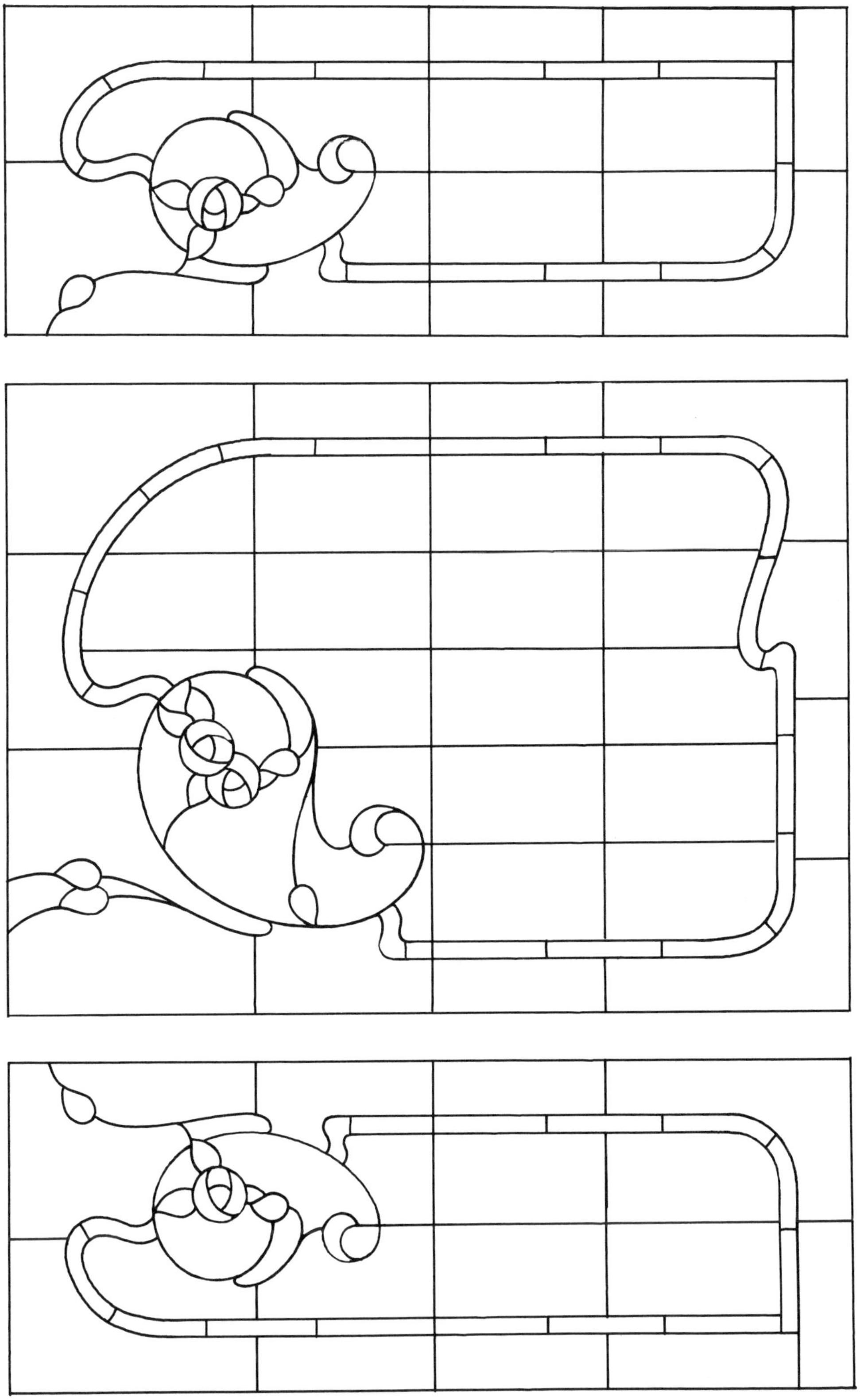

CONTEMPORARY DOOR AND FRONT ENTRY PANELS

CONTEMPORARY FRONT ENTRY PANELS

CONTEMPORARY WINDOW
(see colour plates)

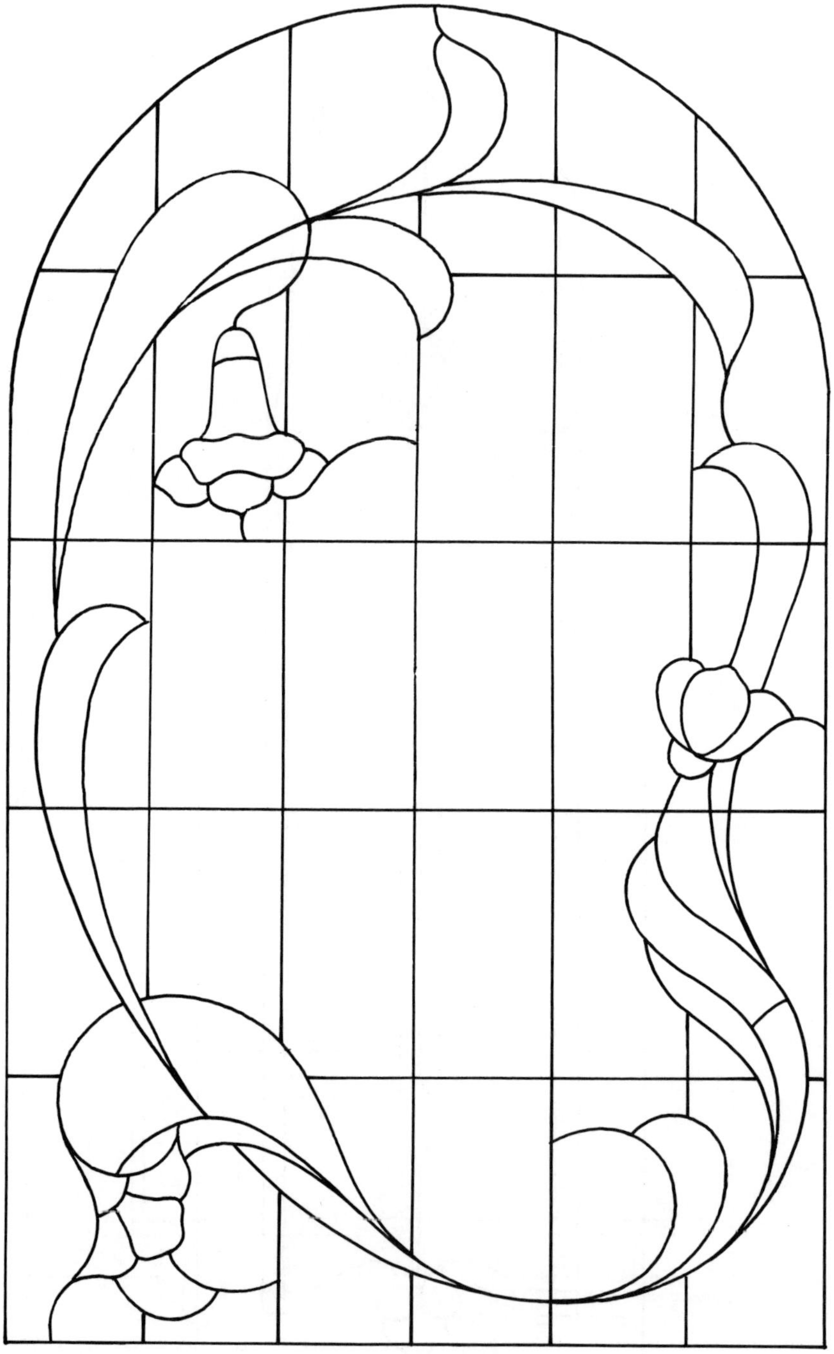

CONTEMPORARY WINDOW

CONTEMPORARY WINDOW
(see colour plates)

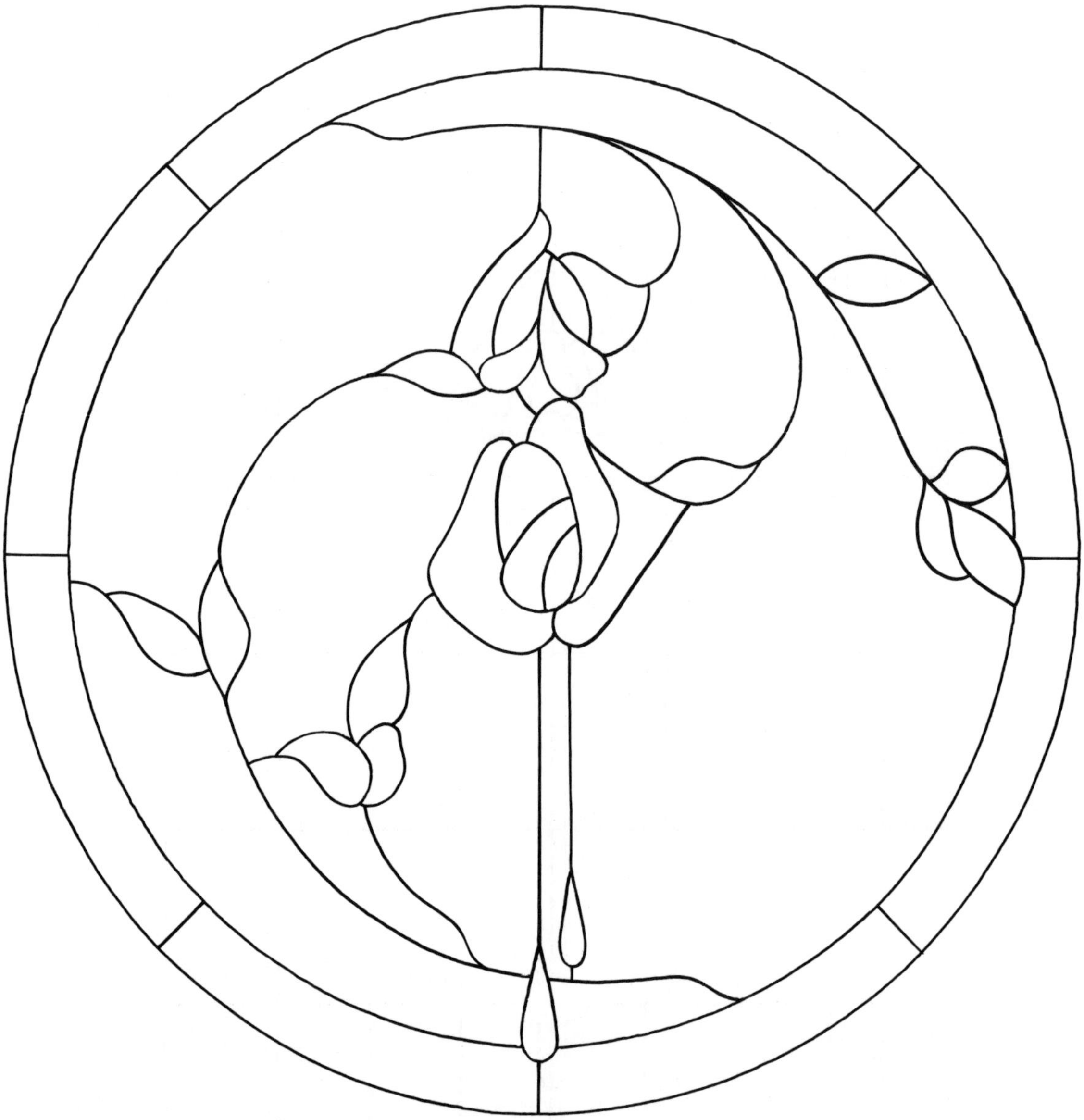

CONTEMPORARY PORTHOLE WINDOW

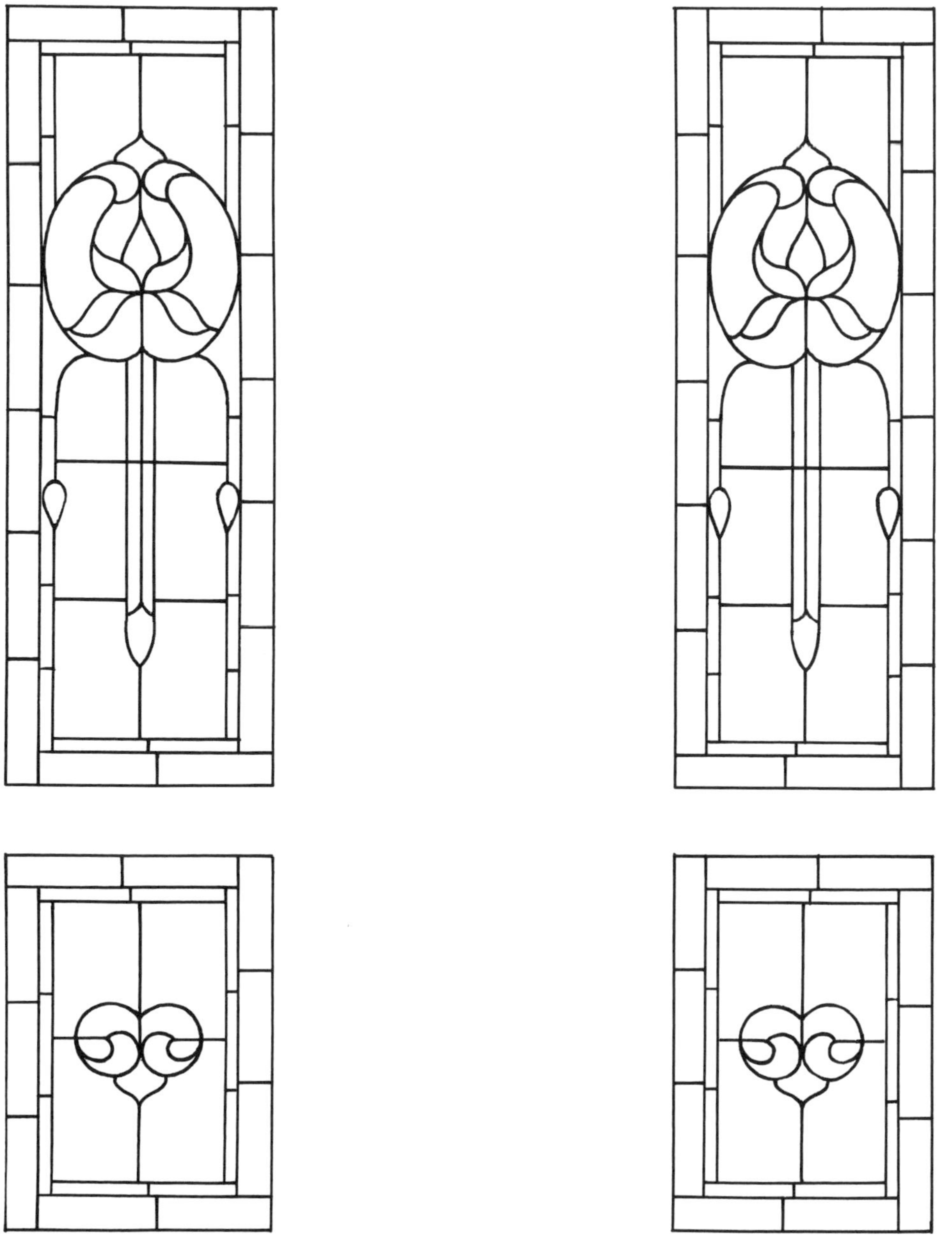

CONTEMPORARY DOOR OR WINDOW PANELS

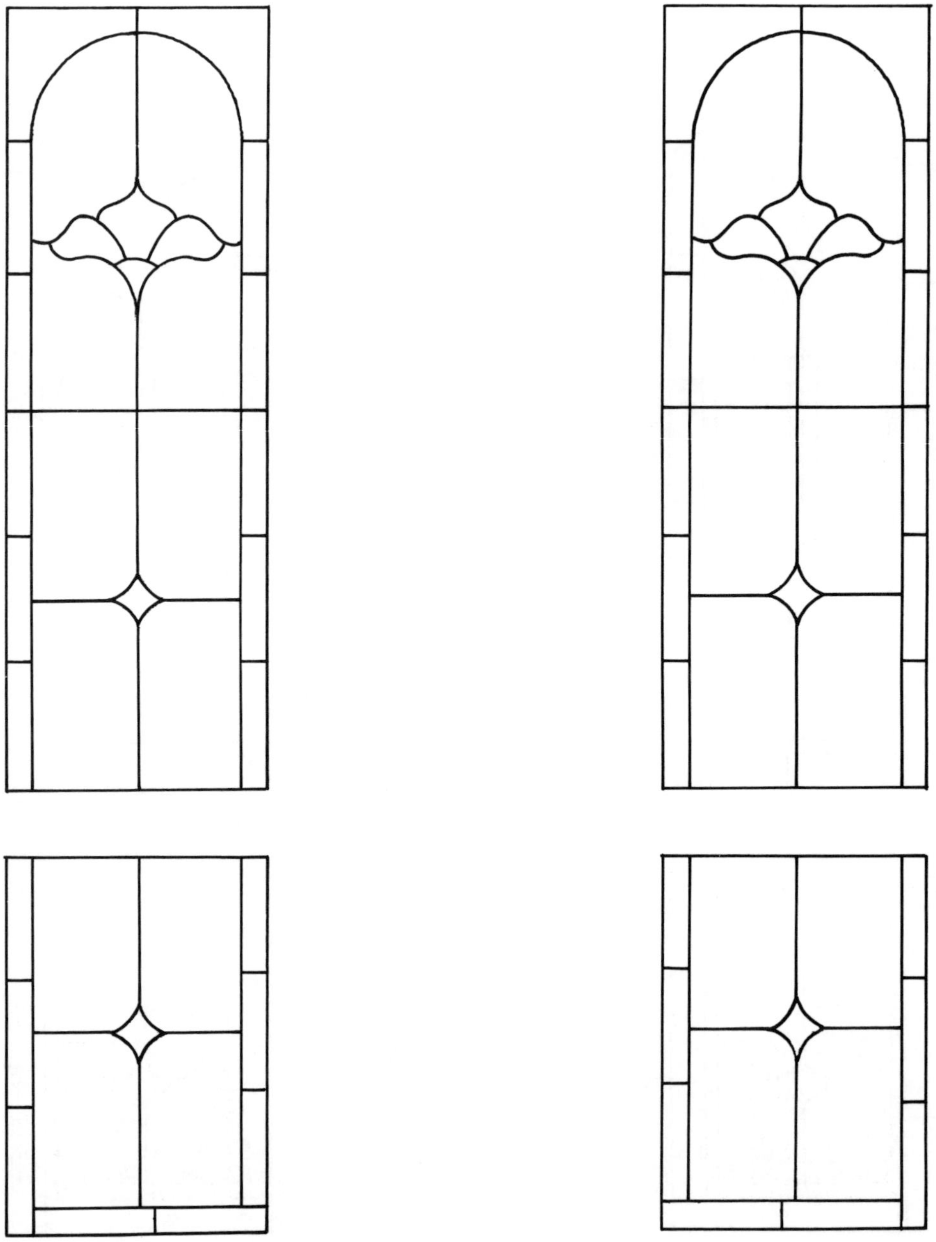

CONTEMPORARY DOOR OR WINDOW PANELS

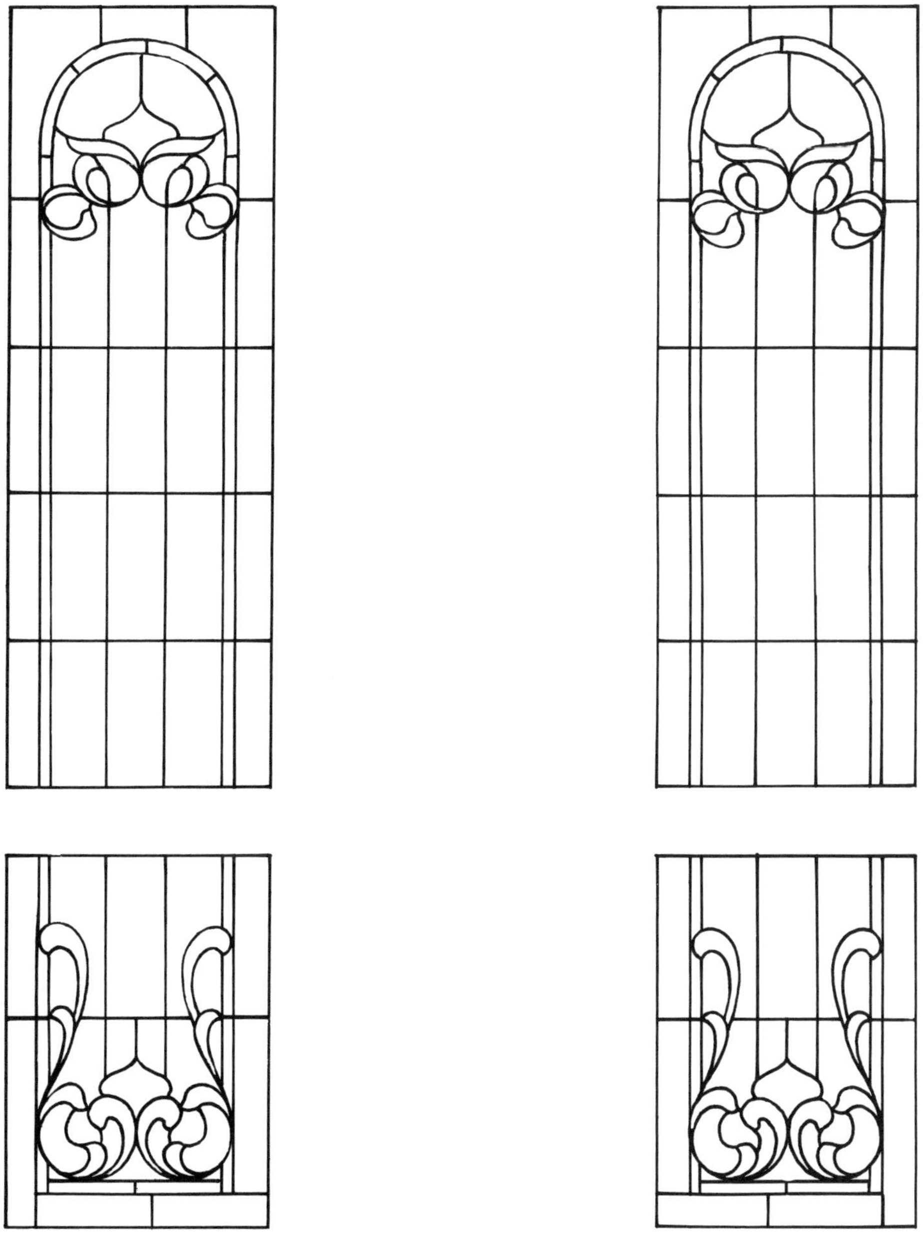

CONTEMPORARY FRONT ENTRY PANELS

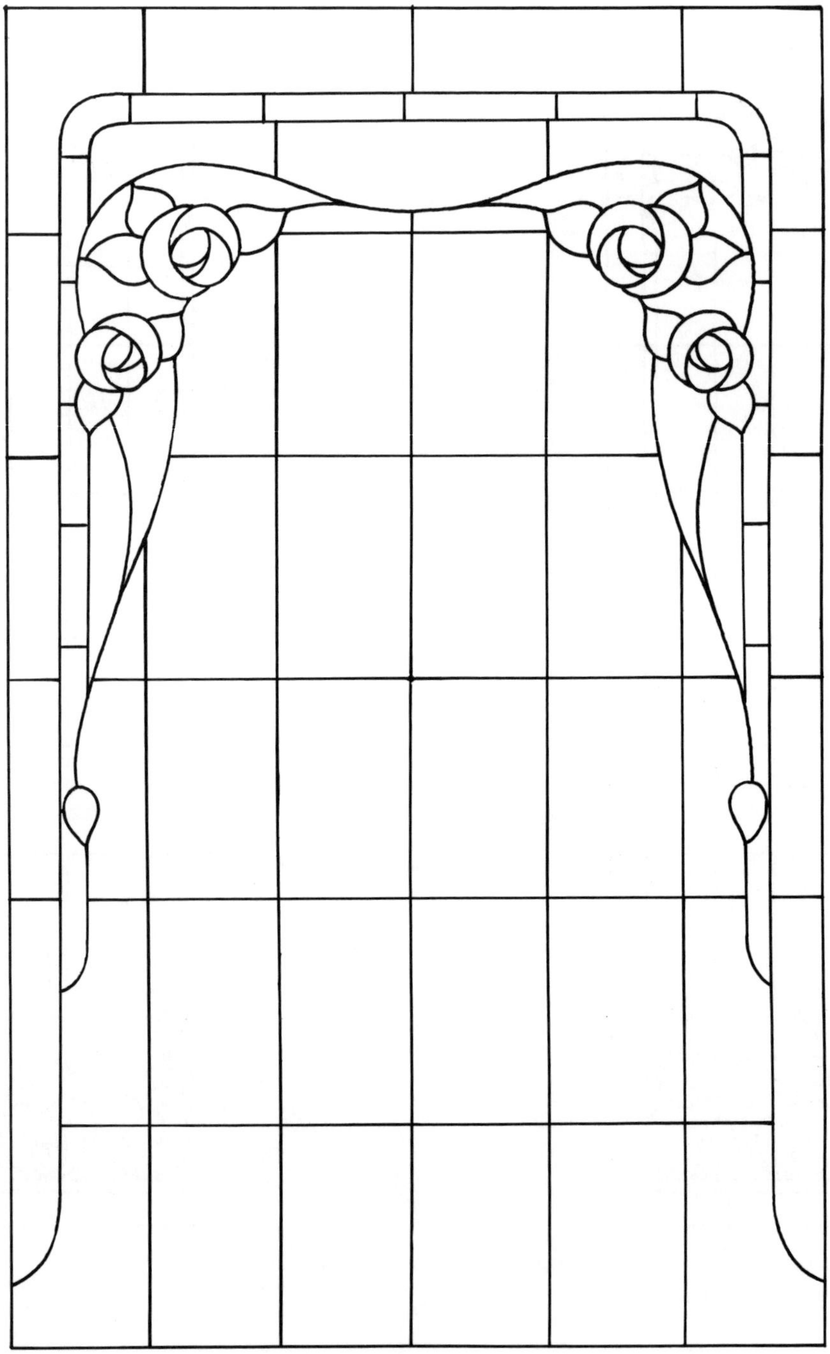

CONTEMPORARY WINDOW OR MIRROR SURROUND

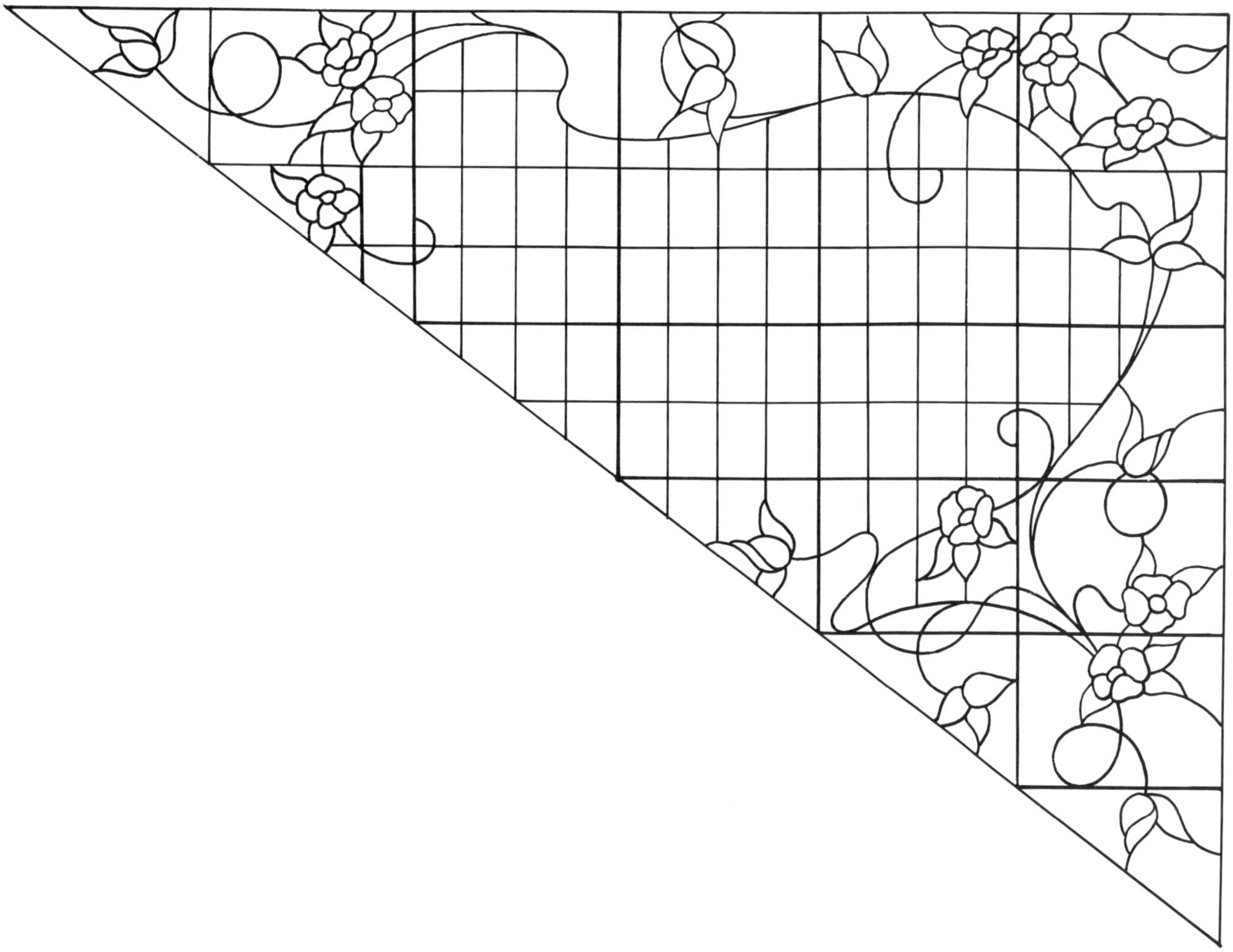

CONTEMPORARY WINDOW

CONTEMPORARY WINDOW

CONTEMPORARY WINDOW OR TRANSOM

CONTEMPORARY FRONT ENTRY PANELS

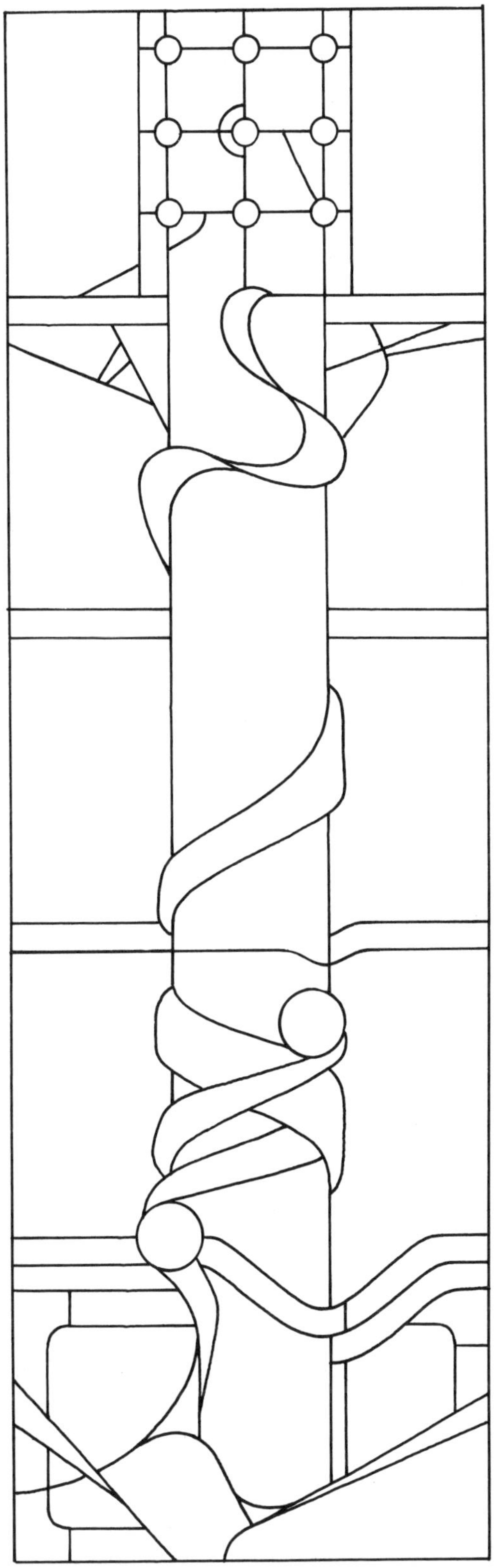

CONTEMPORARY FRONT ENTRY PANEL

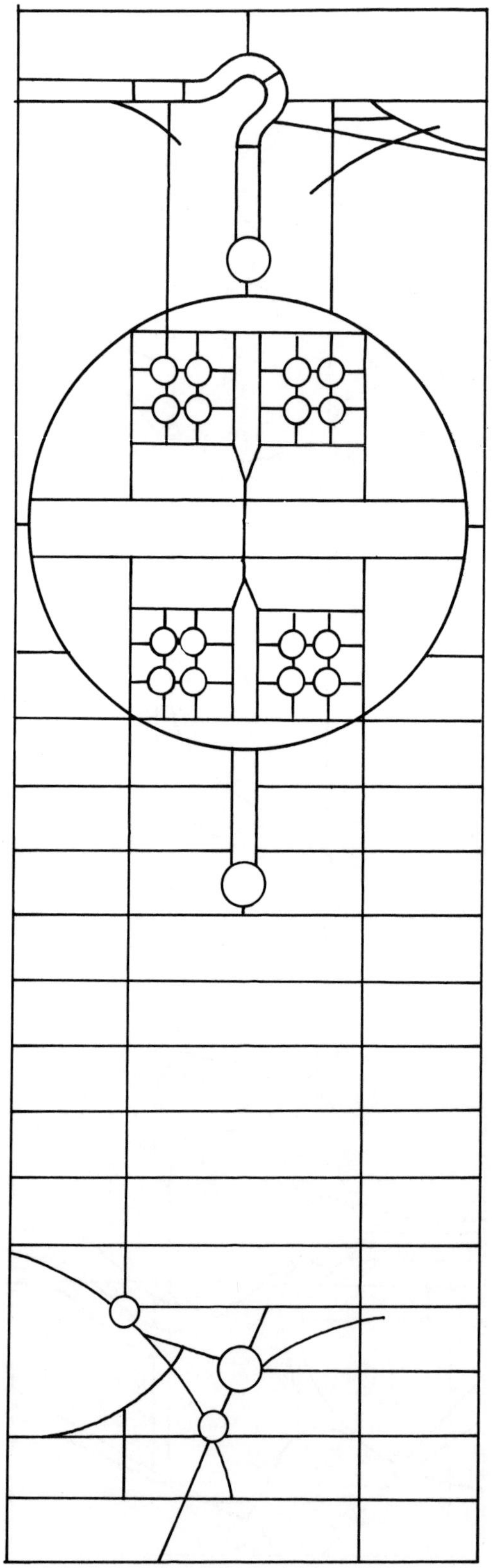

CONTEMPORARY FRONT ENTRY PANEL

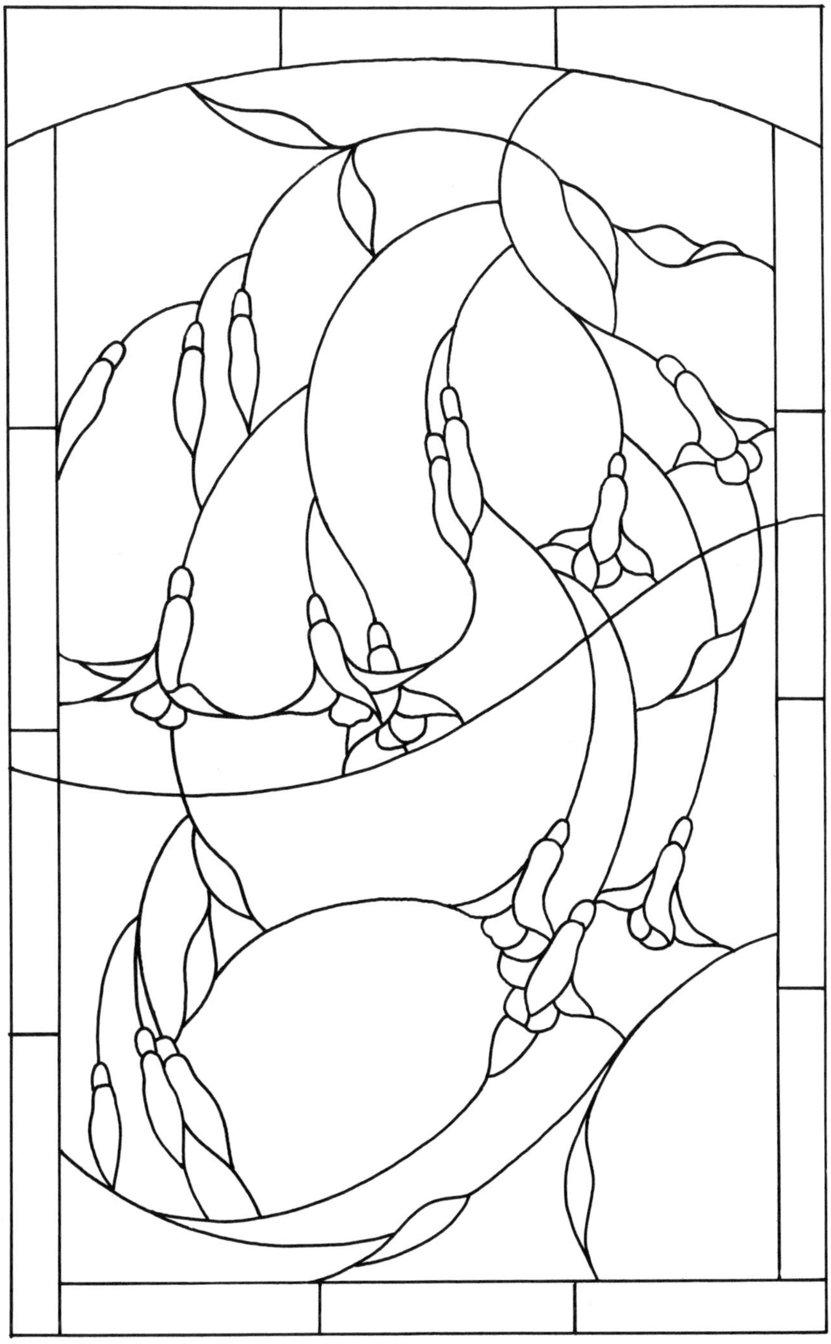

CONTEMPORARY DOOR PANEL OR WINDOW

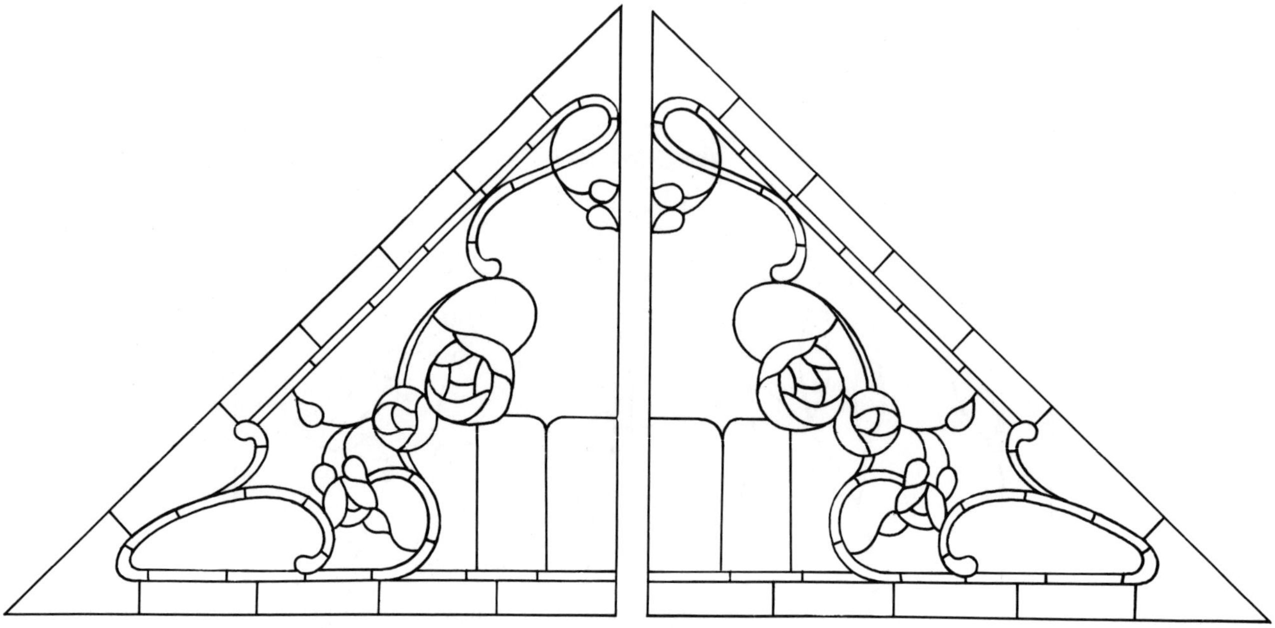

CONTEMPORARY WINDOW

Glossary

Antique glass Mouth-blown glass.

Beading Raised and rounded finish obtained with solder in copper foil work.

Came (lead came) or calme Extruded lead in various profiles.

Cartoon Usually full-size working drawing or pattern.

Cathedral glass Machine-made glass.

Cementing Application of black putty – forced between glass and lead to waterproof and strengthen leadlight windows.

Channel Space formed between the leaves of lead, into which the glass is placed.

Cutline Line shown on cartoon denoting thickness of heart of lead came or copper foil.

False lead Used to repair cracked glass. Half section of lead is soldered either side of crack.

Flashed glass Glass with a thin layer of another coloured glass fused on to one side. Usually antique (mouth-blown).

Flux Any substance applied to metals before soldering to remove oxides and enable a proper bond between base metal and solder.

Foiling Wrapping copper foil around glass edges.

Grinding Method of smoothing rough edges of glass using electric glass grinder and diamond grit grinding head.

Grozing Nibbling away excess glass.

Heart Central section of lead.

Jewels Ornamental glass pieces – sometimes faceted, available in a range of colours and sizes.

Lathekin Plastic or wooden tool, useful for manipulating lead channels.

Lead vice Mounted to your workbench, designed to cramp one end of the lead while straightening.

Leading or leading up Assembly process whereby lead is placed between the different pieces of glass.

Machined antiqued glass Cathedral glass made to resemble antique glass.

Oleic acid A liquid flux for lead.

Opalescent glass Machine-made glass consisting of a mixture of base white opal with an additional colour.

Patina Applied to beaded finish on copper foil items to change colour of solder.

Pot colour Glass with colour through entire thickness of glass (not flashed).

Puttying See *Cementing.*

Reamy See *Streaky.*

Rondells Circles of glass either pressed or spun. Machine-made or mouth-blown: range of sizes and colours.
See also *Jewels.*

Score Mark left on glass by the wheel of a glass cutter.

Seeds Bubbles trapped inside glass.

Solder Alloy of tin and lead.

Stearine Flux with waxy consistency.

Streaky Glass manufactured to give swirled effect, usually a two or more colour mixture.

Striations Lines captured within or on the surface of antique glass during manufacture, giving the glass a crystalline effect.

Tacking Temporary soldering of copper foiled pieces either during or after assembly, but prior to beading.

Tapping To assist the glass in breaking along the scoreline.

Template Shape made of thick paper or cardboard corresponding to the size of glass required.

Tinning Application of thin smooth coat of solder on copper tip of soldering iron.

Whiting Calcium carbonate powder, sprinkled over a window after puttying and scrubbed in to remove grease and excess putty from glass and lead.

❖

Index

❖